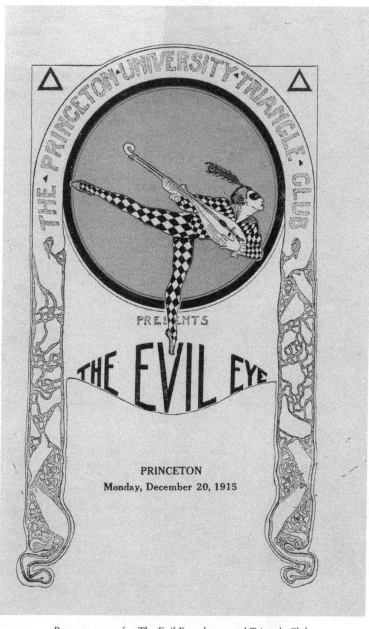

Program cover for *The Evil Eye*, the second Triangle Club
production for which Fitzgerald wrote the lyrics.
Princeton University Libraries.

SPIRES AND GARGOYLES

Early Writings, 1909–1919

* * *

F. SCOTT FITZGERALD

Edited by
JAMES L. W. WEST III

CAMBRIDGE
UNIVERSITY PRESS

CAMBRIDGE
UNIVERSITY PRESS

Shaftesbury Road, Cambridge CB2 8EA, United Kingdom

One Liberty Plaza, 20th Floor, New York, NY 10006, USA

477 Williamstown Road, Port Melbourne, VIC 3207, Australia

314–321, 3rd Floor, Plot 3, Splendor Forum, Jasola District Centre, New Delhi – 110025, India

103 Penang Road, #05–06/07, Visioncrest Commercial, Singapore 238467

Cambridge University Press is part of Cambridge University Press & Assessment,
a department of the University of Cambridge.

We share the University's mission to contribute to society through the pursuit of
education, learning and research at the highest international levels of excellence.

www.cambridge.org
Information on this title: www.cambridge.org/9781009279741

First published 2010
Reprinted 2021
First paperback edition 2022

A catalogue record for this publication is available from the British Library

Library of Congress Cataloging-in-Publication data
Fitzgerald, F. Scott (Francis Scott), 1896–1940.
Spires and gargoyles: early writings, 1909–1919 / F. Scott Fitzgerald ; edited by
James L. W. West III.
p. cm. – (The Cambridge edition of the works of F. Scott Fitzgerald)
ISBN 978-0-521-76592-3 (hardback)
I. West, James L. W. II. Title. III. Series: Fitzgerald, F. Scott (Francis Scott),
1896–1940. Works. 1991.
PS3511.I9S65 2010
813'.52 – dc22 2009047390

ISBN 978-0-521-76592-3 Hardback
ISBN 978-1-009-27974-1 Paperback

CONTENTS

ST. PAUL ACADEMY, 1909–1911

THE NEWMAN SCHOOL, 1911–1913

PRINCETON UNIVERSITY, 1914–1919

Triangle Show Lyrics

Prose and Verse

Contents

Contents

ix

ACKNOWLEDGMENTS

I thank Eleanor Lanahan, Thomas P. Roche, Jr., and Chris Byrne, the Trustees of the F. Scott Fitzgerald Estate, for their continuing support and interest. Phyllis Westberg of Harold Ober Associates, Inc., has given valuable advice and assistance.

The illustrations in this volume are reproduced with permission from originals in the F. Scott Fitzgerald Papers, Manuscript Division, Department of Rare Books and Special Collections, Princeton University Libraries, and from archival materials in the Mudd Manuscript Library, Princeton University. Don Skemer, Charles Greene, and AnnaLee Pauls at the Manuscript Division and Christine A. Lutz at the Mudd Library were most helpful to me in my various labors and searches.

The Cambridge Edition of the Works of F. Scott Fitzgerald is supported at Penn State by Susan Welch, dean of the College of the Liberal Arts, and Robin Schulze, head of the Department of English. I am grateful to Jeanne Alexander Nettles and Gregg Baptista for diligent assistance with transcription, collation, annotation, and proofing.

J. L. W. W. III

ILLUSTRATIONS
(Beginning on p. 277.)

Frontispiece. Program cover for *The Evil Eye.*

INTRODUCTION

When I lived in St. Paul and was about twelve I wrote all through every class in school in the back of my geography book and first year Latin and on the margins of themes and declensions and mathematic problems. Two years later a family congress decided that the only way to force me to study was to send me to boarding school. This was a mistake. It took my mind off my writing. I decided to play football, to smoke, to go to college, to do all sorts of irrelevant things that had nothing to do with the real business of life, which, of course, was the proper mixture of description and dialogue in the short story.

"Who's Who—and Why" (*1920*)

I. BACKGROUND

Young F. Scott Fitzgerald of St. Paul, Minnesota, had a busy and productive literary apprenticeship. His first appearance in print, a short story entitled "The Mystery of the Raymond Mortgage," was published in October 1909, shortly after his thirteenth birthday. It appeared in the *St. Paul Academy Now and Then*, the student magazine at the private school he attended in his home town. Over the next ten years Fitzgerald produced a stream of additional publications—in the *Now and Then* during 1910 and 1911; in the *Newman News*, a student magazine at the Newman School in Hackensack, New Jersey, from 1911 to 1913; and in the *Daily Princetonian*, the *Princeton Tiger*, the *Nassau Literary Magazine*, and the Triangle Club publications at Princeton University from 1914 to 1919.

During this apprenticeship Fitzgerald discovered his calling. He found that he liked writing, enjoyed seeing his words in print, and was pleased by the attention that came to him as a fledgling author. He began to develop a literary style and to discover the kind of writer he wanted to be: one with a readership. Fitzgerald did not aspire, early or late, to be a coterie author; he wanted popularity, notice, and (eventually) money from his writings. He meant to amuse and entertain but also to treat serious subjects—the strivings of the American middle and upper classes, the impact of the First World War on his generation, and the effect of money and privilege on human behavior. These concerns are apparent already in his apprentice writings.

Fitzgerald wrote in a great variety of genres. He produced fiction, poetry, satire, parodies, song lyrics, drama scripts, and book reviews. He was quickened in his literary ambitions at the Newman School by Monsignor Sigourney Fay, who would later be the model for Monsignor Thayer Darcy in *This Side of Paradise* (1920), and by Fay's friend, the Anglo-Irish writer Shane Leslie, who would provide an introduction at Charles Scribner's Sons, Leslie's own American publisher and the eventual publisher of Fitzgerald's work. At Princeton, Fitzgerald took encouragement from three fellow students: Edmund Wilson, who later became one of the most influential critics of his generation; John Peale Bishop, who had a successful career as a poet and literary journalist; and John Biggs, Jr., who published two novels, became a judge, and eventually served as the executor of Fitzgerald's literary estate after his death in 1940.

Fitzgerald's greatest successes at Princeton came from the lyrics he composed for three productions of the Triangle Club, the student musical-comedy group that each fall put together a show and took it on an extended tour over the Christmas holidays to such cities as New York, Baltimore, Cleveland, Detroit, Chicago, and St. Louis. Fitzgerald's lyrics for *Fie! Fie! Fi-Fi!* (1914), *The Evil Eye* (1915), and *Safety First!* (1916) brought him much notice at the university; this campus fame, however, was undercut by the fact that, owing to low marks in his academic work, he was forbidden to travel or perform with the student troupe. Fitzgerald's stories, poems, and parodies were published in the *Nassau Lit*, one of the oldest undergraduate literary magazines in the country, founded in 1842. His satire, jokes, and gags appeared in the *Princeton Tiger*, the campus humor magazine. One item, an athletic fight song, was published in the *Daily Princetonian*, the student newspaper.

Perhaps with his future bibliographers in mind, Fitzgerald removed tearsheets of many of his apprentice writings from the original issues in which they had appeared and preserved them in two thin volumes of juvenilia that he had bound in red leather. These two volumes, which bear the gold-stamped titles *Various Contributions of Scott Fitzgerald to the Nassau Literary Magazine of Princeton, 1915–1917*, and *Other Contributions of Scott Fitzgerald to School and College Magazines, 1909–1919*, are among the Fitzgerald Additional Papers at Princeton University Library. They have been essential in assembling this collection, as have Fitzgerald's personal scrapbooks (also at Princeton), into which he pasted clippings of several other items from his student days.

The present volume of the Cambridge edition includes all public writings from Fitzgerald's literary apprenticeship—that is, all works that he prepared for print. The volume does not include three play scripts that he wrote for summer productions by the Elizabethan Dramatic Club, a local theatre group in St. Paul, nor does it include such writings as his adolescent "Thoughtbook," a diary of sorts that he kept during his thirteenth and fourteenth years, or the surviving fragments of "The Romantic Egotist," his first attempt at a novel. None of these writings was published during Fitzgerald's lifetime; all of them are available today in reliable scholarly editions.[1]

2. SUBSEQUENT APPEARANCES

The work published by Fitzgerald in the *Nassau Literary Magazine* set the stage for his entry into the literary marketplace. In fact

[1] *F. Scott Fitzgerald's St. Paul Plays, 1911–1914*, ed. Alan Margolies (Princeton: Princeton University Library, 1978); *Thoughtbook of Francis Scott Key Fitzgerald*, ed. John R. Kuehl (Princeton: Princeton University Library, 1965). The surviving pages of "The Romantic Egotist" are facsimiled in *This Side of Paradise: The Manuscripts and Typescripts*, vol. I, parts 1 and 2 of *F. Scott Fitzgerald Manuscripts*, ed. Matthew J. Bruccoli (New York and London: Garland Publishing, Inc., 1990).

he recycled the best of his work from the *Nassau Lit* in order to jump-start his professional career. "Babes in the Woods" and "The Debutante" were revised and published in H. L. Mencken's *The Smart Set* in September and November 1919; they were Fitzgerald's initial two appearances in a paying magazine. Both were then revised further and included in *This Side of Paradise*. The poems "Princeton—The Last Day," "On a Play Twice Seen," and "The Cameo Frame" also appear in *This Side of Paradise*, as do sentences and phrases from the short stories "The Spire and the Gargoyle" and "Sentiment—and the Use of Rouge." Material from "The Ordeal" was incorporated into "Benediction," published first in the February 1920 issue of *The Smart Set* and collected in *Flappers and Philosophers* (1920), Fitzgerald's first volume of short stories. "Jemina" was revised from its *Nassau Lit* appearance for publication in *Vanity Fair* in January 1921 and was included, with "Tarquin of Cheapside," in *Tales of the Jazz Age* (1922), Fitzgerald's second collection of short fiction.

This volume of the Cambridge edition includes the earliest extant texts of these writings, the versions that saw print before Fitzgerald became a professional. The later versions have appeared in the Cambridge editions of *This Side of Paradise* (1995), *Flappers and Philosophers* (2000), and *Tales of the Jazz Age* (2002).

3. EDITORIAL PRINCIPLES

With one exception, every piece of writing in this volume survives in only one editorially significant text—its first appearance in print. The exception is a partial holograph for "Babes in the Woods," preserved at Princeton. Substantively this holograph is almost identical to the version in the *Nassau Lit*; it has been useful in establishing the accidental texture for the story published here. An incomplete carbon typescript of "The Debutante" is extant because Fitzgerald incorporated it, with extensive holograph revisions, into the manuscript of *This Side of Paradise*. But this typescript is not of the *Nassau Lit* version; it is a different text, produced by Fitzgerald for submission to *The Smart Set*. He retained this carbon copy and spliced it into the manuscript of his novel, changing the names of some characters and adding numerous alterations and additions in his own hand. Thus this typescript of "The Debutante" bears only a distant relationship to the version published in the *Nassau Lit* and has not been employed in establishing the Cambridge text.[2]

Nearly all of the material in this volume has been reprinted. Three gatherings of the author's early work have been published: *The Apprentice Fiction of F. Scott Fitzgerald, 1909–1917*, ed. John Kuehl (New Brunswick, N.J.: Rutgers University Press, 1965); *F. Scott Fitzgerald in His Own Time: A Miscellany*, ed. Matthew J. Bruccoli and Jackson R. Bryer (Kent, Ohio: Kent State University Press, 1971); and *F. Scott Fitzgerald, the Princeton Years: Selected Writings, 1914–1920*, ed. Chip Deffaa (Fort Bragg, Calif.: Cypress House Press, 1996).[3] In both *The Apprentice Fiction of F. Scott Fitzgerald* and *F. Scott Fitzgerald in His Own Time*, the texts are presented without emendation; misspellings and typographical errors in the original appearances are preserved. This practice, usually employed for private writings such as letters and diaries, is perhaps appropriate for the reprinting of a writer's early efforts, but it creates an impression of inconsequentiality and invites condescension from readers. For the Cambridge edition, the writings are treated as public texts and are emended for accuracy in spelling, capitalization, and punctuation. A few readings have been altered for factual correctness—for example, titles of books and other publications. These emendations, all of which involve single words, are without exception minor and have no effect on meaning or style. Emendations are recorded in the apparatus.

The arrangement of items in this volume is chronological by date of publication except for the Triangle Club lyrics, which are placed together in a separate section. Fiction, nonfiction, drama, humor, and book reviews are intermixed in the other sections of the volume to show the many genres in which Fitzgerald was writing during his apprentice years.

---

[2] A facsimile of the first page of this typescript is included in the illustrations section as Figure 3.

[3] See also the limited edition facsimile of *Fie! Fie! Fi-Fi* published by the Thomas Cooper Library, University of South Carolina Press, Columbia, S.C., 1996.

4. REGULARIZED FEATURES

Like most writers, Fitzgerald was inconsistent in orthography, word division, and punctuation, a problem compounded by the fact that such matters were treated with indifference in the student publications to which he contributed. The most common word divisions and spellings from Fitzgerald's early holographs have been used as guides here. He usually employed American spellings, but for some words he preferred British forms—"grey," for example, and "sombre" and "glamour." These British spellings are preserved. Fitzgerald typically used italics only for emphasis in dialogue, placing the titles of newspapers and books within quotation marks. He often did not use a comma between two adjectives of equal weight, and he sometimes left out the comma between the final two elements in a series. These features of punctuation have been allowed to stand when they appear in the original texts but have not been imposed on the volume as a whole.

Numbers of the avenues in New York City (Fifth Avenue) are spelled out; street numbers (42nd Street) are given in Arabic numerals. The comma is sometimes missing before the conjunction in a compound sentence; if that omission might cause confusion for the reader, the comma is supplied. Structural space breaks in the original texts are preserved. Three ellipsis points appear within sentences, four at the ends of sentences. "Mother" and "Father" as proper nouns are capitalized. Question marks and exclamation points following italicized words are italicized. Years are rendered in Arabic numerals, seasons of the year in lower-case. Dashes are one-em in length. Lines of dialogue in the original texts are sometimes punctuated in this fashion: "You cannot proceed," he insisted, "it's too dangerous." In such readings, the second comma has been emended to a full stop and, when necessary, the initial word of the second clause has been capitalized.

No attempt has been made to create a consistent system of punctuation and to impose that system on the texts published here. Such a policy would in effect subject the texts to house-styling. The accidentals of the original texts are followed as faithfully as possible, with the exceptions noted above and with further emendations recorded in the apparatus.

5. DATES OF PUBLICATION

Given below are the dates of first appearance in print for all items in this collection, divided by the publications in which the items appeared. Dates are given by month or holiday, according to the (sometimes incomplete) designation on the original.

The St. Paul Academy Now and Then:
    "The Mystery of the Raymond Mortgage," 2 (October 1909): 4–8.
    "Reade, Substitute Right Half," 2 (February 1910): 10–11.
    "A Debt of Honor," 2 (March 1910): 9–11.
    "S.P.A. Men in College Athletics," 3 (December 1910): 7.
    "The Room with the Green Blinds," 3 (June 1911): 6–9.

Newman News:
    "'Football,'" 9 (Christmas 1911?): 19.
    "Election Night" (1912): 18.
    "A Luckless Santa Claus," 9 (Christmas 1912): 1–7.
    "Pain and the Scientist" (1913): 5–10.
    "The Trail of the Duke," 9 (June 1913): 5–9.
    "A School Dance" (1913): 18.

Triangle Club lyrics:
    Fie! Fie! Fi-Fi (Cincinnati, New York, and London: John Church Co., 1914).
    The Evil Eye (Cincinnati, New York, and London: John Church Co., 1915).
    Safety First! (Cincinnati, New York, and London: John Church Co., 1916).

The Princeton Tiger:
    "There was once...," 25 (December 1914): 5.
    "May Small Talk," 26 (June 1915): 10.
    "How They Head the Chapters," 26 (September 1915): 10.
    "The Conquest of America," 26 (Thanksgiving 1915): 6.

"Little Minnie McCloskey," 27 (1 December 1916): 6–7.
"One from Penn's Neck," 27 (18 December 1916): 7.
"A Litany of Slang," 27 (18 December 1916): 7.
"'Triangle Scenery by Bakst,'" 27 (18 December 1916): 7.
"Futuristic Impressions of the Editorial Boards," 27 (18 December 1916): 7.
"'A glass of beer kills him,'" 27 (18 December 1916): 7.
"'Oui, le backfield...,'" 27 (18 December 1916): 7.
"'When you find...,'" 27 (18 December 1916): 7.
"Things That Never Change! Number 3333," 27 (18 December 1916): 7.
"The Old Frontiersman," 27 (18 December 1916): 11.
"'Boy Kills Self...,'" 27 (3 February 1917): 12.
"Things That Never Change. No. 3982," 27 (3 February 1917): 12.
"Precaution Primarily," 27 (3 February 1917): 13–14.
"'McCaulay Mission...,'" 27 (17 March 1917): 10.
"Popular Parodies—No. 1," 27 (17 March 1917): 10.
"The Diary of a Sophomore," 27 (17 March 1917): 11.
"Undulations of an Undergraduate," 27 (17 March 1917): 20.
"The Prince of Pests: A Story of the War," 27 (28 April 1917): 7.
"'These rifles...,'" 27 (28 April 1917): 8.
"'It is assumed...,'" 27 (28 April 1917): 8.
"Ethel had her shot of brandy...," 27 (28 April 1917): 8.
"'Yale's swimming team...,'" 27 (28 April 1917): 8.
"The Staying Up All Night," 28 (10 November 1917): 6.
"Intercollegiate Petting-Cues," 28 (10 November 1917): 8.
"Our American Poets," 28 (10 November 1917): 11.
"Cedric the Stoker," 28 (10 November 1917): 12.

The Daily Princetonian:
"A Cheer for Princeton," 28 October 1915: 1. The news item (not written by Fitzgerald) in which the cheer is printed is entitled "Mass Meeting To-Night to Practice New Song."

The Nassau Literary Magazine:

"'Shadow Laurels,'" 71 (April 1915): 1–10.

"The Ordeal," 71 (June 1915): 153–59.

"To My Unused Greek Book," 72 (June 1916): 137.

"Our Next Issue," 72 (December 1916): unpaginated.

"Jemina," 72 (December 1916): 210–15.

"The Vampiest of the Vampires," 72 (December 1916): 126.

"The Usual Thing," 72 (December 1916): 223–28.

"The Debutante," 72 (January 1917): 241–52.

Review of "Penrod and Sam," 72 (January 1917): 291–92.

"The Spire and the Gargoyle," 72 (February 1917): 297–307.

"Rain before Dawn," 72 (February 1917): 321.

Review of "David Blaize," 72 (February 1917): 343–44.

"Tarquin of Cheapside," 73 (April 1917): 13–18.

"Babes in the Woods," 73 (May 1917): 55–64.

"Princeton—The Last Day," 73 (May 1917): 95.

Review of "The Celt and the World," 73 (May 1917): 104–5.

"Sentiment—and the Use of Rouge," 73 (June 1917): 107–23.

"On a Play Twice Seen," 73 (June 1917): 149.

Review of "Verses in Peace and War," 73 (June 1917): 152–53.

Review of "God, The Invisible King," 73 (June 1917): 153.

"The Cameo Frame," 73 (October 1917): 169–72.

"The Pierian Springs and the Last Straw," 73 (October 1917): 173–85.

"City Dusk," 73 (April 1918): 315.

"My First Love," 74 (February 1919): 102.

"Marching Streets," 74 (February 1919): 103–4.

"The Pope at Confession," 73 (February 1919): 105.

6. LACUNAE AND ATTRIBUTIONS

Problems of completeness and attribution are nearly always found in compilations of apprentice writings such as this one. It is probable that not everything Fitzgerald published during his early years has survived or been identified. It is certain that not everything he wrote is extant. No complete run of the *Now and Then* or the *Newman News* has been discovered; Fitzgerald might have published work in issues of these magazines that have not survived. Much of the writing in the *Princeton Tiger* during his years at the university is unsigned; some of it has been attributed to him by its presence in his scrapbooks, but this is not the strongest of evidence. It is possible that other unsigned work by him was published in the *Tiger*.

In a 9 August 1939 letter to Morton Kroll, Fitzgerald wrote, "My mother did me the disservice of throwing away all but two of my very young efforts—way back at twelve and thirteen, and later I found that the surviving fragments had more quality than some of the stuff written in the tightened-up days of seven or eight years later."[4] Whether Fitzgerald's mother destroyed published writing or unpublished manuscripts is not known.

For other writings from the *Tiger* that might have been written or "conceived" by Fitzgerald, including four cartoons, see Matthew J. Bruccoli, *F. Scott Fitzgerald: A Descriptive Bibliography*, rev. edn. (Pittsburgh: University of Pittsburgh Press, 1987), entries C19, C43, C47, C49, C63, and C64.[5] Some of these items were included by Deffaa in *F. Scott Fitzgerald, the Princeton Years*. "Cedric the Stoker" from the 10 November 1917 *Tiger* was signed "F.S.F. and J.B."; the co-author was John Biggs, Jr., who was the editor of the *Tiger* in 1917–18. Five limericks and a humorous poem, all probably by Fitzgerald, are included in the appendix of this volume.

---

[4] *The Letters of F. Scott Fitzgerald*, ed. Andrew Turnbull (New York: Charles Scribner's Sons, 1963): 593.

[5] Bruccoli treats "The Vampiest of the Vampires" as a bibliographical ghost (entry C24), but Fitzgerald included it in the first of the two leather-bound volumes of his juvenilia and listed it in his own table of contents for that volume. It is therefore judged to be by Fitzgerald and is included in this volume.

ST. PAUL ACADEMY
1909–1911

THE MYSTERY OF THE RAYMOND MORTGAGE

When I first saw John Syrel of the "New York Daily News," he was standing before an open window of my house gazing out on the city. It was about six o'clock and the lights were just going on. All down 33rd Street was a long line of gaily illuminated buildings. He was not a tall man, but thanks to the erectness of his posture, and the suppleness of his movement, it would take no athlete to tell that he was of fine build. He was twenty-three years old when I first saw him, and was already a reporter on the "News." He was not a handsome man; his face was clean-shaven, and his chin showed him to be of strong character. His eyes and hair were brown.

As I entered the room he turned around slowly and addressed me in a slow, drawling tone: "I think I have the honor of speaking to Mr. Egan, chief of police." I assented, and he went on: "My name is John Syrel and my business,—to tell you frankly, is to learn all I can about that case of the Raymond mortgage."

I started to speak but he silenced me with a wave of his hand. "Though I belong to the staff of the 'Daily News,'" he continued, "I am not here as an agent of the paper."

"I am not here," I interrupted coldly, "to tell every newspaper reporter or adventurer about private affairs. James, show this man out."

Syrel turned without a word and I heard his steps echo up the driveway.

However, this was not destined to be the last time I ever saw Syrel, as events will show.

The morning after I first saw John Syrel, I proceeded to the scene of the crime to which he had alluded. On the train I picked up a newspaper and read the following account of the crime and theft, which had followed it:

"EXTRA"

"Great Crime Committed in Suburbs of City"
"Mayor Proceeding to Scene of Crime"

On the morning of July 1st, a crime and serious theft were committed on the outskirts of the city. Miss Raymond was killed and the body of a servant was found outside the house. Mr. Raymond of Santuka Lake was awakened on Tuesday morning by a scream and two revolver shots which proceeded from his wife's room. He tried to open the door but it would not open. He was almost certain the door was locked from the inside, when suddenly it swung open disclosing a room in frightful disorder. On the center of the floor was a revolver and on his wife's bed was a bloodstain in the shape of a hand. His wife was missing, but on a closer search he found his daughter under the bed, stone dead. The window was broken in two places. Miss Raymond had a bullet wound on her body, and her head was fearfully cut. The body of a servant was found outside with a bullet hole through his head. Mrs. Raymond has not been found.

The room was upset. The bureau drawers were out as if the murderer had been looking for something. Chief of Police Egan is on the scene of the crime, etc., etc.

Just then the conductor called out "Santuka!" The train came to a stop, and getting out of the car I walked up to the house. On the porch I met Gregson, who was supposed to be the ablest detective in the force. He gave me a plan of the house, which he said he would like to have me look at before we went in.

"The body of the servant," he said, "is that of John Standish. He has been with the family twelve years and was a perfectly honest man. He was only thirty-two years old."

"The bullet which killed him was not found?" I asked.

"No," he answered; and then, "Well, you had better come in and see for yourself. By the way, there was a fellow hanging around here, who was trying to see the body. When I refused to let him in, he went around to where the servant was shot and I saw him go down on his knees on the grass and begin to search. A few minutes later he stood up and leaned against a tree. Then he came up to the house and asked to see the body again. I said he could if he would go away afterwards. He assented, and when he got inside the room he went down on his knees under the bed and hunted around. Then he went over to the window and examined the broken pane carefully.

After that he declared himself satisfied and went down toward the hotel."

After I had examined the room to my satisfaction, I found that I might as well try to see through a millstone as to try to fathom this mystery. As I finished my investigation I met Gregson in the laboratory.

"I suppose you heard about the mortgage," said he, as we went downstairs. I answered in the negative, and he told me that a valuable mortgage had disappeared from the room in which Miss Raymond was killed. The night before, Mr. Raymond had placed the mortgage in a drawer and it had disappeared.

On my way to town that night I met Syrel again, and he bowed cordially to me. I began to feel ashamed of myself for sending him out of my house. As I went into the car the only vacant seat was next to him. I sat down and apologized for my rudeness of the day before. He took it lightly and, there being nothing to say, we sat in silence. At last I ventured a remark.

"What do you think of the case?"

"I don't think anything of it as yet. I haven't had time yet."

Nothing daunted I began again. "Did you learn anything?"

Syrel dug his hand into his pocket and produced a bullet. I examined it.

"Where did you find it?" I asked.

"In the yard," he answered briefly.

At this I again relapsed into my seat. When we reached the city, night was coming on. My first day's investigation was not very successful.

My next day's investigation was no more successful than the first. My friend Syrel was not at home. The maid came into Mr. Raymond's room while I was there and gave notice that she was going to leave. "Mr. Raymond," she said, "there was queer noises outside my window last night. I'd like to stay, sir, but it grates on my nerves." Beyond this nothing happened, and I came home worn out. On the morning of the next day I was awakened by the maid who had a telegram in her hand. I opened it and found it was from Gregson. "Come at once," it said, "startling development." I dressed hurriedly and took the first car to Santuka. When I reached the Santuka station, Gregson was waiting for me in a runabout. As soon as I got into the carriage Gregson told me what had happened. "Someone was in the house last night. You know Mr. Raymond asked me to sleep there. Well, to continue, last night, about one, I began to be very thirsty. I went into the hall to get a drink from the faucet there, and as I was passing from my room (I sleep in Miss Raymond's room) into the hall I heard somebody in Mrs. Raymond's room. Wondering why Mr. Raymond was up at that time of night I went into the sitting room to investigate. I opened the door of Mrs. Raymond's room. The body of Miss Raymond was lying on the sofa. A man was kneeling beside it. His face was away from me, but I could tell by his figure that he was not Mr. Raymond. As I looked he got up softly and I saw him open a bureau drawer. He took something out and put it into his pocket. As he turned around he saw me, and I saw that he was a young man. With a cry of rage he sprang at me, and having no weapon I retreated. He snatched up a heavy Indian club and swung it over my head. I gave a cry which must have alarmed the house, for I knew nothing more till I saw Mr. Raymond bending over me."

"How did this man look?" I asked. "Would you know him if you saw him again?"

"I think not," he answered. "I only saw his profile."

"The only explanation I can give is this," said I. "The murderer was in Miss Raymond's room and when she came in he overpowered her and inflicted the gash. He then made for Mrs. Raymond's room and carried her off after having first shot Miss Raymond, who attempted to rise. Outside the house he met Standish, who attempted to stop him and was shot."

Gregson smiled. "That solution is impossible," he said.

As we reached the house I saw John Syrel, who beckoned me aside. "If you come with me," he said, "you will learn something that may be valuable to you." I excused myself to Gregson and followed Syrel. As we reached the walk he began to talk.

"Let us suppose that the murderer or murderess escaped from the house. Where would they go? Naturally they wanted to get away. Where did they go? Now, there are two railroad stations nearby. Santuka and Lidgeville. I have ascertained that they did not go by

Santuka. So did Gregson. I supposed, therefore, that they went by Lidgeville. Gregson didn't; that's the difference. A straight line is the shortest distance between two points. I followed a straight line between here and Lidgeville. At first there was nothing. About two miles farther on I saw some footprints in a marshy hollow. They consisted of three footprints. I took an impression. Here it is. You see this one is a woman's. I have compared it with one of Mrs. Raymond's boots. They are identical. The others are mates. They belong to a man. I compared the bullet I found, where Standish was killed, with one of the remaining cartridges in the revolver that was found in Mrs. Raymond's room. They were mates. Only one shot had been fired and, as I had found one bullet, I concluded that either Mrs. or Miss Raymond had fired the shot. I preferred to think Mrs. Raymond fired it because she had fled. Summing these things up and also taking into consideration that Mrs. Raymond must have had some cause to try to kill Standish, I concluded that John Standish killed Miss Raymond through the window of her mother's room, Friday night. I also conclude that Mrs. Raymond, after ascertaining that her daughter was dead, shot Standish through the window and killed him. Horrified at what she had done she hid behind the door when Mr. Raymond came in. Then she ran down the back stairs. Going outside she stumbled upon the revolver Standish had used and picking it up took it with her. Somewhere between here and Lidgeville she met the owner of these footprints either by accident or design and walked with him to the station where they took the early train for Chicago. The station master did not see the man. He says that only a woman bought a ticket, so I concluded that the young man didn't go. Now you must tell me what Gregson told you."

"How did you know all this!" exclaimed I, astonished. And then I told him about the midnight visitor. He did not appear to be much astonished, and he said, "I guess that the young man is our friend of the footprints. Now you had better go get a brace of revolvers and pack your suitcase if you wish to go with me to find this young man and Mrs. Raymond, who I think is with him."

Greatly surprised at what I had heard I took the first train back to town. I bought a pair of fine Colt revolvers, a dark lantern, and two changes of clothing. We went over to Lidgeville and found that a young man had left on the six o'clock train for Ithaca. On reaching Ithaca we found that he had changed trains and was now halfway to Princeton, New Jersey. It was five o'clock, but we took a fast train and expected to overtake him halfway between Ithaca and Princeton. What was our chagrin when, on reaching the slow train, to find he had gotten off at Indianous and was now probably safe. Thoroughly disappointed we took the train for Indianous. The ticket seller said that a young man in a light grey suit had taken a bus to the Raswell Hotel. We found the bus which the station master said he had taken, in the street. We went up to the driver and he admitted that he had started for the Raswell Hotel in his cab.

"But," said the old fellow, "when I reached there, the fellow had clean disappeared, an' I never got his fare."

Syrel groaned; it was plain that we had lost the young man. We took the next train for New York and telegraphed to Mr. Raymond that we would be down Monday. Sunday night, however, I was called to the phone and recognized Syrel's voice. He directed me to come at once to 534 Chestnut Street. I met him on the doorstep.

"What have you heard?" I asked.

"I have an agent in Indianous," he replied, "in the shape of an Arab boy whom I employ for ten cents a day. I told him to spot the woman and today I got a telegram from him (I left him money to send one), saying to come at once. So come on." We took the train for Indianous. "Smidy," the young Arab, met us at the station.

"You see, sur, it's dis way. You says, 'Spot de guy wid dat hack,' and I says I would. Dat night a young dude comes out of er house on Pine Street and gives the cabman a ten-dollar bill. An den he went back into the house and a minute after he comes out wid a woman, an' den dey went down here a little way an' goes into a house farther down the street. I'll show you de place."

We followed Smidy down the street until we arrived at a corner house. The ground floor was occupied by a cigar store, but the second floor was evidently for rent. As we stood there a face appeared at the window and, seeing us, hastily retreated. Syrel pulled a picture from his pocket. "It's she!" he exclaimed, and calling us to follow he dashed into a little side door. We heard voices upstairs, a shuffle of feet and a noise as if a door had been shut.

"Up the stairs!" shouted Syrel, and we followed him, taking two steps at a bound. As we reached the top landing we were met by a young man.

"What right have you to enter this house?" he demanded.

"The right of the law," replied Syrel.

"I didn't do it," broke out the young man. "It was this way. Agnes Raymond loved me—she did not love Standish—he shot her; and God did not let her murder go unrevenged. It was well Mrs. Raymond killed him, for his blood would have been on my hands. I went back to see Agnes before she was buried. A man came in. I knocked him down. I didn't know until a moment ago that Mrs. Raymond had killed him."

"I forgot Mrs. Raymond!" screamed Syrel. "Where is she?"

"She is out of your power forever," said the young man.

Syrel brushed past him and, with Smidy and I following, burst open the door of the room at the head of the stairs. We rushed in.

On the floor lay a woman, and as soon as I touched her heart I knew she was beyond the doctor's skill.

"She has taken poison," I said. Syrel looked around; the young man had gone. And we stood there aghast in the presence of death.

READE, SUBSTITUTE RIGHT HALF

"Hold! Hold! Hold!" The slogan thundered up the field to where the battered Crimson warriors trotted wearily into their places again. The Blues' attack this time came straight at center and was good for a gain of seven yards.

"Second down, three!" yelled the referee, and again the attack came straight at center. This time there was no withstanding the rush and the huge Hilton full-back crushed through the Crimson line again and, shaking off his many tacklers, staggered on toward the Warrentown goal.

The midget Warrentown quarter-back ran nimbly up the field and, dodging the interference, shot in straight at the full-back's knees, throwing him to the ground. The teams sprang back into line again, but Hearst, the Crimson right tackle, lay still upon the ground. The right half was shifted to tackle and Berl, the captain, trotted over to the sidelines to ask the advice of the coaches.

"Who have we got for half, sir?" he inquired of the head coach.

"Suppose you try Reade," answered the coach, and calling to one of the figures on the pile of straw, which served as a seat for the substitutes, he beckoned to him. Pulling off his sweater, a light-haired stripling trotted over to the coach.

"Pretty light," said Berl as he surveyed the form before him.

"I guess that's all we have, though," answered the coach. Reade was plainly nervous as he shifted his weight from one foot to the other and fidgeted with the end of his jersey.

"Oh, I guess he'll do," said Berl. "Come on, kid," and they trotted off on the field.

The teams quickly lined up and the Hilton quarter gave the signal "6 – 8 – 7G." The play came between guard and tackle, but before the full-back could get started a lithe form shot out from the Warrentown line and brought him heavily to the ground.

"Good work, Reade," said Berl, as Reade trotted back into his place, and blushing at the compliment he crouched low in the line and waited for the play. The center snapped the ball to quarter, who, turning, was about to give it to the half. The ball slipped from his grasp and he reached for it, but too late. Reade had slipped in between the end and tackle and dropped on the ball.

"Good one, Reade," shouted Mirdle, the Warrentown quarter, as he came racing up, crying signals as he ran. Signal "48 – 10G – 37."

It was Reade around left end, but the pass was bad and the quarter dropped the ball. Reade scooped it up on a run and raced around left end. In the delay which had been caused by the fumble Reade's interference had been broken up and he must shift for himself. Even as he rounded the end he was thrown with a thud by the Blues' full-back. He had gained but a yard. "Never mind, Reade," said the quarter. "My fault." The ball was snapped, but again the pass was bad and a Hilton lineman fell on the ball.

Then began a steady march up the field toward the Warrentown goal. Time and time again Reade slipped through the Hilton line and nailed the runner before he could get started. But slowly Hilton pushed down the field toward the Warrentown goal. When the Blues were on the Crimson's ten-yard line their quarter-back made his only error of judgment during the game. He gave the signal for a forward pass. The ball was shot to the full-back, who turned to throw it to the right half. As the pigskin left his hand, Reade leaped upward and caught the ball. He stumbled for a moment, but, soon getting his balance, started out for the Hilton goal with a long string of Crimson and Blue men spread out behind him. He had a start of about five yards on his nearest opponent, but this distance was decreased to three before he had passed his own forty-five-yard line. He turned his head and looked back. His pursuer was breathing heavily and Reade saw what was coming. He was going to try a diving tackle. As the man's body shot out straight for him he stepped out of the way and the man fell harmlessly past him, missing him by a foot.

From there to the goal line it was easy running, and as Reade laid the pigskin on the ground and rolled happily over beside it he could just hear another slogan echo down the field: "One point—two points—three points—four points—five points. Reade! Reade! Reade!"

A DEBT OF HONOR

"Prayle!"

"Here."

"Martin!"

"Absent."

"Sanderson!"

"Here."

"Carlton, for sentry duty!"

"Sick."

"Any volunteers to take his place?"

"Me, me," said Jack Sanderson eagerly.

"All right," said the captain and went on with the roll.

It was a very cold night. Jack never quite knew how it came about. He had been wounded in the hand the day before and his grey jacket was stained a bright red where he had been hit by a stray ball. And "number six" was such a long post. From way up by the general's tent to way down by the lake. He could feel a faintness stealing over him. He was very tired and it was getting very dark—very dark.

They found him there, sound alseep, in the morning, worn out by the fatigue of the march and the fight which had followed it. There was nothing the matter with him save the wounds, which were slight, and military rules were very strict. To the last day of his life, Jack always remembered the sorrow in his captain's voice as he read aloud the dismal order.

Camp Bowling Green, C. S. A.

Jan. 15, 1863, U. S.

For falling asleep while in a position of trust at a sentry post, private John Sanderson is hereby condemned to be shot at sunrise on Jan. 16, 1863.

By order of

ROBERT E. LEE,

Lieutenant General Commanding.

Jack never forgot the dismal night and the march which followed it. They tied a hankerchief over his head and led him a little apart to a wall which bounded one side of the camp. Never had life seemed so sweet.

General Lee in his tent thought long and seriously upon the matter.

"He is so awfully young and of good family too; but camp discipline must be enforced. Still it was not much of an offense for such a punishment. The lad was over-tired and wounded. By George, he shall go free if I risk my reputation. Sergeant, order private John Sanderson to be brought before me."

"Very well, sir," and saluting, the orderly left the tent.

Jack was brought in, supported by two soldiers, for a reaction had set in after his narrow escape from death.

"Sir," said General Lee sternly, "on account of your extreme youth you will get off with a reprimand but see that it never happens again, for, if it should, I shall not be so lenient."

"General," answered Jack, drawing himself up to his full height; "the Confederate States of America shall never have cause to regret that I was not shot." And Jack was led away, still trembling, but happy in the knowledge of a newfound life.

Six weeks after with Lee's army near Chancellorsville. The success of Fredericksburg had made possible this advance of the Confederate arms. The firing had just commenced when a courier rode up to General Jackson.

"Colonel Barrows says, sir, that the enemy have possession of a small frame house on the outskirts of the woods and it overlooks our earthworks. Has he your permission to take it by assault?"

"My compliments to Colonel Barrows and say that I cannot spare more than twenty men but that he is welcome to charge with that number," answered the general.

"Yes, sir," and the orderly, setting spurs to his horse, rode away.

Five minutes later a column of men from the 3rd Virginia burst out from the woods and ran toward the house. A galling fire broke out from the Federal lines and many a brave man fell, among whom was their leader, a young lieutenant. Jack Sanderson sprang to the front and waving his gun encouraged the men onward. Halfway between the Confederate lines and the house was a small mound, and behind this the men threw themselves to get a minute's respite.

A minute later a figure sprang up and ran toward the house, and before the Union troops saw him he was halfway across the bullet-swept clearing. Then the Federal fire was directed at him. He staggered for a moment and placed his hand to his forehead. On he ran and reaching the house he quickly opened the door and went inside. A minute later a pillar of flame shot out of the windows of the house and almost immediately afterwards the Federal occupants were in full flight. A long cheer rolled along the Confederate lines and then the word was given to charge and they charged sweeping all before them. That night the searchers wended their way to the half-burned house. There on the floor, beside the mattress he had set on fire, lay the body of he who had once been John Sanderson, private, 3rd Virginia. He had paid his debt.

S.P.A. MEN IN COLLEGE ATHLETICS

For a school of from forty to sixty pupils the S.P.A. has more than held its own in supplying athletes to the colleges in all sports, but especially in football and hockey.

Probably the one of whom we have most to be proud is Springer Brooks, left end on the Yale varsity in 1910. Though he is not a graduate of the Academy, he attended school here for some time and received his A in football and hockey. In his junior year at Yale he was substitute left end on the squad and played through most of the West Point game and a large part of the Princeton game. That same year he went out for the skating honors and won his H in hockey. In his senior year he again went out for the football team and made regular left end. He was picked by several eastern newspaper men for the All-American team.

Another alumnus of St. Paul Academy is Carl Schunneman, who went to Yale Sheffield. He made the varsity crew in 1906 and rowed in the Yale–Harvard race, the same year. In 1908 he coached the freshman crew, but on account of ill health was forced to resign this position.

Next in the scale of prominence comes Roger Shepard, '05, who played on the Yale hockey varsity two years ago. This man, together with Conrad Driscoll, made a reputation for himself in hockey, and both were considered two of the best players in the country.

Milton Lightner, '05, was a long-distance man on the Yale track team and was considered one of the fastest men in college.

Hosmer Horton, right half-back on the Academy team of 1909, won his numerals by playing right-half on the Michigan freshman team of this year.

Bob Power, guard on the team of 1909, played guard on the Williams freshmen and acquitted himself very creditably.

"Gis" Wight, 1909, played a half on the Yale second team this year, while Paul Frye played end for awhile last year on the Minnesota freshmen, but quit on account of his studies.

Arthur Driscoll was on his class crew at Yale and his younger brother, Teddy, played half and afterwards full on the Hill football team of 1909.

Preston White was manager of the Football Association at Yale, and the same year Milton Griggs was manager of the Yale track team.

THE ROOM WITH THE GREEN BLINDS

It was ominous-looking enough in broad daylight, with its dull, brown walls, and musty windows. The garden, if it might be called so, was simply a mass of overgrown weeds, and the walk was falling to pieces, the bricks crumbling from the touch of time. Inside it was no better. Rickety old three-legged chairs, covered with a substance that had once been plush, were not exactly hospitable-looking objects. And yet this house was part of the legacy my grandfather had left me. In his will had been this clause: "The house, as it now stands, and all that is inside it, shall go to my grandson, Robert Calvin Raymond, on his coming to the age of twenty-one years. I furthermore desire that he shall not open the room at the end of the corridor on the second floor until Carmatle falls. He may fix up three rooms of the house as modern as he wishes, but let the others remain unchanged. He may keep but one servant."

To a poor young man with no outlook in life, and no money, but a paltry eight hundred a year, this seemed a windfall when counted with the twenty-five thousand dollars that went with it. I resolved to fix up my new home, and so started South to Macon, Georgia, near which my grandfather's house was situated. All the evening on the Pullman I had thought about that clause, "He shall not open the room at the end of the corridor on the second floor until Carmatle falls." Who was Carmatle? And what did it mean when it said, "until Carmatle falls?" In vain I supposed and guessed and thought; I could make no sense of it.

When I finally arrived at the house, I lighted one of a box of candles which I had brought with me and walked up the creaking stairs to the second floor and down a long, narrow corridor covered with cobwebs and bugs of all sorts till I finally came to a massive oaken door which barred my further progress. On the door I could just make out with the aid of the candle the initials J. W. B. in red paint. The door was barred on the outside by heavy iron bars, effectually barricaded against anybody entering or going out. Suddenly, without even a warning flicker, my candle went out, and I found myself in complete darkness. Though I am not troubled with weak nerves, I confess I was somewhat startled by this, for there was not a breath of air stirring. I relit the candle and walked out of the corridor down to the room of the three-legged chairs. As it was now almost nine o'clock and as I was tired after my day of traveling, I soon fell off to sleep.

How long I slept I do not know. I awoke suddenly and sat bolt upright on the lounge. For far down the downstairs hall I heard approaching footsteps, and a second later saw the reflection of a candle on the wall outside my door. I made no noise but as the steps came closer I crept softly to my feet. Another sound and the intruder was directly outside and I had a look at him. The flickering flame of the candle shone on a strong, handsome face, fine brown eyes and a determined chin. A stained grey Confederate uniform covered a magnificent form and here and there a bloodstain made him more weird as he stood looking straight ahead with a glazed stare. His clean-shaven face seemed strangely familiar to me, and some instinct made me connect him with the closed door on the right wing.

I came to myself with a start and crouched to leap at him, but some noise I made must have alarmed him, for the candle was suddenly extinguished and I brought up against a chair, nursing a bruised shin. I spent the rest of the night trying to connect the clause in my uncle's will with this midnight prowler.

When morning came, things began to look clearer, and I resolved to find out whether I had been dreaming or whether I had had a Confederate officer for a guest. I went into the hall and searched for any sign which might lead to a revelation of the mystery. Sure enough, just outside my door was a tallow stain. About ten yards further on was another, and I found myself following a trail of spots along the hall, and upstairs toward the right wing of the house. About twenty feet from the door of the forbidden room they stopped; neither was there any trace of anyone having gone further.

I walked up to the door and tried it to make sure that no one could possibly go in or out. Then I descended and, sauntering out, went around to the east wing to see how it looked from the outside. The room had three windows, each of which was covered with a green blind, and with three iron bars. To make sure of this I went around to the barn, a tumbly old structure and, by dint of much exertion, succeeded in extracting a ladder from a heap of debris behind it. I placed this against the house, and climbing up, tested each bar carefully. There was no deception. They were firmly set in the concrete sill.

Therefore, there could be but one explanation. The man concealed there must have a third way of getting out, some sort of secret passageway. With this thought in mind I searched the house from garret to cellar, but not a sign could I see of any secret entrance. Then I sat down to think it over.

In the first place there was somebody concealed in the room in the east wing. I had no doubt of that. Who was in the habit of making midnight visits to the front hall? Who was Carmatle? It was an unusual name, and I felt if I could find its possessor I could unravel this affair.

Aha! now I had it. Carmatle, the governor of Georgia; why had I not thought of that before? I resolved that that afternoon I would start for Atlanta to see him.

II

"Mr. Carmatle, I believe?"

"At your service."

"Governor, it's rather a personal matter I have come to see you about and I may have made a mistake in identity. Do you know anything about 'J. W. B.' or did you ever know a man with those initials?"

The governor paled.

"Young man, tell me where you heard those initials and what brought you here."

In as few words as possible I related to him my story, beginning with the will and ending with my theories regarding it.

When I had finished, the governor rose to his feet.

"I see it all; I see it all. Now with your permission I shall spend a night with you in your house in company with a friend of mine who is in the Secret Service. If I am right, concealed in that house is—well," he broke off. "I had better not say now, for it may be only a remarkable coincidence. Meet me at the station in half an hour, and you had better bring a revolver."

Six o'clock found us at the manor; and the governor and I, with the detective he had brought along, a fellow by the name of Butler, proceeded at once to the room.

After half an hour's labor we succeeded in finding no such thing as a passageway, secret or otherwise. Being tired I sat down to rest and in doing so my hand touched a ledge projecting from the wall. Instantly a portion of the wall swung open, disclosing an opening about three feet square. Instantly the governor, with the agility of a cat, was through it and his form disappeared from view. We grasped the situation and followed him. I found myself crawling along on hard stone in black darkness. Suddenly a shot resounded, and another. Then the passageway came to an end. We were in a room magnificently hung with oriental draperies, the walls covered with medieval armor and ancient swords, shields and battle axes. A red lamp on the table threw a lurid glare over all and cast a red glow on a body which lay at the foot of a Turkish divan. It was the Confederate officer, shot through the heart, for the life blood was fast staining his grey uniform red. The governor was standing near the body, a smoking revolver in his hand.

"Gentlemen," said he, "let me present to you John Wilkes Booth, the slayer of Abraham Lincoln."

III

"Mr. Carmatle, you will explain this I hope."

"Certainly," and drawing up a chair the governor began:

"My son and I served in Forrest's cavalry during the Civil War, and being on a scouting expedition did not hear of Lee's surrender at Appomattox until about three months afterwards. As we were riding southward along the Cumberland Pike we met a man riding down the road. Having struck up an acquaintance, as travelers do, we camped together. The next morning the man was gone, together with my son's old horse and my son's old uniform, leaving his new horse and new civilian suit instead. We did not know what to make of this, but never suspected who this man was. My son and I separated and I never saw him again. He was bound for his aunt's in western Maryland and one morning he was shot by some Union soldiers in a barn where he had tried to snatch a minute's rest on the way. The story was given out to the public that it was Booth that was shot but I knew and the government knew that my innocent son had been shot by mistake and that John Wilkes Booth, the man who had taken his horse and clothes, had escaped. For four years I hunted Booth, but until I heard you mention the initials J. W. B. I had heard no word of him. As it was, when I found him he shot first. I think that his visit to the hall in the Confederate uniform was simply to frighten you away. The fact that your grandfather was a Southern sympathizer probably had protected him all these years. So now, gentlemen, you have heard my story. It rests with you whether this gets no farther than us three here and the government, or whether I shall be proclaimed a murderer and brought to trial."

"You are as innocent as Booth is guilty," said I. "My lips shall be forever sealed."

And we both pressed forward and took him by the hand.

THE NEWMAN SCHOOL
1911–1913

"FOOTBALL"

Now they're ready, now they're waiting,
Now he's going to place the ball.
There, you hear the referee's whistle,
As of old the baton's fall.
See him crouching. Yes, he's got it;
Now he's off around the end.
Will the interference save him?
Will the charging line now bend?
Good, he's free; no, see that half-back
Gaining up behind him slow.
Crash! they're down; he threw him nicely,—
Classy tackle, hard and low.
Watch that line, now crouching waiting,
In their jerseys white and black;
Now they're off and charging, making
Passage for the plunging back.
Buck your fiercest, run your fastest,
Let the straight-arm do the rest.
Oh, they got him; never mind, though,
He could only do his best.
What is this? A new formation.
Look! their end acts like an ass.
See, he's beckoning for assistance,
Maybe it's a forward pass.
Yes, the ball is shot to full-back,
He, as calmly as you please,
Gets it, throws it to the end; he
Pulls the pigskin down with ease.
Now they've got him. No, they haven't.
See him straight-arm all those fools.

Look, he's clear. Oh, gee! don't stumble.
Faster, faster, for the school.
There's the goal, now right before you,
Ten yards, five yards, bless your name!
Oh! you Newman, 1911,
You know how to play the game.

ELECTION NIGHT

If a stranger had approached the school on election night, he would have come upon a strange scene. His first thought would have been that the long buried New Jersey Indians had risen from their graves and were commemorating the burning of an enemy. In the glare of a huge bonfire, merrily blazing in the crisp November night, danced sixty-five boys arrayed in sweaters, jerseys and all manner of old clothes. Some sang, some yelled, some talked, but all managed to show by some form of vocal expression that there were sixty-five of them, and that they were working off two months of pent-up energy. When the first wild rush around the fire is over, wrestling matches are organized, a ring formed, and the air resounds with cries of "Get him, Fat!" "We're for you, Red!" "Gosh, but he's ferocious!" and the two contestants, plainly seen in the glare of the fire, edge around, feeling each other cautiously, and finally rolling over and over in a mass of arms and legs. The precious minutes speed on. Too soon a whistle is heard, and there is a rush for the houses, for it is half-past nine and the election-night revel is over.

A LUCKLESS SANTA CLAUS

Miss Harmon was responsible for the whole thing. If it had not been for her foolish whim, Talbot would not have made a fool of himself, and—but I am getting ahead of my story.

It was Christmas Eve. Salvation Army Santa Clauses with highly colored noses proclaimed it as they beat upon rickety paper chimneys with tin spoons. Package-laden old bachelors forgot to worry about how many slippers and dressing gowns they would have to thank people for next day, and joined in the general air of excitement that pervaded busy Manhattan.

In the parlor of a house situated on a dimly lighted residence street, somewhere east of Broadway, sat the lady who, as I have said before, started the whole business. She was holding a conversation half frivolous, half sentimental, with a faultlessly dressed young man who sat with her on the sofa. All of this was quite right and proper, however, for they were engaged to be married in June.

"Harry Talbot," said Dorothy Harmon, as she rose and stood laughing at the merry young gentleman beside her, "if you aren't the most ridiculous boy I ever met, I'll eat that terrible box of candy you brought me last week!"

"Dorothy," reproved the young man, "you should receive gifts in the spirit in which they are given. That box of candy cost me much of my hard-earned money."

"Your hard-earned money, indeed!" scoffed Dorothy. "You know very well that you never earned a cent in your life. Golf and dancing—that is the sum total of your occupations. Why you can't even spend money, much less earn it!"

"My dear Dorothy, I succeeded in running up some very choice bills last month, as you will find if you consult my father."

"That's not spending your money. That's wasting it. Why, I don't think you could give away twenty-five dollars in the right way to save your life."

"But why on earth," remonstrated Harry, "should I want to give away twenty-five dollars?"

"Because," explained Dorothy, "that would be real charity. It's nothing to charge a desk to your father and have it sent to me, but to give money to people you don't know is something."

"Why, any old fellow can give away money," protested Harry.

"Then," exclaimed Dorothy, "we'll see if you can! I don't believe that you could give twenty-five dollars in the course of an evening if you tried."

"Indeed, I could."

"Then try it!" And Dorothy, dashing into the hall, took down his coat and hat and placed them in his reluctant hands. "It is now half-past eight. You be here by ten o'clock."

"But, but," gasped Harry.

Dorothy was edging him towards the door.

"How much money have you?" she demanded.

Harry gloomily put his hand in his pocket and counted out a handful of bills.

"Exactly twenty-five dollars and five cents."

"Very well! Now listen! These are the conditions. You go out and give this money to anybody you care to whom you have never seen before. Don't give more than two dollars to any one person. And be back here by ten o'clock with no more than five cents in your pocket."

"But," declared Harry, still backing toward the door, "I *want* my twenty-five dollars."

"Harry," said Dorothy sweetly, "I am *surprised!*" And with that, she slammed the door in his face.

"I insist," muttered Harry, "that this is a most unusual proceeding."

He walked down the steps and hesitated.

"Now," he thought, "where shall I go?"

He considered a moment and finally started off toward Broadway. He had gone about half a block when he saw a gentleman in a top hat approaching. Harry hesitated. Then he made up his mind, and, stepping toward the man, emitted what he intended for a pleasant laugh but what sounded more like a gurgle, and loudly vociferated, "Merry Christmas, friend!"

"The same to you," answered he of the top hat, and would have passed on, but Harry was not to be denied.

"My good fellow—" he cleared his throat. "Would you like me to give you a little money?"

"What?" yelled the man.

"You might need some money, don't you know, to—er—buy the children—a—a rag doll," he finished brilliantly.

The next moment his hat went sailing into the gutter, and when he picked it up the man was far away.

"There's five minutes wasted," muttered Harry, as, full of wrath toward Dorothy, he strode along his way. He decided to try a different method with the next people he met. He would express himself more politely.

A couple approached him,—a young lady and her escort. Harry halted directly in their path and, taking off his hat, addressed them.

"As it is Christmas, you know, and everybody gives away—er—articles, why—"

"Give him a dollar, Billy, and let's go on," said the young lady.

Billy obediently thrust a dollar into Harry's hand, and at that moment the girl gave a cry of surprise.

"Why, it's Harry Talbot," she exclaimed, "begging!"

But Harry heard no more. When he realized that he knew the girl he turned and sped like an arrow up the street, cursing his foolhardiness in taking up the affair at all.

He reached Broadway and started slowly down the gaily lighted thoroughfare, intending to give money to the street Arabs he met. All around him was the bustle of preparation. Everywhere swarmed people happy in the pleasant concert of their own generosity. Harry felt strangely out of place as he wandered aimlessly along. He was used to being catered to and bowed before, but here no one spoke to him, and one or two even had the audacity to smile at him and wish him a "Merry Christmas." He nervously accosted a passing boy.

"I say, little boy, I'm going to give you some money."

"No you ain't," said the boy sturdily. "I don't want none of your money."

Rather abashed, Harry continued down the street. He tried to present fifty cents to an inebriated man, but a policeman tapped him on the shoulder and told him to move on. He drew up beside a ragged individual and quietly whispered, "Do you wish some money?"

"I'm on," said the tramp. "What's the job?"

"Oh! there's no *job!*" Harry reassured him.

"Tryin' to kid me, hey?" growled the tramp resentfully. "Well, get somebody else." And he slunk off into the crowd.

Next Harry tried to squeeze ten cents into the hand of a passing bellboy, but the youth pulled open his coat and displayed a sign "No Tipping."

With the air of a thief, Harry approached an Italian bootblack, and cautiously deposited ten cents in his hand. At a safe distance he saw the boy wonderingly pocket the dime, and congratulated himself. He had but twenty-four dollars and ninety cents yet to give away! His last success gave him a plan. He stopped at a newsstand where, in full sight of the vender, he dropped a two-dollar bill and sped away in the crowd. After several minutes' hard running he came to a walk amidst the curious glances of the bundle-laden passers-by, and was mentally patting himself on the back when he heard quick breathing behind him, and the very newsie he had just left thrust into his hand the two-dollar bill and was off like a flash.

The perspiration streamed from Harry's forehead and he trudged along despondently. He got rid of twenty-five cents, however, by dropping it into a children's aid slot. He tried to get fifty cents in, but it was a small slot. His first large sum was two dollars to a Salvation Army Santa Claus, and, after this, he kept a sharp lookout for them, but it was past their closing time, and he saw no more of them on his journey.

He was now crossing Union Square, and, after another half hour's patient work, he found himself with only fifteen dollars left to give away. A wet snow was falling which turned to slush as it touched the pavements, and the light dancing pumps he wore were drenched, the water oozing out of his shoes with every step he took. He reached Cooper Square and turned into the Bowery. The number of people on the streets was fast thinning and all around him shops were closing up and their occupants going home. Some boys jeered at him, but, turning up his collar, he plodded on. In his ears rang the saying, mocking yet kindly, "It is more blessed to give than to receive."

He turned up Third Avenue and counted his remaining money. It amounted to three dollars and seventy cents. Ahead of him he perceived, through the thickening snow, two men standing under a lamp post. Here was his chance. He could divide his three dollars and seventy cents between them. He came up to them and tapped one on the shoulder. The man, a thin, ugly-looking fellow, turned suspiciously.

"Won't you have some money, you fellow?" he said imperiously, for he was angry at humanity in general and Dorothy in particular. The fellow turned savagely.

"Oh!" he sneered, "you're one of these stiffs tryin' the charity gag, and then gettin' us pulled for beggin'. Come on, Jim, let's show him what we are."

And they showed him. They hit him, they mashed him, they got him down and jumped on him, they broke his hat, they tore his coat. And Harry, gasping, striking, panting, went down in the slush. He thought of the people who had that very night wished him a Merry Christmas. He was certainly having it.

Miss Dorothy Harmon closed her book with a snap. It was past eleven and no Harry. What was keeping him? He had probably given up and gone home long ago. With this in mind, she reached up to turn out the light, when suddenly she heard a noise outside as if someone had fallen.

Dorothy rushed to the window and pulled up the blind. There, coming up the steps on his hands and knees, was a wretched caricature of a man. He was hatless, coatless, collarless, tieless, and covered with snow. It was Harry. He opened the door and walked into the parlor, leaving a trail of wet snow behind him.

"Well?" he said defiantly.

"Harry," she gasped, "can it be you?"

"Dorothy," he said solemnly, "it is me."

"What—what has happened?"

"Oh, nothing. I've just been giving away that twenty-five dollars." And Harry sat down on the sofa.

"But Harry," she faltered, "your eye is all swollen."

"Oh, my eye? Let me see. Oh, that was on the twenty-second dollar. I had some difficulty with two gentlemen. However, we afterward struck up quite an acquaintance. I had some luck after that. I dropped two dollars in a blind beggar's hat."

"You have been all evening giving away that money?"

"My dear Dorothy, I have decidedly been all evening giving away that money." He rose and brushed a lump of snow from his shoulder. "I really must be going now. I have two—er—friends outside waiting for me." He walked towards the door.

"Two friends?"

"Why—a—they are the two gentlemen I had the difficulty with. They are coming home with me to spend Christmas. They are really nice fellows, though they might seem a trifle rough at first."

Dorothy drew a quick breath. For a minute no one spoke. Then he took her in his arms.

"Dearest," she whispered, "you did this all for me."

A minute later he sprang down the steps, and arm in arm with his friends, walked off in the darkness.

"Good-night, Dorothy," he called back, "and a Merry Christmas!"

PAIN AND THE SCIENTIST

Walter Hamilton Bartney moved to Middleton because it was quiet and offered him an opportunity of studying law, which he should have done long ago. He chose a quiet house rather out in the suburbs of the village, for, as he reasoned to himself, "Middleton is a suburb and remarkably quiet at that. Therefore a suburb of a suburb must be the very depth of solitude, and that is what I want." So Bartney chose a small house in the suburbs and settled down. There was a vacant lot on his left, and on his right Skiggs, the famous Christian Scientist. It is because of Skiggs that this story was written.

Bartney, like the very agreeable young man he was, decided that it would be only neighborly to pay Skiggs a visit, not that he was very much interested in the personality of Mr. Skiggs, but because he had never seen a real Christian Scientist and he felt that his life would be empty without the sight of one.

However, he chose a most unlucky time for his visit. It was one night, dark as pitch, that, feeling restless, he set off as the clock struck ten to investigate and become acquainted. He strode out of his lot and along the path that went by the name of a road, feeling his way between bushes and rocks and keeping his eye on the solitary light that burned in Mr. Skiggs' house.

"It would be blamed unlucky for me if he should take a notion to turn out that light," he muttered through his clenched teeth. "I'd be lost. I'd just have to sit down and wait until morning."

He approached the house, felt around cautiously, and, reaching for what he thought was a step, uttered an exclamation of pain, for a large stone had rolled down over his leg and pinned him to the earth. He grunted, swore, and tried to move the rock, but he was held powerless by the huge stone, and his efforts were unavailing.

"Hello!" he shouted. "Mr. Skiggs!"

There was no answer.

34

"Help in there," he cried again. "Help!"

A light was lit upstairs and a head, topped with a conical-shaped night-cap, poked itself out of the window like an animated jack-in-the-box.

"Who's there?" said the night-cap in a high-pitched querulous voice. "Who's there? Speak, or I fire."

"Don't fire! It's me—Bartney, your neighbor. I've had an accident, a nasty ankle wrench, and there's a stone on top of me."

"Bartney?" queried the night-cap, nodding pensively. "Who's Bartney?"

Bartney swore inwardly.

"I'm your neighbor. I live next door. This stone is very heavy. If you would come down here—"

"How do I know you're Bartney, whoever he is?" demanded the night-cap. "How do I know you won't get me out there and blackjack me?"

"For heaven's sake," cried Bartney, "look and see. Turn a search-light on me, and see if I'm not pinned down."

"I have no searchlight," came the voice from above.

"Then you'll have to take a chance. I can't stay here all night."

"Then go away. I am not stopping you," said the night-cap with a decisive squeak in his voice.

"Mr. Skiggs," said Bartney in desperation, "I am in mortal agony and—"

"You are not in mortal agony," announced Mr. Skiggs.

"What? Do you still think I'm trying to entice you out here to murder you?"

"I repeat, you are not in mortal agony. I am convinced now that you really think you are hurt, but I assure you, you are not."

"He's crazy," thought Bartney.

"I shall endeavor to prove to you that you are not, thus causing you more relief than I would if I lifted the stone. I am very moderate. I will treat you now at the rate of three dollars an hour."

"An hour?" shouted Bartney fiercely. "You come down here and roll this stone off me, or I'll skin you alive!"

"Even against your will," went on Mr. Skiggs. "I feel called upon to treat you; for it is a duty to everyone to help the injured, or rather those who fancy themselves injured. Now, clear your mind of all sensation, and we will begin the treatment."

"Come down here, you mean, low-browed fanatic!" yelled Bartney, forgetting his pain in a paroxysm of rage. "Come down here, and I'll drive every bit of Christian Science out of your head."

"To begin with," began the shrill falsetto from the window, "there is no pain—absolutely none. Do you begin to have an inkling of that?"

"No," shouted Bartney. "You, you—" his voice was lost in a gurgle of impotent rage.

"Now, all is mind. Mind is everything. Matter is nothing—absolutely nothing. You are well. You fancy you are hurt, but you are not."

"You lie!" shrieked Bartney.

Unheeding, Mr. Skiggs went on.

"Thus, if there is no pain, it cannot act on your mind. A sensation is not physical. If you had no brain, there would be no pain, for what you call pain acts on the brain. You see?"

"Oh-h," cried Bartney, "if you saw what a bottomless well of punishment you were digging for yourself, you'd cut out that monkey business."

"Therefore, as so-called pain is a mental sensation, your ankle doesn't hurt you. Your brain may imagine it does, but all sensation goes to the brain. You are very foolish when you complain of hurt—"

Bartney's patience wore out. He drew in his breath, and let out a yell that echoed and re-echoed through the night air.

He repeated it again and again, and at length he heard the sound of footsteps coming up the road.

"Hello!" came a voice.

Bartney breathed a prayer of thanksgiving.

"Come here! I've had an accident," he called, and a minute later the night watchman's brawny arms had rolled the stone off him and he staggered to his feet.

"Good-night," called the Christian Scientist sweetly. "I hope I have made some impression on you."

"You certainly have," called back Bartney as he limped off, his hand on the watchman's shoulder, "one I won't forget."

Two days later, as Bartney sat with his foot on a pillow, he pulled an unfamiliar envelope out of his mail and opened it. It read:

WILLIAM BARTNEY.

TO HEPEZIA SKIGGS, DR.

Treatment by Christian Science—$3.00. Payment by check or money order.

* * * * * * * * *

The weeks wore on. Bartney was up and around. Out in his yard he started a flower garden and became a floral enthusiast. Every day he planted, and the next day he would weed what he had planted. But it gave him something to do, for law was tiresome at times.

One bright summer's day, he left his house and strolled toward the garden, where the day before he had planted in despair some "store-bought" pansies. He perceived to his surprise a long, thin, slippery-looking figure bending over, picking his new acquisitions. With quiet tread he approached, and, as the invader turned around, he said severely:

"What are you doing, sir?"

"I was plucking—er—a few posies—"

The long, thin, slippery-looking figure got no further. Though the face had been strange to Bartney, the voice, a thin, querulous falsetto, was one he would never forget. He advanced slowly, eyeing the owner of that voice, as the wolf eyes his prey.

"Well, Mr. Skiggs, how is it I find you on my property?"

Mr. Skiggs appeared unaccountably shy and looked the other way.

"I repeat," said Bartney, "that I find you here on my property—and in my power."

"Yes, sir," said Mr. Skiggs, squirming in alarm.

Bartney grabbed him by the collar, and shook him as a terrier does a rat.

"You conceited imp of Christian Science! You miserable hypocrite! What?" he demanded fiercely, as Skiggs emitted a cry of protest. "You yell. How dare you? Don't you know there is no such thing as pain? Come on, now, give me some of that Christian Science. Say 'mind is everything.' Say it!"

Mr. Skiggs, in the midst of his jerky course, said quaveringly, "Mind is everyth-thing."

"Pain is nothing," urged his tormenter grimly.

"P-Pain is nothing," repeated Mr. Skiggs feelingly.

The shaking continued.

"Remember, Skiggs, this is all for the good of the cause. I hope you're taking it to heart. Remember, such is life, therefore life is such. Do you see?"

He left off shaking, and proceeded to entice Skiggs around by a grip on his collar, the scientist meanwhile kicking and struggling violently.

"Now," said Bartney, "I want you to assure me that you feel no pain. Go on, do it!"

"I f-feel—ouch," he exclaimed as he passed over a large stone in his course, "n-no pain."

"Now," said Bartney, "I want two dollars for the hour's Christian Science treatment I have given you. Out with it."

Skiggs hesitated, but the look of Bartney's eyes and a tightening of Bartney's grip convinced him, and he unwillingly tendered a bill. Bartney tore it to pieces and distributed the fragments to the wind.

"Now, you may go."

Skiggs, when his collar was released, took to his heels, and his flying footsteps crossed the boundary line in less time than you would imagine.

"Good-bye, Mr. Skiggs," called Bartney pleasantly. "Any other time you want a treatment come over. The price is always the same. I see you know one thing I didn't have to teach you. There's no such thing as pain, when somebody else is the goat."

THE TRAIL OF THE DUKE

It was a hot July night. Inside, through screen, window and door, fled the bugs and gathered around the lights like so many humans at a carnival, buzzing, thugging, whirring. From out the night into the houses came the sweltering late summer heat, overpowering and enervating, bursting against the walls and enveloping all mankind like a huge smothering blanket. In the drug stores, the clerks, tired and grumbling, handed out ice cream to hundreds of thirsty but misled civilians, while in the corners buzzed the electric fans in a whirring mockery of coolness. In the flats that line upper New York, pianos (sweating ebony perspiration) ground out ragtime tunes of last winter, and here and there a wan woman sang the air in a hot soprano. In the tenements, shirt-sleeves gleamed like beacon lights in steady rows along the streets in tiers of from four to eight according to the number of stories of the house. In a word, it was a typical, hot New York summer night.

In his house on upper Fifth Avenue, young Dodson Garland lay on a divan in the billiard room and consumed oceans of mint juleps, as he grumbled at the polo that had kept him in town, the cigarettes, the butler, and occasionally breaking the Second Commandment. The butler ran back and forth with large consignments of juleps and soda and finally, on one of his dramatic entrances, Garland turned toward him and for the first time that evening perceived that the butler was a human being, not a living bottle-tray.

"Hello, Allen," he said, rather surprised that he had made such a discovery. "Are you hot?"

Allen made an expressive gesture with his handkerchief, tried to smile but only succeeded in a feeble, smothery grin.

"Allen," said Garland struck by an inspiration, "what shall I do tonight?" Allen again essayed the grin but, failing once more, sank into a hot, undignified silence.

"Get out of here," exclaimed Garland petulantly, "and bring me another julep and a plate of ice."

"Now," thought the young man, "what shall I do? I can go to the theatre and melt. I can go to a roof garden and be sung to by a would-be prima donna, or—or go calling." "Go calling," in Garland's vocabulary meant but one thing: to see Mirabel. Mirabel Walmsley was his fiancée since some three months, and was in the city to receive some nobleman or other who was to visit her father. The lucky youth yawned, rolled over, yawned again and rose to a sitting position where he yawned a third time and then got to his feet.

"I'll walk up and see Mirabel. I need a little exercise." And with this final decision he went to his room where he dressed, sweated and dressed, for half an hour. At the end of that time, he emerged from his residence, immaculate, and strolled up Fifth Avenue to Broadway. The city was all outside. As he walked along the white way, he passed groups and groups clad in linen and lingerie, laughing, talking, smoking, smiling, all hot, all uncomfortable.

He reached Mirabel's house and then suddenly stopped on the doorstep.

"Heavens," he thought, "I forgot all about it. The Duke of Dunsinlane or Artrellane or some lane or other was to arrive today to see Mirabel's papa. Isn't that awful? And I haven't seen Mirabel for three days." He sighed, faltered, and finally walked up the steps and rang the bell. Hardly had he stepped inside the door, when the vision of his dreams came running into the hall in a state of great excitement and perturbation.

"Oh, Doddy!" she burst out, "I'm in an awful situation. The Duke went out of the house an hour ago. None of the maids saw him go. He just wandered out. You must find him. He's probably lost—lost and nobody knows him." Mirabel wrung her hands in entrancing despair. "Oh, I shall die if he's lost—and it's so hot. He'll have a sunstroke surely or a—moonstroke. Go and find him. We've telephoned the police, but it won't do any good. Hurry up! Do! Oh, Doddy, I'm so nervous."

"Doddy" put his hands in his pockets, sighed, put his hat on his head and sighed again. Then he turned toward the door. Mirabel, her face anxious, followed him.

"Bring him right up here if you find him. Oh Doddy you're a life-saver." The life-saver sighed again and walked quickly through the portal. On the doorstep he paused.

"Well, of all outrageous things! To hunt for a French Duke in New York. This is outrageous. Where shall I go? What will I do?" He paused at the doorstep and then, following the crowd, strode toward Broadway. "Now let me see. I must have a plan of action. I can't go up and ask everybody I meet if he's the Duke of —, well of, well—I can't remember his name. I don't know what he looks like. He probably can't talk English. Oh, curses on the nobility."

He strode aimlessly, hot and muddled. He wished he had asked Mirabel the Duke's name and personal appearance, but it was now too late. He would not convict himself of such a blunder. Reaching Broadway he suddenly bethought himself of a plan of action.

"I'll try the restaurants." He started down toward Sherry's and had gone but half a block when he had an inspiration. The Duke's picture was in some evening paper, and his name, too.

He bought a paper and sought for the picture with no result. He tried again and again. On his seventh paper he found it: "The Duke of Matterlane Visits American Millionaire."

The Duke, a man with side whiskers and eye-glasses, stared menacingly at him from the paper. Garland heaved a sigh of relief, took a long look at the likeness and stuck the paper into his pocket.

"Now to business," he muttered, wiping his drenched brow. "Duke or die."

Five minutes later he entered Sherry's, where he sat down and ordered ginger ale. There was the usual summer night crowd, listless, flushed, and sunburned. There was the usual champagne and ice that seemed hotter than the room; but there was no Duke. He sighed, rose, and visited Delmonico's, Martin's, at each place consuming a glass of ginger ale.

"I'll have to cut out the drinking," he thought, "or I'll be inebriated by the time I find his royal nuisance."

On his weary trail, he visited more restaurants and more hotels, ever searching, sometimes thinking he saw an oasis and finding it only a mirage. He had consumed so much ginger ale that he felt a swaying sea-sickness as he walked; yet he plodded on, hotter and hotter, uncomfortable, and, as Alice in Wonderland would have said, uncomfortabler. His mind was grimly and tenaciously set on the Duke's face. As he walked along, from hotel to café, from café to restaurant, the Duke's whiskers remained glued firmly to the insides of his brains. It was half past eight by the City Hall clock when he started on his quest. It was now quarter past ten, hotter, sultrier and stuffier than ever. He had visited every important place of refreshment. He tried the drug stores. He went to four theatres and had the Duke paged, at a large bribe. His money was getting low, his spirits were lower still, but his temperature soared majestically and triumphantly aloft.

Finally, passing through an alley which had been recommended to him as a short cut, he saw before him a man lighting a cigarette. By the flickering match he noticed the whiskers. He stopped dead in his tracks, afraid that it might not be the Duke. The man lit another cigarette. Sure enough, the sideburns, eyeglasses and the whole face proved the question without a doubt.

Garland walked toward the man. The man looked back at him and started to walk in the opposite direction. Garland started to run; the man looked over his shoulder and started to run also. Garland slowed down. The man slowed down. They emerged upon Broadway in the same relative position, and the man started north. Forty feet behind, in stolid determination, walked Garland without his hat. He had left it in the alley.

For eight blocks they continued, the man behind being the pacemaker. Then the Duke spoke quietly to a policeman and when Garland, lost in an obsession of pursuit, was grabbed by the arm by a blue-coated Gorgas, he saw ahead of him the Duke start to run. In a frenzy he struck at the policeman and stunned him. He ran on and in three blocks he had made up what he had lost. For five more blocks the Duke continued, glancing now and then over his shoulder. On the sixth block he stopped. Garland approached him with steady step. He of the side whiskers was standing under a lamp post. Garland came up and put his hand on his shoulder.

"Your Grace."

"What's dat?" said the Duke, with an unmistakable East-Side accent. Garland was staggered.

"I'll grace you," continued the sideburns aggressively. "I saw you was a swell and I'd a dropped you bad only I'm just out of jail myself. Now listen here. I'll give you two seconds to get scarce. Go on, beat it."

Garland beat it. Crestfallen and broken-hearted he walked away and set off for Mirabel's. He would at least make a decent ending to a miserable quest. A half an hour later he rang the bell, his clothes hanging on him like a wet bathing suit.

Mirabel came to the door, cool and fascinating.

"Oh Doddy!" she exclaimed. "Thank you so much. Dukey," and she held up a small white poodle which she had in her arms, "came back ten minutes after you left. He had just followed the mailman."

Garland sat down on the step.

"But the Duke of Matterlane?"

"Oh," said Mirabel, "he comes tomorrow. You must come right over and meet him."

"I'm afraid I can't," said Garland, rising feebly. "Previous engagement." He paused, smiled faintly and set off across the sultry moonlit pavement.

A SCHOOL DANCE

Whenever authority announces that there is soon to be a dance, pandemonium reigns. The corridors and common-room are immediately filled with semi-graceful figures swaying rythmically or unrythmically in time to a one-fingered "Boston" played by some obliging youth. The air resounds with cries of "Look at Bill!" "Keep hopping Bill!" "Show me that step, Jack." "Try it yourself." "Say, Joe's sister is coming out." The boy with pretty sisters is beset with obliging fellows willing to fill out their cards. So the dances are reserved and the hopping becomes softened to a more graceful expression of the terpsichorean art until the dance comes, and reality takes the place of anticipation.

PRINCETON UNIVERSITY
1914–1919

Triangle Show Lyrics

FIE! FIE! FI-FI!

OPENING CHORUS

Chorus of Guests
Cynical, critical, bored and analytical.
Visitors from ev'ry land that sports a millionaire,
Nouveau riche, pedigreed, of a high or petty breed,
Wandering from place to place to get a traveled air.

Guests
Fishing in Sardinia, frightened in Armenia,
Tired to death at Paris, although London makes us glum.
Read a guidebook Litany of Normandy and Brittany;
Since the others bore, to Monte Carlo we have come.

Chorus of Adventuresses
Ou, la, la, love is just a game of chance.
Ou, la, la, love is like Roulette
Ou, la, la, you may find some romance
Play then tho' it bring regret.
Ou, la, la, there's a chance to break the bank,
Ou, la, la, or the hearts of men.
Ou, la, la, if you like excitement
À la mode Parisienne.

Cholmondely
Oh, I'm Tommy, Tommy Atkins of the guards
And I'm strolling up and down the Boulevards
When it comes to the art of breaking a heart,
I'm clever as can be,
For I'm Tommy, Tommy Atkins of the guards.

Full Chorus
Oh he's Tommy, Tommy Atkins of the guards,
And he's strolling up and down the Boulevards,
When it comes to the art of breaking a heart,
He's clever as can be,
For he's Tommy, Tommy Atkins of the guards,
He is, yes, he's Tommy, Tommy Atkins of the guards.

Female Chorus
Come on Tommy and flirt with us,
If you've nothing else to do.

Full Chorus
Ou, la, la, love is just a game of chance,
Ou, la, la, love is like Roulette.
Ou, la, la, you may find some romance
Play then tho' it bring regret.
Ou, la, la, there's a chance to break the bank,
Ou, la, la, or the hearts of men.
Ou, la, la, if you like excitement
À la mode Parisienne.

GENTLEMEN BANDITS WE

Del Monti and Bandit Chorus
Del Monti
Striving 'gainst foul conniving
And base contriving
I'm now a bandit.
This once
My council lusty
So true and trusty
Now roams with me.
Tho' we are burned and browned
Instincts will not be downed.

Roaming thro' grove and gloaming
Like pigeons homing
We've reached the city.
Biding
All safe in hiding
Then slyly gliding
We've come to town.
We've taken quite a chance
Risked all to watch a dance.

Chorus
All
Gentlemen Bandits we
Cultured in Burglary

Del M.
Verily so we are,

All
Merry we, tho' we are lawless!

Del M.
Thieving if done aright
Needn't be impolite

All
So we're gentlemen, gentlemen, gentlemen Bandits,
Yes!

A SLAVE TO MODERN IMPROVEMENTS

Clover
1. Oh my pa's an old physician with a curious ambition
To be a medical celebritie.
He did see his chance and grab it,
So he got into the habit
Of trying all his new ideas on me.

When I foolishly submitted
My ambitious father hit it,
That he might replace my parts with junk and so:
I'm a various collection
Born of modern vivisection.
I must confess I'm false from top to toe.

2. There's the scientific question of our power of digestion,
It worries some, it doesn't worry me.
And of course my father's dictum
Was that I should be the victim,
Get tested for my true capacity.
So they told me at the table "Eat as much as you are able,
So that we can find out what we want to know."
And they brought me in a platter,
What it bore, it doesn't matter,
And then producing watches told me "Go."

Chorus
1. A victim to modern improvements am I,
I've a silver chest and a crystal eye;
A platinum lung and a grafted nose,
Aluminum fingers,
Asbestos toes.
And when I walk I clank and clash,
And rust when damp, you see:
And the wildest lot of anonymous trash
That ever crossed the sea.

2. They fed me a match and a scarlet necktie,
A silver spoon and a croton pie,
Some stuff they called wine but I know they lied,
For I'm pretty sure it was Herpicide
They tried me on ink and LePage's glue
And some goldfish, two or three,
Then they crowded 'round and they said they had found
My full capacity.

IN HER EYES

Celeste and Archie

1. *Arch.*   When you're attached in a friendly way.
   Cel.   To a maid?
  Arch.   To a maid,
   Cel.   I see.
  Arch.   It's the deuce to pay
           When one's this way,
   Cel.   You're staid:
  Arch.   No afraid;
   Cel.   Dear me.
           Then what makes you dumb?
           Do you fear my scorn?
  Arch.   Not at all.
   Cel.   Not at all?
  Arch.   Oh no.
   Cel.   Well perhaps it's my smile,
           Or my frank open style;
  Arch.   It's your eyes,
   Cel.   My eyes?
  Arch.   That's so:

2. *Arch.*   Have you ever met with a villain bold?
   Cel.   I have.
  Arch.   Did you find it true
           That the rascal's eyes
           Were full of lies?
   Cel.   I did, didn't you?
  Arch.   I do.
           There're some eyes I know,
           That where'er I go
           Seem to haunt me in just that way.
   Cel.   Do you mean to imply
           That the light in my eye
           Is a villain's?
  Arch.   Oh, I say:

Chorus
Both
In her eyes, eyes, eyes,
There's a naughty little devil in her eyes
And he lies, lies, lies
Slyly waiting there to take you by surprise.
When she sighs, sighs, sighs
He is up in arms prepared to rise,
So be wise, wise, wise
And beware the little devil in her eyes.

WHAT THE MANICURE LADY KNOWS

Sady and Mrs. Bovine

1. *Sady*   Down behind my screen
             While your nails I clean
             Smiling at you, filing at you all the while
             With a gossip ear
             Many things I hear
             Pretty things and witty things that make you smile.
             While you wield the soap
             You can get the dope
             Pattering and chattering the livelong day.
             Listen to my plea
             Retail some to me;
             Gracious me, sagacious be
             And tell me what they say.

2. *Mrs. B.*   Madame, Major Voe
             Thinks the Count de Trop
   *Sady**   (dum-de-dum-de-dum-de-dum)
             Is that true?
             Madam Tête-à-tête
             Takes her whiskey straight
   Mrs. B.   (dum-de-dum-de-dum-de-dum) so they do.
             Countess Coyne they tell

---

* The parentheses are whispered to the time of the music.

Said to go to (dum)
When she was approached because of daughter's hand.

Sady	Three years on the stage
Mrs. B.	Hates to tell her age;
Sady	Jokes aside, she smokes beside
	And chews to beat the band.

Chorus

1. *Sady*   Count Von Hupp (de-dum) I fear
   Mrs. B. Quite a bit, quite a bit.
   Sady   (dum-de-dum-de-dum) I hear
   Mrs. B. Had a fit? Had a fit?
   Sady   Because the elder Madam (dum)
             Just starves herself for clothes.
   Both   Oh tell me wouldn't you like to hear,
             What the manicure lady knows.

2. *Mrs. B.* (Dum-de-dum-de-dum-de-dum)
   Sady   So I've heard, so I've heard;
   Mrs. B. (dum-de-dum-de-dum-de-dum)
   Sady   Not a word, not a word.
             My dear, don't speak of it, she paints
             And powders up her nose.
   Both   If you want dope on social taints,
             Why the manicure lady knows.

GOOD-NIGHT AND GOOD-BYE

Celeste and Archie

Dreams, sweet dreams of you
Will fill the night and day;
Though the morrow bring us sorrow,
I'll be holding you,
Dream arms enfolding you:
Keep your heart bright for me
And tho' we meet no more
You'll seem real in my dream, dear,
Still mine to adore;

Chorus
Then we'll say Good-Night and Good-Bye,
And never a sigh you'll see
Oh the violin's tune
Only sang in June
But a song was enough for me.
Oh, I dreamed my dream, heart alight,
I laughed for a night to the sky,
But my love's gone
Sped with the dawn;
So I bid you Good-Night and Good-Bye.

'ROUND AND 'ROUND

Celeste, Archie, Sady and Tracy

1. *Arch.*   If Victor's fond of Susie,
           And Susie takes to Sam,
Cel.   And Sam avers that he prefers
           That Mary be his lamb.
Tracy   But Mary quite contrary
           At Sam turns up her nose
Sady   Tho' Victor spurns, for him she yearns,
All   And that is how it goes.

2. *Tracy* If Gwen must marry Peter,
           She straightway takes to Bill,
Cel.   And so one day she runs away,
           To Pete, a bitter pill.
Arch.   But Bill now looks at Gladys
           Whose heart old Pete has got
Sady   But Pete don't care, altho' she's fair
           For Gwen is not forgot.

Chorus
All four
'Round and 'round and 'round and 'round
Goes the chain of love.

Brain a-whirling, all a-twirling,
Chase the dizzy dove:
It's love that makes the world go 'round
So all the sages tell;
But love itself as we have found
Goes 'round and 'round and 'round and 'round
And 'round and 'round and 'round and 'round
And 'round and 'round as well.

CHATTER TRIO

Sady, Mrs. Bovine and Del Monti

Del.   I'd like to hear a reason for this terrible commotion,
But if you try to talk so much I can't get any notion;
So restrain yourselves and take your time and let's discuss
    the question.
You act as though you had a touch of chronic indigestion
And as I need a lot of time for ev'ry mental action;
Kindly ease your flow of English,
Or you'll drive me to distraction.

Sady   He looks as if he needed time for ev'ry mental action:

Mrs. B.   And he must be rather simple if he's driven to distraction.

Sady   I was tearing off some ragtime on her fingers just as pretty,
When she makes a flat remark and I says:
"Gosh! you think you're witty"
Then she slung a lot of con about my plebeian position.
So I told her that she had a rather nasty disposition,
And I said that she would make a shapely stove
If she was thinner;
Then she hit me with a file, and so I stuck the scissors in
    her.

Mrs. B.   It's rather rude to prod a lady just before her dinner.

Del.   And it's not a very kindly thing to stick the scissors in her.

Mrs. B.   We called you in to settle this by peaceful arbitration,
So I wish you wouldn't listen to this woman's fabrication,
For the matter really started in a row about her money.
I said she overcharged me and she started getting funny

And so it's rather fresh of you to think that I'd begin it,
I'm getting very nervous I shall holler in a minute.

Del.   She didn't hurt your finger much,
           She only meant to skin it:

Sady   Well she's going to lose a thumb or two
           In less than half a minute.

FINALE ACT I

Principals and Chorus
Clover
How is it sir, you are with her
When you are pledged to me?

Blossom
Your love inter in sepulchre
We have your promise, see!

Celeste
Do you prefer yon dowager
To one so fair as I?

Archie
Don't make a stir, what they aver
Is some outrageous lie.

Celeste
Oh I dream my dream, heart alight
I laughed for a night to the sky
But my love's gone,
Sped with the dawn,
So I bid you good-night and good-bye!

Chorus
Ah, they are both on love intent
It's quite the height of sentiment
The question is, will she relent
And ruin this romance

They both adore, yet they must part
And nurse a bleeding broken heart
But still it is the height of art
Which nothing could enhance.

Blossom
Come, cheer up, you still have tonight to be gay,
But farewell to love on the break of day.

All
But tonight, tonight
What may occur tonight?
Wine and life, a lover's kiss,
I'd give all my life for this.
Tonight, Tonight.
Ev'rything may come right
So let's rejoice with merry voice,
And Hail the fair tonight.

ROSE OF THE NIGHT

Del Monti and Chorus
Del Monti
The flower of morning, the violet hue
Is blessed by the month of June.
And showered with kisses the whole Spring through
Are the flowers of afternoon.
Alone in a vale,
Without homage or heart, caressed by the stray beams bright:
And worshipped most madly, but worshipped apart,
Blooms the rose of the fairy night.

Ah, my rose, rose, rose of the night
The Spring moon's bright,
You'll be fair, fair, fair
In the spell of midnight air.
So come, come give me just a smile

A kiss under the starry light;
The eve's for play you die with the day,
Little rose of fair tonight.

MEN

Sady
I've lived my life in big hotels
I've seen a lot of men:
From Broadway bums to Newport swells,
From sixty down to ten.
There's the sentimental fellow
Who is rather nice at dusk,
Oh, his voice is sad and mellow
But his manner hints of musk.

To cynics with a manner mild
The ear I turn is deaf;
They think they talk like Oscar Wilde,
But reek of Mutt and Jeff.
There's the ogling man whose attitudes
Don't keep his dullness hid,
He woos you with such platitudes
As "peach" and "oh you kid."

Says the "business" man you read about
"I find I want you." See?
"I'll get you too without a doubt"
It never worked with me.
And the pious youth who dares to say:
I'm anything but slow,
He is toasting me in old Tokay
Before I let him go.

Chorus
Men, men, I've seen a lot of men,
A peculiar kind of insect

You will step on now and then.
A few to love, a few to hate,
You'd better leave them to their fate,
They're harmless
Don't exterminate the men.

IN THE DARK

Dulcette, Giuseppe, Del Monti and Mrs. Bovine

Men   Oh the eve is very dark
        So I'm sure we'll not be seen,
        If you join us for a lark,
        Night will be a perfect screen.
Girls Who you are we do not know,
        But you think convention stuff,
        So a little way we'll go
        If it's only dark enough.
Girls When you're sure you're out of sight,
        Better throw your cares away,
        There are things we do at night
        That we wouldn't do by day.
Men   Just a word and we are gone
        Far away beyond recall,
        We'll be back before the dawn,
        Or we won't be back at all.

Chorus
All

        In the dark, dark, dark,
        For a lark, lark, lark,
        Let's go, let's go.
        Oh the moon's never critical,
        The stars analytical,
        Oh, no, no, no!
        We may never know your pedigree
        Or ever see your face

But if we're sure there's no one 'round to hark
We'll go anywhere with anyone at any time or place,
If it's dark, quite dark.

LOVE OR EUGENICS

Celeste and Clover
Clover

1. My figure discloses no finicky poses
    No curve so soft and fair.
    No fashionable bustle but plenty of muscle,
    And Avoirdupois to spare.

Celeste

   Now I'm a most popular, tippular, toppular
   Maiden born to vex.
   And yet he prefers me and always avers me
   The queen of the feminine sex.

Clover

2. The rouge and the powder that make you look louder
    I always scorn to use.
    I'd rather be lorn with the face I was born with,
    A face never meant to abuse.

Celeste

   You scorn good cosmetics in verses ascetic
   But there's a reason alack!
   For powder looks smart on, with something to start on,
   A something you certainly lack.

Chorus
Both

   Ladies, here's a problem none of you can flee,
   Men, which would you like to come and pour your tea.
   Kisses that set your heart aflame,
   Or love from a prophylactic dame
   Ladies, take your choice of what your style shall be.

REMINISCENCE

Del Monti and Chorus
Del Monti
The shadows of evening have fallen at last
And memories sweet recall
The dream's gone forever, the joys long past,
The girls and the gaieties all
So fill to the brimming the cup of regret
And drink ere your fancies fly
Better to dream than to try and forget,
Tho' your dreams bring a tear to your eye:

Refrain
Solo
Dreams, dreams, dreams,
They're a part
Of the shimmering heart of the wine,
They whisper of past loves,
Of first loves,
Of last loves,
Of memories half divine.
Drink, drink, drink,
To her smile,
'Mid the fancies the years enhance.
The old loves go by,
But we'll pause for a sigh,
O'er the ashes of dead romance.

Male Quartet
Dreams, dreams, dreams,
They're a part of the shimmering heart of the wine:
They whisper of past loves,
Of first loves,
Of last loves.
Of memories half divine.
Drink, drink, drink,

To her smile,
Mid the fancies the years enhance.
The old loves go by
But we'll pause for a sigh,
O'er the ashes of dead romance.

FIE! FIE! FI-FI!

Sady and Company
Sady   *Company*
                                          Fie! Fie! Fi-fi!
                                          We're shocked that you are
                                          married.
                                          Sly, sly, Fi-fi,
                                          Your little plan miscarried.

I only did what I thought best.

                                          The place for you is way out West,
                                          From manicuring take a rest,
                                          For far too long you've tarried.
                                          Fie! Fie! Fi-fi!

It seems I'm in the way;

                                          Bye-bye, Fi-fi!

I guess I'll leave today.

                                          Your looks belie,
                                          Without a sigh, we'll say good-bye,
                                          Fie! Fie! Fi-fi!
                                          Fie! Fie! Fi-fi!
                                          Fie! Fie!

THE MONTE CARLO MOON

Celeste and Archie
Mem'ries calling sweetly to me
In the summer night:
Cupid with his arrows slew me
When the moon was bright.
We were drifting slowly, sweetly

On a half forgotten day
When he turned and whispered neatly:
"Don't you wish 'twould ne'er be day."
"It won't" said the summer breeze:
"It won't" said the whisp'ring trees.

Chorus
Underneath the Monte Carlo moon, dear,
In June dear, we'll stay:
Drifting to a gentle southern tune, dear,
On a sentimental Oriental Bay.
Dreaming in the silver starlight,
'Ere the dawn comes all too soon.
In the summer weather
We'll be there together
Underneath the Monte Carlo moon.

FINALE ACT II

Full Chorus
Underneath the Monte Carlo moonlight
The June night is gay
Laughing, loving, dancing to the music
Of a serenading joy-persuading lay
So the ruby wine is flowing,
Happy we will all be soon
All our woes are over,
Ev'ryone's in Clover,
Underneath the Monte Carlo moon.

THE EVIL EYE

OPENING CHORUS

Night Watchman
When the weary town is sleeping
Bar the watchman and the owl,
All around the streets we're creeping
Where the thieves and scoundrels prowl;
When the weary town is sleeping
We can hear the night winds howl
Till the tip of dawn come peeping
And the night-clouds cease to scowl.

'Neath the stars serenely beaming
With our eyes alert and wide
And our lanterns softly gleaming
Lest the sneaking rascal hide;
'Neath the stars serenely beaming
With our lanterns close beside
While the town is all a-dreaming
And the trick of thieves defied.

Oh, the sleepy-head,
Best get out of bed,
Dream your dreams no more;
See the morn is here,
Night has gone, dear,
Sandman's fled from your door.
He's forsaken you,
We will waken you,
Send us not away;

Shut your eyes and count to ten,
Better get up, 'tis day!

(*Entrance of Fishermen*)
Fishermen of character are we,
Picturesque and sturdy don't you see,
Up in the early morning
Bound for the stormy shore.
First we'll sing and then we'll disappear,
We'll be back directly don't you fear
'Though we be lonely
For the only girls we adore right here.

Ensemble
Come we'll sing a song of Brittany,
Ah! We'll tell our little history
All of a lonely maiden
Sighing in vain for love
Please applaud us till our course be run,
Jacques and Margot,
Claude and ev'ryone;
Dawn bells are ringing,
Time for singing,
On with the play,
'Tis morn!

I'VE GOT MY EYES ON YOU

Margot
Rumor says I'm very catty,
Rumor lies.
I admit I'm rather chatty,
Somewhat wise;
Air all guilt in the beginning,
As the sinners keep on sinning;
What there be to it

I'll see to it
It flies.

I but said that Missus Burt had turned Brunette;
She passed by with head averted
When we met.
Surely taking down a beauty
Should be ev'ry woman's duty;
Soon you'll yearn for it,
You'll burn for it,
I'll bet.

Chorus
So to my cause I'm true
I've got an eye on you
I can tell you I'm a real reformer,
Born to censor the haughty, punish the naughty.
Watch your step
Or you will lose your rep.
Conversation fattens on reputation,
Tho' it's just duty that's all.

ON DREAMS ALONE

Claude and Dulcinea
Dear heart, tho' night be dreary,
The stars of hope may gleam;
Faint stars make me but weary,
I'm tired of dreaming dreams.
Ah, then ever I'm lonely
For some once longed-for June, dear,
Dream on, I love you only,
And I'll come soon, dear.

Love's own paradise near us,
And yet we answer not;
Love's own ears wait to hear us,
And still our love's forgot.

Doubts, cares, sorrows we'll banish, if only you will wake me;
Else my dreams will all vanish,
And love forsake us.

Chorus
I'm dreaming all the while
My dreams grow bright at your smile.
Oh, I'll dream forever and aye
If dreams bring you some day,
Come live as love has shown.
Enough I call you my own;
For love, it seems
Can live on dreams,
On dreams alone.

THE EVIL EYE

Jacques
When I go harmlessly down the street,
They spread to left and to right.
If ever I'm near
They tremble with fear
And frequently die of fright.
I view a building; it's soon condemned;
I see some ships and they sink.
I look at a wife,
Her husband for life
Immediately takes to drink.
Ha, ha, ha, ha, ha, ha, ha, ha, ha.
A panic begins when I wink.

The Church collection on Sunday morn
Is not passed overly near.
They fear for its fate,
I'll shatter the plate,
And dollars will change to beer;
And all Theatres are closed to me,

The sleight-of-hand shark can't shine;
The lady that stars
On parallel bars
Collapses and breaks her spine.
Ha, ha, ha, ha, ha, ha, ha, ha, ha.
The bald-headed row change to swine.

Chorus
Beware lest I look behind
If anyone's sick
By chance or trick
I'm fined.
The devil also others of my adopted brothers
By comparison are most kind.
Beware of my passing glance
"It's worse than any curse," they cry.
It's all a story but just the same
I wish I had it, I'd play the game.
Beware, Beware, Beware, The Evil Eye.

WHAT I'LL FORGET

The Girl
I'm a girl who hasn't any memory,
It doesn't worry me at all;
Chorus girl or cast girl, prim girl, fast girl,
Dance, or just dance hall.
I've forgotten all the ills the doctor wants,
Appendicitis haunts me not;
Maybe I am ailing, slowly, surely, failing,
But I've quite forgot.

I'll forget the furry shoes they wear about,
Or rather tear about in, now,
Winter Garden dollies,
Cafés, "Follies,"
Dance—I don't know how.

I've forgotten all the stone-age sentiment
That used to find a vent in me;
When they say I'm pretty, then I think they're witty,
Such simplicity!

Chorus
I've forgotten all the fashions and the passions
That are current in the present century,
All my past, perhaps a hot one, husband if I've got one,
And maybe I'm a refugee;
I've forgotten all the Balkan situation,
I've forgotten whether hoops are stylish yet;
But the wonderful sensation of
This mental dislocation,
That's the only thing I can't forget.

I've forgotten all the hints to beauty seekers
Which the Sunday supplement will give you free,
All my past, perhaps a hot one, husband if I've got one,
And maybe I'm a refugee;
I've forgotten if my age is worth concealing,
I've forgotten ev'ry bill and ev'ry debt;
But the wonderful sensation of
This mental dislocation,
That's the only thing I can't forget.

OVER THE WAVES TO ME

Jacques and The Girl
I've dreamt alone on the ocean track
When the stars were pale and cold
And the night clouds gathered scowling black
Of a face I should once behold,
A whisper sweet in a midnight blow,
A smile on a twilight wave;
But who was a fisher to dream on so
I, a dreamer to dreams a slave.

The sea that sang to a heart of stone on the cliff-side years ago
Sang its hope to one who was lost alone
With the surge of its breakers low;
"Oh, bring my love and my life," I cried,
"And bring back my heart to me";
And here as its answer you're by my side;
You're a wonderful friend,
Oh sea.

Chorus
Over the waves,
O sea,
Bring my true love to me;
Promise to seek her far away,
Seek her where'er your billows play.
Then while I dream alone
She whom I call my own
Over the seas, borne by the breeze,
Comes to my heart, to me.

ON HER EUKALALI

The Mayor, Margot, Boileau, Dulcinea
William Jones to Honolulu went and on the beach
Feeling tender
Spied a slender
Hula Honolulu peach.
Tho' he knew no
Honolulu talk, her heart knew best;
She kept strumming, softly humming things he guessed.

Bye and bye they married by the sea and care defied;
Surf board riding,
Seaward gliding,
She was always by his side.
His fiancée back in Bangor, Maine, could vainly call.
Tho' he missed her like a sister, that was all.

Chorus
Oh upon her Eukalali
She'd chatter to him gaily;
He could almost guess the things she meant,
She was from the Orient.
She knew that he was saying,
"My boat has gone, I'm staying."
She smiled and just kept playing;
And they managed to find a way.

JUMP OFF THE WALL

Boileau
I'm very fond of fisher maids,
They're innocent and demure;
But still they say the city gay has such a mighty lure.
You'd like to try the Moulin Rouge and rule the feast alone;
But safe and high against the sky,
You'd better keep your throne.
With compliments inane
The city calls in vain.

The Paris lights, on August nights,
Keep humming your heart a tune;
But simple maids, in caps and braids, prefer the harvest moon.
Au "Dansant Boire" the café noir is stronger far than wine;
So bob your hair, I'll pay your fare,
Romance is next in line.
The belles of Brittany
Have rung their last for me.

Chorus
Fisher maids as brown as copper,
You'll get lonesome bye and bye,
Paris tho' is quite improper
Country walls are safe and high.
Come, we'll take a look at Maxim's

Some night we'll do them all.
On the boulevards, dears,
You'll be drawing-cards, dears,
Little girls jump off the wall.

FINALE ACT I

Chorus
Jacques we're very sorry for the company you're keeping,
And you'd better go to prison or you'll stab us while we're
    sleeping,
For we're much afraid you're sinking to a lower, lower level
When you spend your time in country roads and gossip with the
    devil.
We knew "La Rire" was written for the devil's humor, drat
    him!
You were reading all the risqué jokes and maybe laughing
    at 'em;
The scales will soon be growing on your chest and on your tummy;
But the scales will give you character,
You're such an awful rummy.
Soon Satan will commence to golf and bridge with all the fellows,
And next install a telephone and flirt with all the "Hellos";
The highbrow social register will want at once to list him,
And the débutantes of Naiserie will brag because they've kiss'd
    him;
And such an awful state of things will drive us to distraction
You'd better try the jail awhile and muse upon your action.
So stick to your level
And herd with the devil, go 'way.

Jacques
True to me now, oh sea,
Take not my love from me,
Mine when I kept her safe from harms,
Mine when I held her in my arms.
And tho' I stand alone,

She is my love, my own;
Tho' we may part,
Here in my heart
She will be mine, mine, mine.

Ensemble
Oh, Jacques, you're really to blame,
These things are truly a shame,
Our town will lose its good name,
For you have reached your level
When you gossip with the devil,
We feel for Miss I-don't-know;
She's no experience, so
She had better take the fellow while she can,
True love is so beautiful,
Happy and dutiful;
He looks good to me
She'd better let it be.

ACT II

OPENING CHORUS

Dulcinea
Out of the sea returning,
Worn with their weary stay,
Now to their homes they are turning
Just at the close of day,
Draw in your nets full laden,
Hoist when the sun meets sea,
Here is a lonely maiden,
Waiting for thee, for thee,
Here is a lonely maiden,
Waiting for thee, waiting for thee, waiting for thee.

(*Entrance of Fishermen*)
Sail on,
Sail on,

While the lapping wavelets kiss the side
Sail on,
Sail on,
Mermaids will ride beside
Sail on,
Sail on,
Lucky blows the homing wind, good men
Sail on,
Sail on,
Westward ho!
We're drifting home again.

HARRIS FROM PARIS

Mr. Harris
You're looking at a man
Who's modelled on a plan,
The up-to-date detective.
In Sunday magazines,
You've read of my machines
For making jails selective.
The intimate affairs
Of multi-millionaires
Are vested safe within me;
For money in advance,
I'll find the King of France
And prove his ancestry.

The crooks of other times
Were judged upon their crimes;
It's now their circulation;
Deduction will not serve,
You test their pressure curve
And try their chest inflation.
Craig Kennedy's the King;
The lab'ratory thing
Is getting quite au fait,

The burglar is so wise
He laughs at your disguise;
This progress makes me grey.

Chorus
Harris from Paris,
The dread of the crook,
Sleuth-hound from Broadway,
You're down in his book.
Knifers and lifers
Turn pale at his call;
Gangmen thereabout learn to care about Harris,
That's all.

TWILIGHT

A Gypsy
Come, wander where the firefly gleams;
Night's mingling with day.
Come soon for all the summer beams
Fade slowly away.
Night will burn you with its kisses;
Day will charm you with its eyes,
I'm waiting for the twilight time
Where mystery lies.

Love's sweeter in the afterglow
Born over the years;
Red roses when their beauties go
Hold laughter and tears.
Gold is fading in the yellow,
Yellow melting into grey;
Eve's perfumed with the Jessamine,
Farewell to the day.

Chorus
Twilight, shylight,
Thro' the shadow land we'll stroll

Dreaming,
Dreaming,
While the mellow night-bells toll
Softly,
Softly
Fades the summer daylight while
I'm peace at last obtaining
In the waning twilight time.

"THE NEVER, NEVER LAND"

Jacques, The Girl, Claude, Dulcinea
(*Men*)

> Just listen, I'll tell you of a plan, dear,
> A hunch for a gay honeymoon;

(*Girls*)

> I'll listen and listen all I can, dear,
> Keep talking from now till June;

(*Men*)

> Discovered an undiscovered country,
> On shores of the sea I-don't-know.

(*Girls*)

> You haven't told us yet;

(*Men*)

> The truth is, we forget;

(*All*)

> But we know how to get there when we go.

(*Men*)

> Its lure is forever calling you, dear;
> Enchanted the fair skies above;

(*Girls*)

> The laws are but one, that you'll be true, dear,
> The password is only Love.

(*Men*)

> The song of the nation is an old one,
> It's only, I love you alone.

(*Girls*)

> This land preserves, you see,
> Its own neutrality

(*All*)

> And even guards of lovers are unknown.

Refrain
To the land of the never, never
Where we can love forever,
We will sail away;
So put the ring where it ought to linger,
On your engagement finger,
Pack your little grip, we'll leave today;
And there's no room for care and sorrow,
We'll not be back tomorrow,
Carefully we've planned;
There'll be no one around when we're departing, starting
For the never, never land.

MY IDEA OF LOVE

Mme. Mirliflore and Mr. Harris
A drug clerk, "Mike," from Yonkers
Loved Esmerelda Sage;
One evening he proposed that she
Should share his humble wage;

And when he'd gotten calmer,
She cooly answered, "Mike,
I'll meet someday my fiancée,
I'll tell you what he's like."

Young Stuyvesant, worth millions,
Came touring through the town;
He met Miss Sage, and asked her age,
And wished to settle down.
The day that they were married,
He said with fond appeal,
"My eyes so blue have won me you";
She told him her ideal.

Chorus
Give him a swell name like Astor,
Give him a great big limousine,
Show me the mansion where he's master,
Add just the touch that keeps the
Brain from tinkling, clothes from wrinkling,
Give him a face that won't scare you
Fringed with a little hair above;
Hand me the silken halter
That will lead him to the altar,
That's my idea of love.

OTHER EYES

Jacques and Quartet
When one at last
Denies his past
To honor and obey
With fervor and sighs
You swear that her eyes
Are brighter than you can say
She says, "How nice!"
And she blushes twice;

On compliments she's fed;
But you know well
You'll never tell
Of ghosts that aren't quite dead
A lot of things you've left unsaid.

The loves of old
That once unfold,
The heart with tender bliss
Are folded away
With dreams of the day
That smiled on another kiss
The songs and sighs
To the other eyes
Have sung and sighed their last;
But in your breast,
Tho' unconfessed,
Your heart could still beat fast
For all the youthful romance past.

Chorus
Solo
    Tell her of the other eyes
    That call you in the night,
Tenors and Basses
    Tell her of the other eyes
    That call you in the night, dark night.
Solo
    Eyes of sadness,
    Eyes of gladness, past delight,
Tenors and Basses
    Eyes of sadness,
    Eyes of gladness, past delight, her tears still shining,
Solo
    Ne'er forgetting, half regretting other sunny skies
Tenors and Basses
    Ne'er forgetting, half regretting other sunny skies ne'er fading

All
> How they haunt you,
> Seem to want you,
> Other eyes.

THE GIRL OF THE GOLDEN WEST

Jacques
Cowboys are what I can dote upon,
Like those Puccini wrote upon
Roaming the plains of the golden west;
Girls who are quick with the gun or knife,
Tho' they're still quicker to be your wife.
I'm going to start upon a merry quest.
I know that soon I'll flit,
Out where Puccini got it.

Fair ladies staged so dramatic'ly,
Brave deeds done operatic'ly
Give me a wonderful thrill for fair;
Bad men who rampage and run about,
Carelessly swinging a gun about,
Add such a bristle to my curly hair.
High are the horse-thieves hung;
I want to hear the deed sung.

Chorus
Ride your horse right to my heart,
(*All a-whirl, all a-whirl, for my little girl.*)
Tied am I by cowgirl art
(*To a tree, to a tree, hanging over me.*)
We await the hour
When we can round 'em up again
In that operatic style.
I'm happy while Caruso twirls his rope
(*While the hills, while the hills, ring with tenor trills.*)
You could swear he had the dope

(*On the names, on the names, such as Jesse James.*)
Don't know whether to bide or go
To the borders of Idaho
Oh—Puccini, do it some more.

WITH ME

The Girl, Mme. Mirliflore, Mr. Harris and Boileau
There's a proverb I have heard:
"Two heads are better than one";
Two together in any old weather
Have ever so much more fun;
So don't be stingy with yourself,
Show generosity;
No solo you get can beat a duet,
Come form a trust with me.

Solo dancing's all the rage;
Nevertheless it is true,
Give me a lady who's never old-maidy
But saves up a lot for you.
I'd rather dance with Mary Brown
Than look at Miss Deslys;
So give me your hand and signal the band,
You're going to dance with me.

Chorus
Play, play, play with me,
Promise you'll come and stay with me.
I could love you, dear, quite a bit,
Even tho' we should fight a bit.
Hide, ride, bide with me,
Merry we two shall be
And ev'ry single thing you do,
Promise you'll do with me.

SAFETY FIRST!

(A) PROLOGUE

Spirit of the Future
Hail to the spirit of the muse of Youth,
Dear to the hardest heart!
Hail to the sunny seekers after Truth,
That herald modern art!
Hail to the century of foolish fads,
Best century and worst!
Be this the gist of our satire,
To make your rule Safety First!
Eyes up!
We're off!

(B) GARDEN OF ARDEN

Spirit of the Future, Ralph, Bill, Betty and Cynthia

Garden of Arden in fairyland,
When love and art linger hand in hand;
Far from the passions, the hobbies and fashions,
Glad beyond measure, rich in our search for pleasure,
You are invited to wander there.
We'll be delighted you know;
Always it's June, 'neath the Calcium Moon,
To the Garden of Arden we'll go.

ACT I
OPENING CHORUS

Howard, Percy and Chorus
Art Students (first whistling, then singing)
Prettily painting,

82

Frequently painting,
Weak with art,
Braving the yawning
Depths of the dawning,
Set apart,
Trying to roll in some of our soul
In pictures that don't come true;
Work! work! the gallery waits for all we do.
Hail, Cubo!
Jitney muse of post-impression!
We make confession
You're all for show,
You're a very gentle grafter;
Bouillon cubes they named you after;
Excuse our laughter,
Ha ha ha, Cubo!

SEND HIM TO TOM

The Convicts
Dear old Ding Ding, home of the blest,
Invalid's rest, after leaving the court,
You're my summer resort;
Since my father Shermy, the worm, finished his term,
Osborne Merry has made it very seductive to one sport:

We're so bored with people who dare not to prepare,
Men who worship their purse, women probably worse;
Someday soon we'll send them away, send them to stay,
Up the river to help their liver. They seem to need a nurse:

When the Allies finally win, capture Berlin,
Here's the problem they'll get, one they'll never forget;
What to do with William the King, nasty old thing,
This solution will suit the "Roosian" as well as any yet:

Chorus
Send him to Tom,
Send him to Tom,

There he'll better his ways.
Kings of the trust,
Bankers that bust,
Pass the rest of their days,
Knitting neckties for Belgians
Cutting down their aplomb,
There they will cure, weep for the poor
Just send them to Tom.

Send them to Tom,
Send them to Tom,
Far from whispers of war.
Needles and Thread,
Early to bed,
Paper dollies galore,
Parsons pink and pacific
Bryan bearing his palm,
Ivory domes, nobody homes
Just send them to Tom.

Send him to Tom,
Send him to Tom,
Sword and speeches and "Hochs,"
Give him a year,
Serve him no beer,
Start him darning his socks,
Read him stories by Henry
Keep him quiet and calm,
Put him to work chained to a Turk
Just send him to Tom.

ONE-LUMP PERCY

Percy
Snakes were once despised of beasts
And unappreciated,
They were not invited to the feasts,
To eat alone were fated;

But now a diff'rent brand of snake
Does Cleopatra handle,
For it feeds on tea and angel cake
And knows the latest scandal.

Some girls like them "big and strong"
And some prefer them mental,
But I'd rather listen all day long,
When you grow sentimental;
Your line is stocked with artifice
And other people's humor,
For you draw conclusions from a kiss
And scandal from a rumor.

Chorus
One-lump Percy, Percy, the parlor snake,
Please have mercy, Percy, for mercy's sake,
Tender hearts you're breaking,
Someone forsaking;
When upon your knee your tea you balance,
We lose sight of other gallants,
King of parlor talents,
Percy the parlor snake.

WHERE DID BRIDGET KELLY
GET HER PERSIAN TEMPERAMENT?

Ralph and Chorus
I'm oh so very blue today;
I haven't got a thing to say!
My Bridget has torn my loving heart in two,
I don't know what I shall do!

I couldn't sleep a wink last night;
I'm looking for a man to fight!
Tony with his curly muspistachios,
I'll get him and spoil his clothes!

Chorus
Where did Bridget Kelly get her Persian temp'rament?
I'm a very angry man at her,
For she left her cop,
Goes with that Tony wop,
Eats his peanuts in his dirty shop,
Soon she'll dress up in jewels and veils;
All her beautiful vermillion hair
Is dyed away,
Now she's got an oriental air;
She's smoking Meccas
Murads and Fatimas,
Since my Bridget got her temp'rament.

IT IS ART

Percy
We're kneeling at the shrine of post-impression,
The art whose patron saint is Doctor Cook;
Our chief and only patrons,
Are feebleminded Matrons,
And dilettantes who have to have a cook.
There are no strict requirements for a cubist,
You only need a dipperful of paint,
A little distance bring it
And at your canvas fling it,
Then shut your eyes and name it what it ain't.

For anything's a subject if it's ugly,
And anything's a picture if it hangs;
I'm using as a sitter,
A young banana fritter,
And painting her in pantalettes and bangs.
We try to sketch the passion in the onion,
We never do the hair, we paint the part;
We've passed through ev'ry stage

And reached the golden age
When anything and ev'rything is art.

Refrain
Art, Art, the period is o'er
When your standards stand apart;
Mister Comstock's indignation
Gives a picture reputation
And doubles its sale as Art.

Art, Art, you're getting rather deep,
Common Sense and you must part;
For a complex cubist dimple
Makes the "Mona Lisa" simple,
There's no "Safety First" in Art.

SAFETY FIRST

Ralph, Bill, Betty and Cynthia
Sages for ages have said to hasten slowly,
To stay away from phoney tricks
And never hit a cop,
When one rocks the boat a bit
The undertakers gloat a bit
They'll place you in a two-by-six
And they'll hammer down the top.

Fair ones are rare ones for never picking winners,
They like the man with wavy hair
Who looks like Bruce McRae,
Who's able to walk about
And competent to talk about
Their color and their baby stare
And why New York is gay.

Chorus
Oh, you might be careful
If you won't be good,

The aeroplane is beautiful and new,
But Mother Earth is good enough for you,
'Though you like her dancing
And you know her name,
This love is just a game of chance,
She'll try to do her worst;
So hide your watch before you dance,
For Safety First!

For the men who thrill you
May be clerks by day,
So wed a man who's prosperous tho' meek
Or else you'll take in washing by the week;
Though he's most entrancing
And he knows new steps,
And calls himself a Duke or Count
Or Baron at the worst,
Just ask to see his bank account,
For Safety First!

CHARLOTTE CORDAY

Ralph, Cynthia and Chorus
Back where Robespierre ruled
In frivolous fickle France,
That's when someone was fooled
And fooled in a bold way, fooled in the old way.
Young Miss Charlotte Corday
Of the "Follies of Ninety-three,"
Asked old Marat to buy her a hat,
Oh, mercy on me!
So Marat he had it sent,
And to her little flat it went.

Poor old Mister Marat,
He never was more surprised,
For he ordered the hat
To get him in strong there,

He was in wrong there.
When she looked in the glass,
For, oh, she was very trim,
Found it too big, it mussed up her wig;
So she showed him;
She had him at her nod and beck
And so he got it in the neck,
Oh!

Chorus
Oh! Charlotte Corday, Charlotte Corday,
You had them all on the string;
Gee, they were mean to guillotine
A sweet, little innocent thing!
Got the hat when you wanted it,
Tried it on, but it didn't fit,
Then you joined the wrath club,
Stabbed him in his bathtub,
Served him just right, he was a fright,
You were impulsive through life.
Many a dame, does just the same,
But stabs with her eyes, not a knife;
Still we've thought upon it,
And we wear your bonnet;
Charlotte Corday, Charlotte Corday,
You were some girl in your day!

UNDERNEATH THE APRIL RAIN

Bill, Cynthia and Chorus
One day ere May had brought one wonderful flower,
'Twas in a stummering shower, I saw her pass by,
I stared, I dared to be an impudent fellow,
To spread my big umbrella, tell her that she was welcome.

We walked, we talked and thought no more of the weather;
We stayed so closely together we didn't get wet,

The rain in vain dripped on attempting to drown us;
But drops that fell around us found us quite unobserving.

Chorus
April rain,
Dripping happily,
Once again catch my love and me;
Beneath our own umbrella cosy,
The world will still seem gay and rosy.
Drip, drip, drop, while we're strolling down
Through the stunning town;
And since it's turning colder,
I'll hold her, enfold her
Under the Thunder with love and the rain.

FINALE ACT I

"DANCE, LADY, DANCE"

Ralph and Chorus
Ralph
Afar in the distance again
A violin takes up the strain,
So you to the waltz as the leaf to the rose,
Come dance with me in dreams that dances will disclose!

Chorus
1st time: Ralph
2nd time: Ensemble
So dance, dance, Lady, dance,
Weaving in the same design
With eyes and lips that cling to mine;
And love, love, love while you may,
For the rose in the day will wither.
Dear, dear, hold me near,
Mine the hour ere the dawn,
For youth and love will soon be gone;

[1]We'll glide, glide into the night,
While the waning moon is bright.
[2]And as soft violins sigh, as the violins sigh,
As the waning moon is bright.
One long good-bye,
Dance, Lady, dance ere the night goes by!

ACT II

(A) SAFETY FIRST

Chorus
When the 'cello's sighing
And the lights are low,
The new loves seem much nearer than the old
Remember all that glitters isn't gold;
Tho' the wine forgetful
Turns your soul aglow,
The chilly dawn will quench the fire,
And thunderstorms may burst;
So keep enough for taxi hire
For Safety First.

(B) HELLO TEMPTATION

Ralph and Chorus
Ralph
  I've a friend who doesn't know tomorrow.
Girls
  (He's very nice very nice.)
Ralph
  Lives his life today for fun and fame.
Girls
  (What a thrill what a thrill what a thrill!)
Ralph
  Makes a hit with all of us

And plays a bit with all of us
And Lord Temptation's his name.
Ralph
  Miss Temptation's just as nice as Mister.
Girls
  (She's quite a kid quite a kid.)
Ralph
  Takes her suitors old and rather bald.
Girls
  (Pretty bald pretty bald pretty bald.)
Ralph
  Dances like Pavlova does
  And charms you like a boa does
  And Miss Temptation she's called.

Chorus
Hello Temptation I'll play with you
Tempt me with something I shouldn't do,
Stolen sweets are best,
We've stolen much, we'll steal the rest
Before we leave you;
Take me and make me your fav'rite child,
Lead me
Let's go!
Oh, resist you I can't, Sir,
Just page me, I'll answer,
Temptation, hello!

WHEN THAT BEAUTIFUL CHORD CAME TRUE

The Pianist and Chorus
One day I sat, took a pat
At my baby grand, my Chickering
Glued to the stool, like a fool,
I was musically bickering;
Played something pash with a dash,

That was Spanish in its temp'rament
Then all those keys came true,
Each one a maid, a laughing maid.

Often I've dreamed that it seemed
Ev'ry melody must have a heart,
Were all the notes from the throats
Of a chorus in a world apart?
Sprites from above or perhaps
Little Demons from a place below
Even a blonde or so?
And soon I knew it could be true.

Chorus
When that joyful chord came true,
And the notes hurried out, ran about,
Then that room turned sickly blue,
And I reeled almost keeled from the stool.
A was a Persian petter,
B natural knew no better,
Little C was sentimental
She was horribly oriental,
Each in harmony agrees
(Little G pours my tea ev'ry day),
As they dance upon the keys
Gleaming bright, black and white, in the night;
I've acted like the dickens
With those harmonic chickens,
Beautiful chord, now that you've come true.

RAGTIME MELODRAMA

Convicts, Detectives and Chorus
Convicts
Surprise will fell you
When we will tell you
In strictest confidence

We are not really masquerading,
But rather Uncle Sam evading.
The clothes we've got on
Are really not on
To help the merriment
But for protection
From life election
Back to the cell we'll be sent!

Detectives
Oh, here we come, we're going some!
The cops are strolling up the avenue
In little Fords
With running boards to hold our captives
Who will have a new number of their own,
Not a telephone;
For they have no bells in their private cells.
Whom have we here Horatio?

Convicts
Ah!
Detectives
Oh! Clue!
Convicts
No!
Detectives
We can't be wrong,
The clues are strong,
We'd better take them into custody!
Convicts
Oh, we've got a date,
We're sorry to run away,
Yes we're late.
Tut, Tut! put your gun away!
See you soon, Good-bye!
Detectives
What's the rush!

Convicts
Good-day!
Ensemble
Got a date, got a date, got a date, got a date,
Got to see a fellow who is terribly sick!
Better wait, better wait, better wait, better wait!
Stick around a minute and we'll show you a trick!
Convicts
Handcuffs weren't made for me,
Just give me liberty.
Ensemble
Got a date, got a date, got a date, got a date,
Must hurry along!

SCENE II

Spirit of the Future
Stop! what's the row? what's all
This commotion
In our colony formed for quietude?
Cease now, let's have peace now!
You have shocked my sober sobrietude!
Why this scurry and hateful hurry?
The tree trunks themselves are all nervous and quivery.
Hush your clatter, your childish chatter!
You act like a boy with a Special Delivery!
What's all this commotion
In our colony formed for quietude?
Cease now, let's have peace now!
You have shocked my sober sobrietude!

TAKE THOSE HAWAIIAN SONGS AWAY

Bill, Cynthia and Chorus
Now'days from giddy Piccadilly
Back to the snores of sleepy Philly,
You can hear the strum of the eukalali,

Mingled with the sliding guitar;
I'm not too strong for Claude Debussy
Or for this Russian Charlotte "Russey,"
But now they push Hawaii too far;
I'm tired of hearing:

Once all the world was growing dippy
For Alabam' and Mississippi,
Franz Lehár once kept us in time with him
With his waltzes dreamy and loud;
Next ev'ry debutante was whirlin'
Round at the will of Irving Berlin,
Lately he's joined the popular crowd
And now he writes like:

Chorus
Oo-ley Bool-ey wool-ey-ing
By the Cool-ey ool-ey-ing
On her Eu-ki-wak-i-wee,
She would ick-y ick to me
This is all they sing about,
Stuff like this they fling about,
When will they shift to a new locality?
Iona Bologna is her name,
Each Hula dame
Is named the same
As the others.
Honolulu go away,
You have more than had your day!
Take those Hawaiian songs away,
Eu-ka-la-li-oo-li-ay!

THE VAMPIRES WON'T VAMPIRE FOR ME

Percy and Sal
Often I have seen on the screen,
Pictures living and snappy,

Girls quite a fistful, ingénues wistful,
Loving I look at that makes me unhappy;
Tell me why are girls that I meet,
Always simple and slow?
I want a brunette like those I met,
Back in the seven-reel show.

Liking striking blondes as I do,
Hair that's golden and rippling,
Why don't I meet a few that aren't sweet but
Act very much like the ladies in Kipling?
Dolls are very numerous now,
Many wonders I've seen;
But I'd like a wife early in life,
Someone who learned on the screen.

Chorus
Theda Bara they say,
Drives depression away,
What Olga Petrova knows
Won't go in the censored shows!
Why are ladies I meet
Never more than just sweet?
Girls seem to be Vampires,
But they won't vampire for me.

THE HUMMIN' BLUES

Ralph, Bill, Percy and Guild Master
My love has gone away,
She wouldn't stay,
She left today,
I'm feelin' mighty lonely,
For I want her, want her only!
The little bird she knew
Has gone along away and left me too;
He's not returnin',

I miss the yearnin'
Hummin' songs he used to sing.

The shadows gather near,
The stars appear,
Why don't I hear,
The song we heard together,
In some other summer weather?
Oh, little bird I know
You wouldn't go away, we loved you so.
I know you want me,
Your hummins haunt me,
Hum a sadder melody.

Chorus
Oh Hummin' bird, Hummin' bird,
Hummin' thro' the lingerin' twilight,
Singin' sad for your lad
'Cause he's got the blues, melodious blues;
Seems as tho'
You must know
My longin' heart is a-yearnin',
Lovin' bird, I need you with your hummin' blues!
My little ever lovin' blues!

DOWN IN FRONT

*Ralph, Bill, Percy, Howard, the Guild Master
and the Convicts*
I've been around Triangling,
I'm used to angling, you know;
I've travelled o'er this ground before,
As you'll have found out before I go.
Once while singing something clinging,
Beheld the girl
I'd been seeking,
Primly peeking at me.

So, like a fool I married her,
Ha! ha! And carried her away,
Drew out a check on Father dear,
Then settled down prepared to stay.
Since she'd known me as a pony in Triangle plays,
Hooking dresses, I confess, is my job.

Refrain
Down in front, there the lady sat
Gazing on me, eyes upon me, just like that!
Watched me act,
That's a fact,
Heard her laughter, met her after,
Tipped my hat;
Liked her fine,
Liked her lilac eyes entrancing,
Liked her line,
Liked her face and liked her dancing,
She's my wife, mine for life,
I loved her when she was down in front.

Down in front, 'round and up in back,
Thus I hooked her till she looked her very best;
Night and day, that's the way;
Such a deadlock in the wedlock, never rest!
I was rash,
Her dressmakers must be gluttons,
Belt and sash,
Hooks and eyes and holes and buttons!
"Oswald" dear, hurry here!
You've got to hook my dress down in front.

FINALE

Entire Cast and Chorus
Oh, the play is over
And the song is sung,

The paint comes off,
The wig is put away,
The violin's dumb until another day;
For the pony ballet
With their figures trim
Can stand no more this awful pest,
Their corsets most accursed
And now they'll give themselves a rest
For Safety First!

Good-bye, Temptation,
We're tired of you;
Tempt us
No more for we're really through.
You have said your say,
Just go away
We've won the day
And you're resisted;
Time was we courted and welcomed you
Nor were you shy;
But since we outdid you,
We cheerfully bid you,
Temptation, good-bye.

Prose and Verse

"THERE WAS ONCE . . ."

There was once a second group student who lived in Holder. He thought that solitude would give him a first group. So he moved to Patton, where he lent an unwilling ear to the following:

1:30–2:30 P. M.—Shrill soprano shrieks of soccer team.
2:30–3:30 " " Session of the gun club.
3:30–4:30 " " Interclass baseball game on Brokaw. (Continuous cheering.)
4:30–5:30 " " Engines puffing up and down for their afternoon exercise.
7:00–8:00 " " Mandolin or banjo practice in Brokaw.
8:00–9:00 " " Triangle practice in Casino.

* * *

The next day the student moved back to Holder.

"SHADOW LAURELS"

(*The scene is the interior of a wine shop in Paris. The walls are lined on all sides by kegs, piled like logs. The ceiling is low and covered with cobwebs. The mid-afternoon sun filters dejectedly through the one-barred window at the back. Doors are on both sides; one, heavy and powerful, opens outside; the other, on the left, leads to some inner chamber. A large table stands in the middle of the room backed by smaller ones set around the walls. A ship's lamp hangs above the main table.*

As the curtain rises there is knocking at the outside door—rather impatient knocking—and almost immediately Pitou, the wine dealer, enters from the other room and shuffles toward the door. He is an old man with unkempt beard and dirty corduroys.)

Pitou—Coming, coming—Hold tight! (*The knocking stops. Pitou unlatches the door and it swings open. A man in a top hat and opera cloak enters. Jacques Chandelle is perhaps thirty-seven, tall and well groomed. His eyes are clear and penetrating; his chin, clean-shaven, is sharp and decisive. His manner is that of a man accustomed only to success but ready and willing to work hard in any emergency. He speaks French with an odd accent as of one who knew the language well in early years but whose accent had grown toneless through long years away from France.*)

Pitou—Good afternoon, Monsieur.

Chandelle—(*looking about him curiously*) Are you perhaps Monsieur Pitou?

Pitou—Yes, Monsieur.

Chandelle—Ah! I was told that one would always find you in at this hour. (*He takes off his overcoat and lays it carefully on a chair.*) I was told also that you could help me.

Pitou—(*puzzled*) I could help you?

Chandelle—(*sitting down wearily on a wooden chair near the table*) Yes, I'm a—a stranger in the city—now. I'm trying to trace someone—someone who has been dead many years. I've been informed that you're the oldest inhabitant (*he smiles faintly*).

Pitou—(*rather pleased*) Perhaps—and yet there are older than I, ah yes, older than I. (*He sits down across the table from Chandelle.*)

Chandelle—And so I came for you. (*He bends earnestly over the table toward Pitou.*) Monsieur Pitou, I am trying to trace my father.

Pitou—Yes.

Chandelle—He died in this district about twenty years ago.

Pitou—Monsieur's father was murdered?

Chandelle—Good God, no! What makes you think that?

Pitou—I thought perhaps in this district twenty years ago, an aristocrat—

Chandelle—My father was no aristocrat. As I remember, his last position was that of waiter in some forgotten café. (*Pitou glances at Chandelle's clothes and looks mystified.*) Here, I'll explain. I left France twenty-eight years ago to go to the States with my uncle. We went over in an immigrant ship, if you know what that is.

Pitou—Yes: I know.

Chandelle—My parents remained in France. The last I remember of my father was that he was a little man with a black beard, terribly lazy—the only good I ever remember his doing was to teach me to read and write. Where he picked up that accomplishment I don't know. Five years after we reached America we ran across some newly landed French from this part of the city, who said that both my parents were dead. Soon after that my uncle died and I was far too busy to worry over parents whom I had half forgotten anyway. (*He pauses.*) Well to cut it short I prospered and—

Pitou—(*deferentially*) Monsieur is rich—'tis strange—'tis very strange.

Chandelle—Pitou, it probably appears strange to you that I should burst in on you now at this time of life, looking for traces of a father who went completely out of my life over twenty years ago.

Pitou—Oh—I understood you to say he was dead.

Chandelle—Yes, he's dead, but (*hesitates*) Pitou, I wonder if you can understand if I tell you why I am here.

Pitou—Yes, perhaps.

Chandelle—(*very earnestly*) Monsieur Pitou, in America the men I see now, the women I know, all had fathers, fathers to be ashamed of, fathers to be proud of, fathers in gilt frames, and fathers in the family closet, Civil War fathers, and Ellis Island fathers. Some even had grandfathers.

Pitou—I had a grandfather. I remember.

Chandelle—(*interrupting*) I want to see people who knew him, who had talked with him. I want to find out his intelligence, his life, his record. (*impetuously*) I want to sense him—I want to know him—

Pitou—(*interrupting*) What was his name?

Chandelle—Chandelle, Jean Chandelle.

Pitou—(*quietly*) I knew him.

Chandelle—You knew him?

Pitou—He came here often to drink—that was long ago when this place was the rendezvous of half the district.

Chandelle—(*excitedly*) Here? He used to come here? To this room? Good Lord, the very house he lived in was torn down ten years ago. In two days' search you are the first soul I've found who knew him. Tell me of him—everything—be frank.

Pitou—Many come and go in forty years. (*shakes his head*) There are many names and many faces—Jean Chandelle—ah, of course, Jean Chandelle. Yes, yes; the chief fact I can remember about your father was that he was a—a—

Chandelle—Yes.

Pitou—A terrible drunkard.

Chandelle—A drunkard—I expected as much. (*He looks a trifle downcast, but makes a half-hearted attempt not to show it.*)

Pitou—(*rambling on through a sea of reminiscence*) I remember one Sunday night in July—hot night—baking—your father—let's see—your father tried to knife Pierre Courru for drinking his mug of sherry.

Chandelle—Ah!

Pitou—And then—ah, yes, (*excitedly standing up*) I see it again. Your, father is playing *vingt-et-un* and they say he is cheating so he breaks Clavine's shin with a chair and throws a bottle at someone and Lafouquet sticks a knife into his lung. He never got over that. That was—was two years before he died.

Chandelle—So he cheated and was murdered. My God, I've crossed the ocean to discover that.

Pitou—No—no—I never believed he cheated. They were laying for him—

Chandelle—(*burying his face in his hands*) Is that all? (*He shrugs his shoulders; his voice is a trifle broken.*) I scarcely expected a— saint but—well: so he was a rotter.

Pitou—(*laying his hand on Chandelle's shoulder*) There Monsieur, I have talked too much. Those were rough days. Knives were drawn at anything. Your father—but hold—do you want to meet three friends of his, his best friends? They can tell you much more than I.

Chandelle—(*gloomily*) His friends?

Pitou—(*reminiscent again*) There were four of them. Three come here yet—will be here this afternoon—your father was the fourth and they would sit at this table and talk and drink. They talked nonsense—everyone said; the wine room poked fun at them— called them "les Académicians Ridicules." Night after night would they sit there. They would slouch in at eight and stagger out at twelve—

(*The door swings open and three men enter. The first, Lamarque, is a tall man, lean and with a thin straggly beard. The second, Destage, is short and fat, white-bearded and bald. The third, François Meridien, is slender, with black hair streaked with grey and a small moustache. His face is pitifully weak, his eyes small, his chin sloping. He is very nervous. They all glance with dumb curiosity at Chandelle.*)

Pitou—(*including all three with a sweep of his arm*) Here they are, Monsieur; they can tell you more than I. (*turning to the others*) Messieurs, this gentleman desires to know about—

Chandelle—(*rising hastily and interrupting Pitou*) About a friend of my father's. Pitou tells me you knew him. I believe his name was—Chandelle.

(*The three men start and François begins to laugh nervously.*)

Lamarque—(*after a pause*) Chandelle?

François—Jean Chandelle? So he had another friend besides us?

Destage—You will pardon me, Monsieur; that name—no one but us had mentioned it for twenty-two years.

Lamarque—(*trying to be dignified, but looking a trifle ridiculous*) And with us it is mentioned with reverence and awe.

Destage—Lamarque exaggerates a little perhaps. (*very seriously*) He was very dear to us. (*Again François laughs nervously.*)

Lamarque—But what is it that Monsieur wishes to know? (*Chandelle motions them to sit down. They take places at the big table and Destage produces a pipe and begins to fill it.*)

François—Why, we're four again!

Lamarque—Idiot!

Chandelle—Here, Pitou! Wine for everyone. (*Pitou nods and shuffles out.*) Now, Messieurs, tell me of Chandelle. Tell me of his personality.

(*Lamarque looks blankly at Destage.*)

Destage—Well, he was—was attractive—

Lamarque—Not to everyone.

Destage—But to us. Some thought him a sneak. (*Chandelle winces.*) He was a wonderful talker—when he wished, he could amuse the whole wine room. But he preferred to talk to us. (*Pitou enters with a bottle and glasses. He pours and leaves the bottle on the table. Then he goes out.*)

Lamarque—He was educated. God knows how.

François—(*draining his glass and pouring out more*) He knew everything, he could tell anything—he used to tell me poetry. Oh, what poetry! And I would listen and dream—

Destage—And he could make verses and sing them with his guitar.

Lamarque—And he would tell us about men and women of history—about Charlotte Corday and Fouquet and Molière and St. Louis and Mamine, the strangler, and Charlemagne and Mme. du Barry and Machiavelli and John Law and François Villon—

Destage—Villon! (*enthusiastically*) He loved Villon. He would talk for hours of him.

François—(*pouring more wine*) And then he would get very drunk and say "Let us fight" and he would stand on the table and say that everyone in the wine shop was a pig and a son of pigs. La! He would grab a chair or a table and Sacré Vie Dieu! but those were hard nights for us.

Lamarque—Then he would take his hat and guitar and go into the streets to sing. He would sing about the moon.

François—And the roses and the ivory towers of Babylon and about the ancient ladies of the court and about "the silent chords that flow from the ocean to the moon."

Destage—That's why he made no money. He was bright and clever—when he worked, he worked feverishly hard, but he was always drunk, night and day.

Lamarque—Often he lived on liquor alone for weeks at a time.

Destage—He was much in jail toward the end.

Chandelle—(*calling*) Pitou! More wine!

François—(*excitedly*) And me! He used to like me best. He used to say that I was a child and he would train me. He died before he began. (*Pitou enters with another bottle of wine; François siezes it eagerly and pours himself a glass.*)

Destage—And then that cursed Lafouquet—stuck him with a knife.

François—But I fixed Lafouquet. He stood on the Seine bridge drunk and—

Lamarque—Shut up, you fool you—

François—I pushed him and he sank—down—down—and that night Chandelle came in a dream and thanked me.

Chandelle—(*shuddering*) How long—for how many years did he come here?

Destage—Six or seven. (*gloomily*) Had to end—had to end.

Chandelle—And he's forgotten. He left nothing. He'll never be thought of again.

Destage—Remembered! Bah! Posterity is as much a charlatan as the most prejudiced tragic critic that ever boot-licked an actor. (*He turns his glass nervously round and round.*) You don't realize—I'm afraid—how we feel about Jean Chandelle, François and Lamarque and I—he was more than a genius to be admired—

François—(*hoarsely*) Don't you see, he stood for us as well as for himself.

Lamarque—(*rising excitedly and walking up and down*) There we were—four men—three of us poor dreamers—artistically uneducated, practically illiterate. (*He turns savagely to Chandelle and speaks almost menacingly.*) Do you realize that I can neither read nor write? Do you realize that back of François there, despite his fine phrases, there is a character weak as water, a mind as shallow as—

(*François starts up angrily.*)

Lamarque—Sit down. (*François sits down muttering.*)

François—(*after a pause*) But, Monsieur, you must know—I leave the gift of—of—(*helplessly*) I can't name it—appreciation, artistic, aesthetic sense—call it what you will. Weak—yes, why not? Here I am, with no chance, the world against me. I lie—I steal perhaps—I am drunk—I—

(*Destage fills up François' glass with wine.*)

Destage—Here! Drink that and shut up! You are boring the gentleman. There is his weak side—poor infant.

(*Chandelle, who has listened to the last, keenly turns his chair toward Destage.*)

Chandelle—But you say my father was more to you than a personal friend; in what way?

Lamarque—Can't you see?

François—I—I—he helped—(*Destage pours out more wine and gives it to him.*)

Destage—You see he—how shall I say it?—he expressed us. If you can imagine a mind like mine, potently lyrical, sensitive without being cultivated. If you can imagine what a balm, what a medicine, what an all in all was summed up for me in my conversations with him. It was everything to me. I would struggle pathetically for a phrase to express a million yearnings and he would say it in a word.

Lamarque—Monsieur is bored? (*Chandelle shakes his head and opening his case selects a cigarette and lights it.*)

Lamarque—Here, sir, are three rats, the product of a sewer—destined by nature to live and die in the filthy ruts where they were born. But these three rats in one thing are not of the sewer—they have eyes. Nothing to keep them from remaining in the sewer but their eyes, nothing to help them if they go out but their eyes—and now here comes the light. And it came and passed and left us rats again—vile rats—and one, when he lost the light, went blind.

François—(*muttering to himself*)—

> Blind! Blind! Blind!
> Then he ran alone, when the light had passed;
> The sun had set and the night fell fast;
> The rat lay down in the sewer at last.
> Blind!

(*A beam of the sunset has come to rest on the glass of wine that François holds in his hand. The wine glitters and sparkles. François looks at it, starts, and drops the glass. The wine runs over the table.*)

Destage—(*animatedly*) Fifteen—twenty years ago he sat where you sit, small, heavy-bearded, black-eyed—always sleepy-looking.

François—(*his eyes closed—his voice trailing off*) Always sleepy, sleepy, slee—

Chandelle—(*dreamily*) He was a poet unsinging, crowned with wreaths of ashes. (*His voice rings with just a shade of triumph.*)

François—(*talking in his sleep*) Ah, well, Chandelle, are you witty tonight, or melancholy or stupid or drunk?

Chandelle—Messieurs—it grows late. I must be off. Drink all of you. (*enthusiastically*) Drink until you cannot talk or walk or see. (*He throws a bill on the table.*)

Destage—Young Monsieur?

(*Chandelle dons his coat and hat. Pitou enters with more wine. He fills the glasses.*)

Lamarque—Drink with us, Monsieur.

François—(*asleep*) Toast, Chandelle, toast.

Chandelle—(*taking a glass and raising it aloft*) Toast. (*His face is a little red and his hand unsteady. He appears infinitely more Gallic than when he entered the wine shop.*)

Chandelle—I drink to one who might have been all; who was nothing—who might have sung; who only listened—who might have seen the sun; who but watched a dying ember—who drank of gall and wore a wreath of shadow laurels—

(*The others have risen, even François, who totters wildly forward.*)

François—Jean, Jean, don't go—don't—till I, François—you can't leave me—I'll be all alone—alone—alone. (*His voice rises higher and higher.*) My God, man, can't you see, you have no right to die—*You are my soul.* (*He stands for a moment, then sprawls across the table. Far away in the twilight a violin sighs plaintively. The last beam of the sun rests on François' head. Chandelle opens the door and goes out.*)

Destage—The old days go by, and the old loves and the old spirit. "Où sont les neiges d'antan?" I guess. (*pauses unsteadily and then continues*) I've gone far enough without him.

Lamarque—(*dreamily*) Far enough.

Destage—Your hand, Jacques! (*They clasp hands.*)

François—(*wildly*) Here—I, too—you won't leave me. (*feebly*) I want—just one more glass—one more—

(*The light fades and disappears.*)

CURTAIN

MAY SMALL TALK

To get a reputation for ability to chatter
You must learn this little system for your common campus patter.
First you ask about exams and how your victim thinks he's doing,
Speak of war and shake your head and say you think there's
    trouble brewing.
A word about your bills, and on the chapel question, too,
Then "Gee, but it was mighty tough—you know about the crew."
"Yes, Charlie Chaplin's at the show—a mighty funny thing";
"Going over Campus now, to hear the Seniors sing?"
"I s'pose since you're a parlor snake you'll bring a girl in June?"
"Oh! eat your soup, for movie show is starting pretty soon."
"Well, these are busy days for me"—"You've always been a bummer,"
"Yes, meet me here at Morey's School," and "What's the dope this summer?"
You must always ask the heeler, how he's coming with the Prince,
And "Coming back here early?" makes the guards and centers wince:
For this is always easier and better far for mine,
Than a continental, trancendental, consequental line!

THE ORDEAL

The hot four o'clock sun beat down familiarly upon the wide stretch of Maryland country, burning up the long valleys, powdering the winding road into fine dust and glaring on the ugly slated roof of the monastery. Into the gardens it poured hot, dry, lazy, bringing with it, perhaps, some quiet feeling of content, unromantic and cheerful. The walls, the trees, the sanded walks, seemed to radiate back into the fair cloudless sky the sweltering late summer heat and yet they laughed and baked happily. The hour brought some odd sensation of comfort to the farmer in a nearby field, drying his brow for a moment by his thirsty horse, and to the lay brother opening boxes behind the monastery kitchen.

The man walked up and down on the bank above the creek. He had been walking for half an hour. The lay brother looked at him quizzically as he passed and murmured an invocation. It was always hard, this hour before taking first vows. Eighteen years before one, the world just behind. The lay brother had seen many in this same situation, some white and nervous, some grim and determined, some despairing. Then, when the bell tolled five, there were the vows and usually the novice felt better. It was this hour in the country when the world seemed gloriously apparent and the monastery vaguely impotent. The lay brother shook his head in sympathy and passed on.

The man's eyes were bent upon his prayer book. He was very young, twenty at the most, and his dark hair in disorder gave him an even more boyish expression. A light flush lay on his calm face and his lips moved incessantly. He was not nervous. It seemed to him as if he had always known he was to become a priest. Two years before, he had felt the vague stirring, the transcendent sense of seeing heaven in everything, that warned him softly, kindly, that the spring of his life was coming. He had given himself every opportunity to resist. He had gone a year to college, four months abroad, and both experiences only increased within him the knowledge of his destiny. There was little hesitation. He had at first feared self-committal with a thousand nameless terrors. He thought he loved the world. Panicky, he struggled, but surer and surer he felt that the last word had been said. He had his vocation—and then, because he was no coward, he decided to become a priest.

Through the long month of his probation he alternated between deep, almost delirious joy and the same vague terror at his own love of life and his realization of all he sacrificed. As a favorite child he had been reared in pride and confidence in his ability, in faith in his destiny. Careers were open to him, pleasure, travel, the law, the diplomatic service. When, three months before, he had walked into the library at home and told his father that he was going to become a Jesuit priest, there was a family scene and letters on all sides from friends and relatives. They told him he was ruining a promising young life because of a sentimental notion of self-sacrifice, a boyish dream. For a month he listened to the bitter melodrama of the commonplace, finding his only rest in prayer, knowing his salvation and trusting in it. After all, his worst battle had been with himself. He grieved at his father's disappointment and his mother's tears, but he knew that time would set them right.

And now in half an hour he would take the vows which pledged him forever to a life of service. Eighteen years of study—eighteen years where his every thought, every idea would be dictated to him, where his individuality, his psychical ego, would be effaced and he would come forth strong and firm to work and work and work. He felt strangely calm, happier in fact than he had been for days and months. Something in the fierce, pulsing heat of the sun likened itself to his own heart, strong in its decision, virile and doing its own share in the work, the greatest work. He was elated that he had been chosen, he from so many unquestionably singled out, unceasingly called for. And he had answered.

The words of the prayers seemed to run like a stream into his thoughts, lifting him up peacefully, serenely; and a smile lingered around his eyes. Everything seemed so easy; surely all life was a prayer. Up and down he walked. Then of a sudden something happened. Afterwards he could never describe it except by saying that some undercurrent had crept into his prayer, something unsought, alien. He read on for a moment and then it seemed to take the form of music. He raised his eyes with a start—far down the dusty road a group of negro hands were walking along singing, and the song was an old song that he knew:

> We hope ter meet you in heavan whar we'll
> Part no mo',
> Whar we'll part no mo'.
> Gawd a'moughty bless you twel we
> Me-et agin.

Something flashed into his mind that had not been there before. He felt a sort of resentment toward those who had burst in upon him at this time, not because they were simple and primitive, but because they had vaguely disturbed him. That song was old in his life. His nurse had hummed it through the dreamy days of his childhood. Often in the hot summer afternoons he had played it softly on his banjo. It reminded him of so many things: months at the seashore on the hot beach with the gloomy ocean rolling around him, playing with sand castles with his cousin; summer evenings on the big lawn at home when he chased fireflies and the breeze carried the tune over the night to him from the negro quarters. Later, with new words, it had served as a serenade—and now—well, he had done with that part of life, and yet he seemed to see a girl with kind eyes, old in a great sorrow, waiting, ever waiting. He seemed to hear voices calling, children's voices. Then around him swirled the city, busy with the hum of men; and there was a family that would never be, beckoning him.

Other music ran now as undercurrent to his thoughts: wild, incoherent music, illusive and wailing, like the shriek of a hundred violins, yet clear and chord-like. Art, beauty, love and life passed in a panorama before him, exotic with the hot perfumes of world-passion. He saw struggles and wars, banners waving somewhere, voices giving hail to a king—and looking at him through it all were the sweet sad eyes of the girl who was now a woman.

Again the music changed; the air was low and sad. He seemed to front a howling crowd who accused him. The smoke rose again around the body of John Wycliffe; a monk knelt at a prie-dieu and laughed because the poor had not bread. Alexander VI pressed once more the poisoned ring into his brother's hand, and the black-robed figures of the Inquisition scowled and whispered. Three great men said there was no God; a million voices seemed to cry, "Why! Why must we believe?" Then as in a crystal he seemed to hear Huxley, Nietzsche, Zola, Kant cry, "I will not"—He saw Voltaire and Shaw wild with cold passion. The voices pleaded "Why?" and the girl's sad eyes gazed at him with infinite longing.

He was in a void above the world—the ensemble, everything called him now. He could not pray. Over and over again he said senselessly, meaninglessly, "God have mercy, God have mercy." For a minute, an eternity, he trembled in the void and then—something snapped. They were still there, but the girl's eyes were all wrong; the lines around her mouth were cold and chiselled and her passion seemed dead and earthy.

He prayed, and gradually the cloud grew clearer; the images appeared vague and shadowy. His heart seemed to stop for an instant and then—he was standing by the bank and a bell was tolling five. The reverend superior came down the steps and toward him.

"It is time to go in."

The man turned instantly.

"Yes, Father, I am coming."

II

The novices filed silently into the chapel and knelt in prayer. The blessed sacrament in the gleaming monstrance was exposed among the flaming candles on the altar. The air was rich and heavy with incense. The man knelt with the others. A first chord of the Magnificat, sung by the concealed choir above, startled him; he looked up. The late afternoon sun shone through the stained glass window of St. Francis Xavier on his left and fell in red tracery on the cassock of the man in front of him. Three ordained priests knelt on the altar. Above them a huge candle burned. He watched it abstractedly. To the right of him a novice was telling his beads with trembling fingers. The man looked at him. He was about twenty-six with fair hair and green-grey eyes that darted nervously around the chapel. They caught each other's eye, and the elder glanced quickly at the altar candle as if to draw attention to it. The man followed his eye, and as he looked he felt his scalp creep and tingle. The same unsummoned instinct filled him that had frightened him half an hour ago on the bank. His breath came quicker. How hot the chapel was. It was too hot, and the candle was wrong—wrong—everything suddenly blurred. The man on his left caught him.

"Hold up," he whispered. "They'll postpone you. Are you better? Can you go through with it?"

He nodded vaguely and turned to the candle. Yes, there was no mistake. Something was there; something played in the tiny flame, curled in the minute wreath of smoke. Some evil presence was in the chapel, on the very altar of God. He felt a chill creeping over him, though he knew the room was warm. His soul seemed paralyzed, but he kept his eyes riveted on the candle. He knew that he must watch it. There was no one else to do it. He must not take his eyes from it. The line of novices rose, and he mechanically reached his feet.

"Per omnia saecula, saeculorum. Amen."

Then he felt suddenly that something corporeal was missing—his last earthly support. He realized what it was. The man on his left had gone out, overwrought and shaken. Then it began. Something before had attacked the roots of his faith; had matched his world-sense against his God-sense; had brought, he had thought, every power to bear against him; but this was different. Nothing was denied, nothing was offered. It could best be described by saying that a great weight seemed to press down upon his innermost soul, a weight that had no essence, mental or physical. A whole spiritual realm, evil in its every expression, engulfed him. He could not think, he could not pray. As in a dream he heard the voices of the men beside him singing, but they were far away, farther away from him than anything had ever been before. He existed on a plane where there was no prayer, no grace; where he realized only that the forces around him were of hell and where the single candle contained the essence of evil. He felt himself alone pitted against an infinity of temptation. He could bring no parallel to it in his own experience or any other. One fact he knew: one man had succumbed to this weight and he must not—must not. He must look at the candle and look and look until the power that filled it and forced him into this plane died forever for him. It was now or not at all.

He seemed to have no body, and even what he had thought was his innermost self was dead. It was something deeper that was he, something that he had never felt before. Then the forces gathered for one final attack. The way that the other novice had taken was open to him. He drew his breath quickly and waited and then the shock came. The eternity and infinity of all good seemed crushed, washed away in an eternity and infinity of evil. He seemed carried helplessly along, tossed this way and that—as in a black limitless ocean where there is no light and the waves grow larger and larger and the sky darker and darker. The waves were dashing him toward a chasm, a maelstrom everlastingly evil, and blindly, unseeingly, desperately he looked at the candle, looked at the flame which seemed like the one black star in the sky of despair. Then suddenly he became aware of a new presence. It seemed to come from the left, seemed consummated and expressed in warm, red tracery somewhere. Then he knew. It was the stained window of St. Francis Xavier. He gripped at it spiritually, clung to it and with aching heart called silently for God.

"*Tantum ergo Sacramentum*
Veneremur cernui."

The words of the hymn gathered strength like a triumphant paean of glory; the incense filled his brain, his very soul; a gate clanged somewhere and *the candle on the altar went out.*

"*Ego te absolvo a peccatis tuis in nomine patris, filii, spiritus sancti.* Amen."

The file of novices started toward the altar. The stained lights from the windows mingled with the candle glow, and the eucharist in its golden halo seemed to the man very mystical and sweet. It was very calm.

The subdeacon held the book for him. He placed his right hand upon it.

"*In the name of the Father and of the Son and of the Holy Ghost*—"

HOW THEY HEAD THE CHAPTERS

A. DETECTIVE STORY

Chapter I.—The Affair at Brownwill.
Chap. II.—In The Dark.
Chap. III.—The Hound Hits The Trail.
Chap. IV.—A Ray Of Light.
Chap. V.—Fresh Developments.
Chap. VI.—Gone!
Chap. VII.—Caught!
Chap. VIII.—Old Jacques Speaks.
Chap. IX.—Solved!

B. CHOBERT RAMBERS STORY

Chap. I.—Auction Bridge.
Chap. II.—At Seabreeze.
Chap. III.—The Shooting Party.
Chap. IV.—A Kiss In The Dark.
Chap. V.—A Gentleman's Gentleman.
Chap. VI.—Rector's.
Chap. VII.—Champagne.
Chap. VIII.—Arms And The Man.

C. ANY BEST SELLER

Chap. I.—Third Avenue.
Chap. II.—Fifth Avenue.
Chap. III.—The Big Man With The Lame Head And The Little
Girl With The Lame Back.
Chap. IV.—A New Start.

A CHEER FOR PRINCETON

Glory, Glory to the Black and Orange,
It's the Tiger's turn today.
Glory, glory, it's the same old story
Soon as Princeton starts to play.
Eli, Eli, all your hopes are dead
For the Tiger's growling in his lair,
Don't you hear him?
You'll learn to fear him,
Try to face him if you dare.

Chorus
Princeton, cheer for Princeton,
Raise your voices, loud and free
Strong and steady
Ever ready
For defeat or victory.
Princeton, cheer for Princeton,
Always sure to win renown,
So we'll raise our praise to Nassau
To the pride of the Tiger town.

NOTE:—Many articles have appeared lately in our current magazines stating how simple it is for Germany to conquer this country. Is it? the TIGER asks. Read on, oh, gentilissimo!

THE CONQUEST OF AMERICA

(as some writers would have it:)

(Mr. Fitzcheesecake, who has written this article, needs no introduction. He has held numerous official positions: he was on three different beats in Trenton, and was for one year Deputy Garbage Man of Bordentown; and we feel that what he writes will be authoritative.)—THE EDITORS.

The American Atlantic fleet had been sunk. The Germans were coming in three thousand transports and were about to land in New York. Admiral Von Noseitch was swimming across with the fleet. Pandemonium reigned in the great city; women and tenors were running frantically up and down their rooms, the men having all left; the police force also, fearing to be called to the colors, had been in Canada for two months. Who was to raise and equip a vast army? The New York Baseball Team had finished in the second division, so Mgr. McGraw gave up all hope and volunteered; the new army, for secrecy, used a subway car to drill in. No help could be had from Boston, for they had won the pennant, and there was nothing on the front pages of the papers to warn the people of the imminent danger. General McGraw entrenched himself in the middle of Brooklyn for, so he thought, not even a German would go there. He was right, but three stray cannon balls came his way, and he struck out. The Statue of Liberty had been invested; New York's six million people were all captured; the Germans were upon them before preparation could be accomplished. Generals Von Limburger, Munchener, and Frankfurter held a consultation in Busty's the first night: General Von Limburger was going to attack General Bryan and his army of the Raritan in New Jersey; General Frankfurter was going to take a Day-Line boat to Albany and thence to Canada, where three-fourths of the citizens of the U.S. capable of bearing arms had fled for a much-needed rest; while General Munchener with thirty picked men would hold New York. Gen. Von Limburger took the 7 P. M. train to Princeton, near which place Bryan was reported to have fled. Meanwhile all the United States had been captured, save this section of New Jersey. The Pacific Squadron, however, was intact; they had been taken for fishing boats and had escaped without any injury. The besieging army was fast approaching the city; preceptors could be seen running madly to and fro, mostly fro. Bryan drew up his army in the TIGER Office; they voted five votes to one not to let a German live.

It was February. Glory Be! And meant all fortune to the United States! The Germans advanced. They were held up at Rocky Hill. They re-advance; they column right around the old mill; they pass the Prep; they leave the outskirts far behind. They cluster round the Chem. Lab. and then—Bei Reichstag, was ist? The Polar's Recess and the poisonous gases of the Lab hit that vast army at one fell swoop! Long had it been since they had heard the sound of guns, and the shock of Polar's Recess made them sore afraid. Some fled to the Nass. It was closed. Some rushed to Joe's. The promise of a small check cashed was too much for them. Some dove toward the Jigger Shop where a raspberry marshmallow nut meringue laid a hundred more beside their graves. Some sank upon the benches on Nassau Street. Both collapsed, each under the strain of seeing the other. Some tried to P-rade around the Cannon, but the prestige of Whig and Clio drove them off to Penn's Neck. And the one man left cried out, "I'm Gish—I touched the Cannon." Bryan's army rushed out of the TIGER Office and stuck him with the point of a joke—a joke preserved for these many years. America was saved, saved, SAVED, yes—saved by the point of a joke. YE GODS!

TO MY UNUSED GREEK BOOK

(Acknowledgments to Keats)

Thou still unravished bride of quietness,
  Thou joyless harbinger of future fear,
Garrulous alien, what thou mightst express
  Will never fall, please God, upon my ear.
What rhyme or reason can invest thy shape
  That is not found in countless syllabi?
What trots and cribs there are, what ponies rich,
  With all thou sing'st and in a clearer key.
Expose thee to a classroom's savage rape?
  Nay! better far remain within thy niche.

Tasks all complete are sweet, but those untried
  Are sweeter, therefore little book, with page
Uncut, stay pure, and live thy life inside,
  And wait for some appreciative age.
Oh, Author, most admired and left alone,
  Thou canst not ever see the garish day.
Editor: never, never wilt thou speak,
  But yellow grow and petrify to stone
Where I shall throw thee after tests next week;
  Yet grieve not—ever thou'lt have much to say.

Oh happy, happy leaves that cannot shed
  Their ink, or ever bid the print adieu;
Oh happy, happy bard who never bled
  At verse of his droned out with meaning new.
No words are penciled in a barbarous tongue
  Above thy dactyls oft misunderstood;
Caesuras are not marked to shame thy taste;
  Thy song is as you sing it, though unsung.
If not of use at least thou'rt noble waste;
  Let stand thy native accent as it should.

OUR NEXT ISSUE

THE JANUARY CHAOPOLITAN'S TREMENDOUS SCOOP.
SEVENTEEN of America's Leading Authors caught with the ink on their fingers.

AMERICA'S GREATEST ENEMY TO LITERATURE.
HARRISON FLAGG'S same old model appears for the first time in red hair.

JACK UNDONE. Author of *Primitive Primordial Primes, The Beer-Hound*, etc., etc., continues *The Soul-Struggle of a Passionate Duckling*, a story of the North Dakota Barnyards.

ELINOR GYN, in her own inimitable and suggestive way, will portray the career of a young Count who kisses with a Viennese accent in her new novel, *Experiences of Egbert Ethelred*.

MAURICE MATTERHORN emerges from his mists of mysticism to discuss whether women have souls.

OUT JULY 15TH.

$1.50 a year $1.50 a copy (unexpurgated)

We cannot begin subscriptions with back numbers. There are no back numbers. In combination with *La Vie Parisienne* and the *Atlantic Monthly*, two dollars a term. Our agent will call every Tuesday and Friday until suppressed.

JEMINA

A STORY OF THE BLUE RIDGE MOUNTAINS
BY JOHN PHLOX, JR.

It was night in the mountains of Kentucky.

Wild hills rose on all sides. Swift mountain streams flowed rapidly up and down the mountains.

Jemina Tantrum was down at the stream brewing whiskey at the family still.

She was a typical mountain girl.

Her feet were bare. Her hands, large and powerful, hung down below her knees. Her face showed the ravages of work. Although but sixteen, she had for over a dozen years been supporting her aged pappy and mappy by brewing mountain whiskey.

From time to time she would pause in her task, and, filling a dipper full of the pure invigorating liquid, would drain it off—then pursue her work with renewed vigor.

She would place the rye in the vat, thresh it out with her feet, and in twenty minutes the completed product would be turned out.

A sudden cry made her pause in the act of draining a dipper and look up.

"Hello," said a voice. It came from a man in hunting costume who had emerged from the wood.

"Hi, thar," she answered sullenly.

"Can you tell me the way to the Tantrums' cabin?"

"Are you uns from the settlements down thar?"

She pointed her hand down to the bottom of the hill where Louisville lay. She had never been there, but once, before she was born, her great-grandfather, old Gore Tantrum, had gone into the settlements in the company of two marshalls, and had never come back. So the Tantrums from generation to generation had learned to dread civilization.

The man was amused. He laughed a light tinkling laugh, the laugh of a Philadelphian. Something in the ring of it thrilled her. She drank off a dipper of whiskey.

"Where is Mr. Tantrum, little girl?" he asked kindly.

She raised her foot and pointed her big toe toward the woods.

"Thar in the cabing behind those thar pines. Old Tantrum air my ole man."

The man from the settlements thanked her and strode off. He was fairly vibrant with youth and personality. As he walked along he whistled and sang and turned handsprings and flapjacks, breathing in the fresh, cool air of the mountains.

The air around the still was like wine.

Jemina Tantrum watched him fascinated. No one like him had ever come into her life before.

She sat down on the grass and counted her toes. She counted eleven. She had learned arithmetic in the mountain school.

Ten years before, a lady from the settlements had opened a school on the mountain. Jemina had no money, but she had paid her way in whiskey, bringing a pailful to school every morning and leaving it on Miss Lafarge's desk. Miss Lafarge had died of delirium tremens after a year's teaching, and so Jemina's education had stopped.

Across the still stream still another still was standing. It was that of the Doldrums. The Doldrums and the Tantrums never spoke.

They hated each other.

Fifty years before old Jem Doldrum and old Jem Tantrum had quarrelled in the Tantrum cabin over a game of slapjack. Jem Doldrum had thrown the king of hearts in Jem Tantrum's face, and the old Doldrum, enraged, had felled the old Tantrum with the nine of diamonds. Other Doldrums and Tantrums had joined in and the little cabin was soon filled with flying cards. Hartsrum Doldrum lay stretched on the floor writhing in agony, the ace of hearts crammed down his throat. Jem Tantrum, standing in the doorway, ran through suit after suit, his face lit with fiendish hatred. Old Mappy Tantrum stood on the table wetting down the Doldrums with hot whiskey. Old Heck Doldrum, having finally run out of trumps, was backed out of the cabin, striking left and right with his tobacco pouch, and, gathering around him the rest of his clan, they mounted their cows and galloped furiously home.

That night old man Doldrum and his sons, vowing vengeance, had returned, put a tick-tock on the Tantrum window, stuck a pin in the doorbell and beaten a retreat.

A week later the Tantrums had put Cod Liver Oil in the Doldrum's still, and so, from year to year, the feud had continued, first one family being entirely wiped out and then the other.

Every day Jemina worked the still on her side of the stream, and Boscoe Doldrum worked the still on his side.

Sometimes, with inborn hatred, the feudists would throw whiskey at each other, and Jemina would come home smelling like a Bowery saloon on election night.

But now Jemina was too thoughtful to look across. How wonderful this stranger had been and how oddly he was dressed! In her innocent way she had never believed that there were any settlements at all, and she had put it down to the credulity of the mountain people.

She turned to go up to the cabin, and as she turned something struck her in the neck. It was a sponge soaked in whiskey, and thrown by Boscoe Doldrum—a sponge soaked in whiskey from his still on the other side.

"Hi thar, Boscoe Doldrum," she shouted in her deep bass voice.

"Yo', Jemina Tantrum. Gosh ding yo'!" he returned.

She continued up to the cabin.

The stranger was talking to her father. Gold had been discovered on the Tantrum land, and the stranger, Edgar Edison, was trying to buy the land for a song.

She sat upon her hands and watched him.

He was wonderful. When he talked his lips moved.

She sat upon the stove and watched him.

Suddenly there came a blood-curdling scream. The Tantrums rushed to the windows.

It was the Doldrums.

They had hitched their cows to trees and concealed themselves behind the bushes and flowers and soon a perfect rattle of stones and bricks beat against the windows, bending them inward.

"Father, Father," shrieked Jemina.

Her father took down his slingshot from his slingshot rack on the wall and ran his hand lovingly over the elastic band. He stepped to a loophole. Old Mappy Tantrum stepped to the coalhole.

The stranger was aroused at last. Furious to get at the Doldrums, he tried to get out of the house by crawling up the chimney. Then he thought there might be a door under the bed, but Jemina told him there was not one. He hunted for doors under the beds and sofas, but each time Jemina pulled him out and told him there were no doors there. Furious with anger, he beat upon the door and hollered at the Doldrums, but, cowed, they could not answer him, but kept up their fusillade of bricks and stones against the windows. Old Pappy Tantrum knew that as soon as they were able to effect an aperture they would pour in and the fight would be over.

Old Heck Doldrum, foaming at the mouth and spitting on the ground left and right, led the attack.

The terrific slingshots of old Pappy Tantrum had not been without their effect. A master shot had disabled one Doldrum, and another, shot three times through the abdomen and once through the stomach, fought feebly on.

Nearer and nearer they approached the house.

"We must fly," shouted the stranger to Jemina. "I will sacrifice myself and bear us both away."

"No," shouted Pappy Tantrum, his face begrimed with cold cream and grease paint. "You stay here and fit on. I will bar Jemina away. I will bar Mappy away. I will bar myself away."

The man from the settlements, pale and trembling with anger, turned to Ham Tantrum, who stood at the door throwing loophole after loophole at the advancing Doldrums.

"Will you cover the retreat?"

But Ham said that he too had Tantrums to bear away, but that he would leave himself here to help the stranger cover the retreat if he could think of a way of doing it.

Soon smoke began to filter through the floor and ceiling. Shem Doldrum had come up and touched a match to old Japhet Tantrum's breath as he leaned from a loophole, and the alcoholic flames shot up on all sides.

The whiskey in the bathtub caught fire. The walls began to fall in.

Jemina and the man from the settlements looked at each other.

"Jemina," he whispered.

"Stranger," she answered in an answering answer.

"We will die together," he said. "If we had lived I would have taken you to the settlements and married you. With your ability to hold liquor, your social success was assured."

She caressed him idly for a moment, counting her toes softly to herself. The smoke grew thicker. Her left leg was on fire. She was a human alcohol lamp.

Their lips met in one long kiss, and then a wall fell on them and blotted them out.

When the Doldrums burst through the ring of flame ten minutes later, they found them dead where they had fallen, their arms around each other.

Old Jem Doldrum was moved.

He took off his hat.

He filled it with whiskey and drank it off.

"They air daid," he said slowly. "They hankered after each other. The fit is over now. We must not separate them."

So they threw them together into the stream and the two splashes they made were as one.

THE VAMPIEST OF THE VAMPIRES

Kneeda Baral in the new screen version of Marie-Odile. An absolutely new interpretation of a much discussed part.

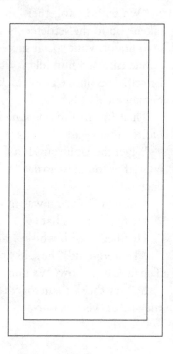

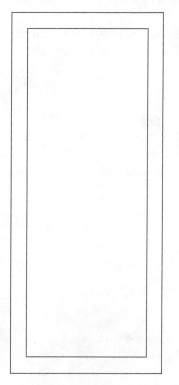

At the age of five. This precocious actress passed from the nursery to such parts as Carmen, Pollyanna, Sapho and Queen Elizabeth. Her first part was that of the Chicken in "Chanticleer."

EDITOR'S NOTE:—We have written for photographs but as yet Miss Baral has sent us none that we can possibly print.

THE USUAL THING

BY ROBERT W. SHAMELESS
SYNOPSIS OF PRECEDING CHAPTERS

John Brabant, adopted son of Jules Brabant, the South American Peccadillo Merchant, reaches New York penniless. He has, however, six letters of introduction, one of them unsigned, unsealed, and in fact unwritten. He presents all five of them, including the sixth, to John Brabant. John Brabant, a young South American, is in love with pretty Babette Lefleur, the daughter of Jules Lefleur, a merchant from South America. Upon Jules presenting four of the six letters of introduction which Babette Brabant has written to Jules Lefleur, John begins to realize that Jules, John, and Babette are in league against Brabant and Lefleur for some sinister purpose. Upon presenting the unwritten letter, he realizes that of the five letters Jules or possibly Babette has given Brabant the only clue to the case of Lefleur and his connection with Babette. At this point Jules and Lefleur meet in Central Park, and Jules, presenting the sixth or fifth letter, finds that Babette has given Brabant the letter that Jules presents to John. Confused by this, and, in fact, not realizing the importance of the third or fourth letter, he takes tea in his boudoir one day with Brabant. Brabant believes that some sinister connection with Lefleur has driven Babette from South America, where John had been employed in Lefleur's peccadillo factory. He takes boat to South America and, on board, sees Brabant also bound South on some secret mission. They decide to combine forces and destroy the second letter. Meanwhile, on the same ship, unknown to the other two, Brabant is disguised as a steward with the first, third and part of the fifth letters of introduction in his possession. As they pass through the Suez Canal a boat rows out from Cairo, and Brabant boards the ship. The other four notice his arrival, but fearful for the safety of the fourth and part of the sixth letter decide among themselves not to mention peccadillos or South America in general. Meanwhile Babette and Lefleur, still in Newport, are falling more and more deeply in love. Lefleur hears of this, and unwilling that Babette should become involved in an affair with this man, leaves his peccadillo factory in the charge of an employee named Brabant and comes North. George meets him in Troy at the business firm of Dulong and Petit, and boarding the train they rush to Tuxedo Park to join the others, and incidentally to seize the sixth letter, if the Countess has not already written it. Arriving in New York they take rooms at the Ritz, and begin the search for Brabant. Babette, in her boudoir, is sorting towels when the door suddenly bursts open and Genevieve comes in.

CHAPTER XXXI

Tea was being served at the VanTynes. On the long lawn the pear trees cast their shadows over the parties of three and four scattered about. Babette and Lefleur had secured a table in a secluded nook, and as the sun glimmered and danced on the burnished silver tea set, she told him the whole story. When she had finished neither spoke for a minute, while he reached into the little mother-of-pearl satchel that hung at his side for cigarettes.

He selected one; he lit a match.

She held it for him.

The cigarette instantly lighted.

"Well?" She smiled up at him, her eyes ringed with those long eyelashes that had evoked Rembrandt's enthusiastic praise in Holland the previous summer.

"Well?" He equivocated, shifting his foot from one knee to the other; the foot that had so often booted Harvard to victory on the gridiron.

"You see I am nothing but a toy after all," she sighed, "and I've wanted to be so much more—for you." Her voice sank to a whisper.

"That night," he exclaimed impetuously. "You did, didn't you?"

She blushed.

"Perhaps."

"And that other time in the Chauncy Widdecombs' limousine when you—"

"Hush," she breathed. "The servants: one is never alone. Oh! I'm tired of it all, the life I lead. I go to breakfast, what do I eat—grapefruit. I ride—where—the same old places. Do I see life? No!"

"Poor girl," he sympathized.

"It's horrible," she went on. "Nothing to eat but food, nothing to wear but clothes, nowhere to live but here and in the city." She flung her hand in a graceful gesture toward the city.

There was a silence. An orange rolled from the table down to the grass, then up again onto a chair where it lay orange and yellow in the sun. They watched it without speaking.

"Why can't you marry me," he began.

She interrupted.

"Don't, don't let's go over that again. Do you think I could ever live on your income? I—live over a stable, with the smelly horses smelling of horses. No—I'm selfish!"

"Not selfish, dear," he interrupted.

"Yes, selfish," she went on. "Do you think I could go around and bear the covert sneers of those who call themselves my friends? Yes, they would sneer at me riding around in your Saxon. No, Gordon— this morning I went downtown in sections in two Pierce-Arrows. I've got to have it."

"But dear," he broke in again, "I—"

"No, don't apologize. You say we do not need a box at the opera. We can sit in the stalls. But I can't sleep except in a box. I should be kept awake the whole time to bear the covert sneers of those who call themselves my friends. Yes, they would sneer at me."

He mused a moment, making the old clanging noise by snapping his lips together that he used to make, when, as two little friends, they played together in Central Park, then his family home.

He took her hand in his, his hand that had won so many baseball games for Yale, when known as Beau Brabant, he had been the pitcher. He thought of the hot languorous days of the previous summer, when they had read Gibbon's history of Rome to each other, and had thrilled over the tender love passages.

Mrs. VanTyne came tripping down the lawn, tripped over the grass, and tripped over the tea table.

"What are you two dears doing here?" she asked kindly, but suspiciously. "The others are waiting." She turned to Jules: "They think you have hidden the polo balls for a joke, and they are furious at you."

He smiled wearily. What had he to do with polo balls and other gilded ornaments of the world he had renounced forever?

"They are in the kitchen," he said slowly, "in the drawer with the soap." He ran slowly toward the walk with the famous dog-trot that had made him captain of the running team at Princeton.

Babette turned angrily to her mother.

"You have hurt him," she cried. "You are cold and cruel, mer- cenary and heartless, big and fat." She pushed her mother into the tea table.

The sun slowly sank out of sight, and long after the others were dressing and undressing for dinner Babette sat and watched the orange roll up and down from the lawn to the table, and wondered if, in its own dumb way, it had solved the secret of things.

CHAPTER XXXII

As Babette left the house, followed by a deferential butler carrying her suitcases, she glanced back and saw the Countess Jenavra silhouetted in the doorway.

"Good trip," shouted the Countess.

Lefleur, his Saxon purring with energy, was waiting at the gates. She stepped in the front seat. Muffled in fur robes, blankets, overcoats, old sacking, and cotton batting, she gazed once more back at the house. The brilliant Cedric I exterior was punctuated by flashes denoting early English windows. In the Elizabethan doorway stood the Colonial figure of Babette's mother.

The butler gave the car a deferential push, and they started bowling down the long highway alone. The trees bent as if to intercept them, swooping back, however, as they burst by. Lefleur, his foot upon the cylinder, felt a wild exhilaration sweeping over him as they bobbed madly up and down, to and fro, toward the city.

"John," she began, "I know—" she paused and seemed to breathe—"that you think," her voice sank to a whisper, then lower still. Nothing could be heard but the rasping of her teeth against her jaws.

"Unghlt," she said, as they passed Bridgeport. It was not until Greenwich that she got his answering "Gthliuup."

The town was a mere speck as they sped by. He increased the speed. Leaning back against his shoulder, she felt a deep, perfect content surge through her. Surely this was living or more than living. The cold air surging by turned her senses cold and tense. Sharp as a whip, everything, all her life, stood out against the background of this ride. She wondered if all things could not be solved in this way, with the sting of the fresh night and the rat-tat of the motor.

Up to this time he had been running on two cylinders. He now threw on two more, and the car, careening up for a second on its front wheels, righted itself and continued with its speed redoubled. However, in the confusion of the change, his right arm had become disengaged and thrown around her. She did not move it.

Faster they went. He pressed harder on the steering gear, and in response to his pressure, the car sprang forward like a well-trained steed. They were late, and realizing it, he threw on the last two cylinders. The car seemed to realize what was demanded of it. It stopped, turned around three times, and then bounded off at twice its former speed.

Along they went. Suddenly the car stopped, and with the instinct of a trained mechanic, he realized that something was the matter. After an inspection, he saw that one of the tires was punctured. He looked to see what damage had been done. They had run over a hairpin, and the rubber was torn and splintered to shreds. They looked around for another tire. They looked in the back seat, they looked under the car, they looked behind the bushes on the edge of the road. There was no tire. They must fix the old one. John put his mouth to the puncture and blew it up, sticking his handkerchief into the hole.

They started off, but after several miles, the grueling strain of the road wore through the handkerchief, little by little, and the car stopped again. They tried everything, leaves and gravel, and pieces of the road. Finally Babette sacrificed her gum to stop up the gaping aperture, but after several miles this too wore out.

There was but one thing to do, to take off the tire, run into town on three wheels, and hire a man to run along beside the car and hold up the fourth side. No sooner had they had this thought than they put it into action. Three whistles, and a cry of "buckwheats," brought a crowd of Yokels in a jiffy; and the most intelligent-looking one of the lot was engaged for the arduous task.

He took his place by the fender, and they again started off. They increased the speed soon, driving along at the rate of forty miles an hour. The Yokel, running beside with a long easy stride, was panting and seemed to have difficulty in keeping up the pace.

It was growing darker. Sitting up close to John's huge rat-skin coat, Babette felt the old longing to see his eyes close to hers, and feel his lips brush her cheek.

"John," she murmured. He turned. Above the clatter of the motor and the harsh plebeian breathing of the peasant, she heard his heart heave with emotion.

"Babette," he said.

She started sobbing softly, her voice mingling with the roar of the fan belt.

He folded her slowly, dignifiedly, and willfully in his arms and ki————.

The next installment of Mr. Shameless' fascinating story will appear in the July number.

LITTLE MINNIE McCLOSKEY

A STORY FOR GIRLS

EDITOR'S NOTE—*Not since "Little Women" have we had so moving a picture of girlhood hopes and dreams.*

It was midnight in Miss Pickswinger's Select Seminary for Young Ladies (country location, hot and cold water, wrestling, bull-baiting, and other outdoor sports; washing, ironing, and Bulgarian extra). A group of girls had gathered in a cozy room. There was going to be a midnight feast. Oh, goody! There was but little light, for, fearing to turn on the acetylene, they had built a bonfire on the table, and one girl was appointed to feed the faint flames with false hair and legs which she wrenched quietly from the chairs and tables. A saddle of venison for their little supper was turning over and over on a spit in the cooking stove in the corner, and the potatoes were boiling noiselessly in the steam radiator. Perched like a little queen on the armchair sat Louise Sangfroid, the hostess; on the mantlepiece lay Mary Murgatroid in red and white striped pajamas, while balancing on the molding sat Minnie McCloskey in a nightshirt of Yaeger flannel. Other girls sat around the room, two on a trunk which they had ingeniously improvised as a chair, one on an empty case of beer and three on a heap of broken glass and tin cans in the corner.

Girls will be girls! Ah, me! They would have their little frolic; a cask of Haig and Haig, stolen from Miss Pickswinger's private stock, was behind the door and the mischievous girls had almost finished it.

Minnie McCloskey was the school drudge; she was working for her education. At three every morning she rose, made the beds, washed the dishes, branded the cattle, cut the grass, and did many other tasks. She was known affectionately to her companions as "Piggy" McCloskey. (All the girls had nicknames. How they got them no one knew.) Amy Gulps was called "Fatty," perhaps because she was fat; Mary Munks was called "Red," conceivably because she had red hair. Phoebe Cohop was called "Boils," possibly because—(but enough, let us continue).

"Girls," said Bridget Mulcahey, a petite little French girl, whose father had been shot at Soissons (for deserting), "let's play a prank."

A chorus of ohs! and ahs! and girlish giggles greeted this suggestion.

"What shall we do?" asked Gumpsa LePage.

"Something exciting," said Bridget. "Let's hang Miss Pickswinger." All assented enthusiastically except Minnie McCloskey.

"'Fraid cat," sneered the others. "'Fraid you'll get punished."

"No," said Minnie. "But think of all she's done for me."

They struck her savagely with chairs, locked her in and rushed off. There was but one chance. Minnie quickly braided a rope out of rugs, lowered herself from the window, quickly wove another rope out of grass, raised herself to Miss Pickswinger's window. They were not there. There was yet time to outwit them. Suddenly she gasped in horror.

* * *

A moment later the rollicking crowd of girls was confronted in front of Miss Pickswinger's door by a slender figure. It was Minnie.

"You cannot pass," she said sternly.

"Do you mean to say we cannot hang Miss Pickswinger if we wish?" cried Louise, indignantly.

Minnie shivered with emotion and sneezed with emotion. Then she spoke.

"There is no need. She has gotten one of her bedroom slippers in her mouth and choked to death."

The girls rushed off shouting "Holiday" and striking each other playfully on the head with stones, but Minnie, in the room above, threw herself down upon the heap of glass in the corner and sobbed as if her heart would break.

ONE FROM PENN'S NECK

Baby Ben, Baby Ben, you annoy a lot of men
With your aggravating tinkle at about eight-ten.
I'm dreaming pretty dreams about the girls who love me—when
I hear your voice a-calling, Baby Ben.

* * *

A LITANY OF SLANG

From "Knockouts"—	Great Von Hindenburg deliver us.
From "dopeless" people—	Great Von, etc.
From "sardines"—	Great Von, etc.
From "trick" things—	Great Von, etc.
From "trick" people—	Great Von, etc.
From "I'll say"—	Great Von, etc.
From lads who "have it"—	Great Von, etc.
From lads who "lack it"—	Great Von, etc.
From "nice fellow you are"—	Great Von, etc.
From "Hotstuff"—	Great Von, etc.
From "Persian Petters"—	Great Von, etc.
From all last year's slang—	Great Von Hindenburg do deliver us if you get time. Amen.

* * *

"TRIANGLE SCENERY BY BAKST"

—*Princetonian.*

We are glad to see that this scene designer has broken his fifty-thousand-dollar contract with the Russian Ballet. The Triangle Club must be prospering. Next year's score by Claude Debussy?

* * *

FUTURISTIC IMPRESSIONS OF THE EDITORIAL BOARDS

The Prince—A merry-go-round game of "who read the proof?" with solid gold-filled radicalism every morning before breakfast.

The Lit—Half a dozen men who agree, at the price of appearing in print, to listen to each others' manuscript.

The Pic—The tall man with the black box who gets in front of the umpire all through May.

THE TIGER—A lot of lo—yes, sir; all right, sir, a collection of artists and side-splitting humorists.

* * *

"A GLASS OF BEER KILLS HIM"

—New York Sun.

brought forth "Ex Princetoniensi non erat"
from the *Yale Record.*
Right again. Probably someone threw it at an Eli.

* * *

"OUI, LE BACKFIELD . . ."

Oui, le backfield est from Paris
Quel les Eli studes adore,
C'est Messieurs Laroche and Neville
Messieurs Jaques et LeGore.
—Maxim of General Joffre.

* * *

"WHEN YOU FIND . . ."

"When you find a man doing a little more than his duty, you find that kind of patriotism not found in Blair or Campbell."
—Oliver Wendell Holmes.
We were under the impression that Mr. Holmes went to Harvard, but he evidently roomed in North Edwards.

* * *

THINGS THAT NEVER CHANGE!
NUMBER 3333

"Oh, you fr-shm-n, where shall we go. Let's go to J—'s. I want to get a sm-ll check c-shed. We g-t g—d M-j-st-c s-ndw-tches there."

THE TIGER's reward for the most complete solution will be a m-j-st-c s-ndw-tch at J—'s.

THE OLD FRONTIERSMAN
A Story of the Frontier

It was the middle of the forest. A figure might have been noticed crawling along, sniffing at the ground. It was Old Davy Underbush, the frontiersman and b'ar hunter. He was completely invisible and inaudible. The only way you could perceive him was by the sense of smell.

He was dressed as a frontiersman (*cf.* "what the men will wear," theatre programs of 1776). On his feet he wore moccasins made from the skin of the wood weasel. Around his legs were coonskin spats which ran into his trousers made of sheepskin; these extended to the waist. He wore a belt made of an old rattlesnake and a long bearskin coat. Around his head was wrapped a fishskin hat. At his hip hung horrible trophies of Indian warfare. One scalp of Object the Ojibway, still wet with Oleaqua, hung there beside the pompadour of Eardrum the Iroquois and the cowlick of Bootblack the Blackfoot. By his side walked "Très Bien," his trusty Eskimo cheesehound.

He carried a muzzle-loading shotgun, an old horse-pistol, and a set of razors. He was on the trail of Sen-Sen the Seneca and Omlette the Omega. They had come into the clearing and drunk all the fire-water from the fire-water factory. As they left they had, in the usual Indian manner, carved their initials on each tree they passed and it was by this that the astute old frontiersman had been sent out to track them.

It was now too dark to read the initials plainly and Davy often got them mixed up with those of other savages who had passed that way before. For three weeks the old b'ar hunter had followed them, living on the berries from the bushes and sometimes, when no berries were to be found, snatching great handfuls of grass and dry leaves and devouring them.

As he crawled along he was thinking. If he did not find the redskins soon he would have to eat his moccasins. His scarred brow was knit with worry.

All around him were the noises of the forest; the long sad "Hoo" of the Huron, the plaintive sigh of the Sioux, and the light cackle of the Apache. Suddenly a new sound broke the stillness. It was the dry harsh cawing of the Seneca. Davy ran forward noiselessly. He was careful to make no sound. He ran with his feet completely off the ground to leave no clue for the watchful redmen. Sure enough the savages were in a little clearing in the forest playing on their primitive musical instruments. Sen-Sen the Seneca sat playing "The Last Rose of Summer" on an old comb wrapped in tissue paper, and Omlette the Omega accompanied him on the snare Tom-Tom. The old frontiersman burst in on them waving his gun at them and threatening their scalps with one of his tempered razors.

The fight which ensued was furious.

The savages pulled his coat over his ears and hit him on the head with their bows and arrows. One would kneel behind Davy and the other would push the old frontiersman over him. Sen-Sen combed all the hair of his sheepskin trousers the wrong way and, frantic with pain, the old b'ar hunter fought on.

Finally Omlette the Omega withdrew to a distance and, taking a station behind the old frontiersman, let fly an arrow at him which passed through his sheepskin trousers and pierced his catskin underwear. The old b'ar hunter expired.

The savages fried him for dinner but found, to their disappointment, that he was all dark meat owing to his lifelong exposure to the sun.

THE DEBUTANTE

The scene is a boudoir, or whatever you call a lady's room which hasn't a bed. Smaller rooms communicate with it, one on each side. There is a window at the left and a door leading into the hall at the back. A huge pier-glass stands in the corner; it is the only object in the room which is not littered with an infinitude of tulle, hat-boxes, empty boxes, full boxes, ribbons and strings, dresses, skirts, suits, lingerie, petticoats, lace, open jewel-cases, sashes, belts, stockings, slippers, shoes—perfectly littered with more than all this. In the very middle of the confusion stands a girl. She is the only thing in the room which looks complete, or nearly complete. She needs to have her belt hooked, and has too much powder on her nose; but, aside from that, looks as though she might be presented to almost anything at almost any time, which is just what is going to happen to her. She is terrifically pleased with herself, and the long mirror is the focus of her activity. Her rather discontented face is consciously flexible to the several different effects. Expression number one seems to be a simple, almost childish, ingenue, upward glance, concentrated in the eyes and the exquisitely angelic eyelashes. When expression number two is assumed, one forgets the eyes, and the mouth is the center of the stage. The lips seem to turn from rose to a positive, unashamed crimson. They quiver slightly—where is the ingenue?

Disappeared. Good evening Sapho, Venus, Madam Du—no! ah! Eve, simply Eve! The pier-glass seems to please. Expression number three:—Now her eyes and lips combine. Can this be the last stronghold? The aesthetic refuge of womanhood; her lips are drawn down at the corners, her eyes droop and almost fill with tears. Does her face turn paler? Does—No! Expression one has dismissed tears and pallor, and again—

HELEN—What time is it?

(*The sewing machine stops in the room at the left.*)

VOICE—I haven't a watch, Miss Helen.

HELEN—(*Assuming expression number three and singing to the mirror*) "Poor butterfly—by the blossoms waiting—poor butter——" What time do you think it is, Narry, old lady? Where's Mother, Narry?

NARRY—(*Rather crossly*) I am sure I haven't the slightest idea.

HELEN—Narry! (*No answer.*) Narry, I called you "old lady," because—(*She pauses. The sewing machine swings into an emphatic march.*) Because it's the last chance I will have.

The machine stops again and Narry comes into the room sniffing. Narry is exactly of the mold with which the collective temperaments of Helen and her family have stamped her. She is absolutely adamant with everyone not a member of the family and absolutely putty in the hands of the least capable of them.

NARRY—You might just not call me "old lady." (*She sniffs, and handkerchiefs herself.*) Goodness gracious! I feel old enough now with you going out.

HELEN—Coming!

NARRY—Coming—

HELEN—(*Her mind wandering to her feet, which carry her around the room to the sound of her voice.*) "The moments pass into hours—the hours pass into years—and as she smiles through—"

Peremptory voice with the maternal rising accent ascends the stairs, and curls into the bedroom.

VOICE—Hel-*en*.

HELEN—(*With more volume than you would imagine could go with such a deliciously useless figure*) Yes, Mother.

MOTHER—(*Drawing near.*) Are you very nearly ready, dear? I am coming up. I have had such a hard time with one of the waiters.

HELEN—I know, Mother. Tight as he could be. Narry and I watched him try to get up when they threw him outside into the yard.

MOTHER—(*Now on the stairway landing*) You and Narry should not have done any such thing, Helen dear. I am surprised at Narry. I— (*She seems to pause and pant.*)

NARRY—(*Almost shouting*) I do declare, Mrs. Halycon. I—

Mrs. Halycon appears in the doorway and becomes the center of the stage. She is distinctly a factor in the family life. Neither her daughter's slang nor her son's bills discourage her in the least. She is jeweled and rouged to the dowager point.

MRS. HALYCON—Now, Narry. Now, Helen. (*She produces a small notebook.*) Sit down and be quiet. (*Narry sits down anxiously on a chair which emerges from the screen of dresses. Helen returns to the pier-glass, and the sequence of expressions passes over her face in regular rotation.*) Now, I've made some notes here—let's see. I've made notes on things you must do. Just as I have thought of them, I have put them down. (*She seats herself somewhere and becomes severely judicial.*) First, and absolutely, you must not sit out with anyone. (*Helen looks bored.*) I've stood for it at your other dances and heaven knows how many dances of other people, but I will not, understand me, I will not endure to look all over for you when some friend of mine, or of your father's, wants to meet you. You must tonight, you must all season—I mean you must stay in the ballroom, or some room where I can find you when I want you. Do you understand?

HELEN—(*Yawning*) Oh, yes! You would think I didn't know what to do.

MRS. HALYCON—Well, do it if you know how. I will not endure finding you in a dark corner of the conservatory, exchanging silliness with anyone, or listening to it.

HELEN—(*Sarcastically*) Yes, listening to it *is* better.

MRS. HALYCON—And you positively cannot give more than two dances to young Cannel. I will not have everyone in town having you engaged before you have had a fair chance.

HELEN—Same old line. You'd think from the way you talk that I was some horrible old man-chaser, or someone so weak and wobbly that you'd think I'd run off with someone. Mother, for heaven's sake—

MRS. HALYCON—My dear, I am doing my very best for you.

HELEN—(*Wearily*) I know. (*She sits down decidedly on another invisible chair.*) Mother, I happen, my dear, to have four dances with John Cannel. He called up, asked me for four of them, and what could I say? Besides, it's a cut-in dance, and he would cut in as much as he wants anyhow. So what's the difference? (*Becoming impatient*) You can't run everything now, the way they did in the early nineties.

MRS. HALYCON—Helen, I've told you before that you can't say early nineties to me.

HELEN—Don't treat me like a child then.

Mr. Halycon comes in. He is a small man with a large appearance and a board-of-directors heartiness.

MR. HALYCON—(*Feeling that the usual thing is expected of him*) Well, how is my little debutante daughter? About to flit into the wide, wide world?

HELEN—No, Daddy, just taking a more licensed view of it.

MR. HALYCON—(*Almost apologetically*) Helen, I want you to meet a particular friend of mine, a youngish man—

HELEN—About forty-five?

MRS. HALYCON—Helen!

HELEN—Oh, I like them forty-five. They know life, and are so adorably tired-looking.

MR. HALYCON—And he is very anxious to meet you. He saw you when you came into my office one day, I believe—and let me tell you, he is a brainy man. Brought up from Providence by the—

HELEN—(*Interrupting*) Yes, Daddy, I'll be delighted to meet him. I'll—

Enter Cecilia, Helen's younger sister. Cecilia is sixteen, but socially precocious and outrageously wise on all matters pertaining to her sister. She has blonde hair, in contrast to her sister's dark brown; and, besides, remarkable green eyes with a wistful trusting expression in them. However, there are very few people whom she trusts.

CECILIA—(*Calmly surveying the disorder around her*) Nice-looking room.

HELEN—Well, what do you expect? Nothing but milliners, dress-makers and clumsy maids all day. (*Narry rises and leaves the room.*) What's the matter with her?

MRS. HALYCON—You've hurt her feelings.

HELEN—Have I? What time is it?

Mrs. Halycon—Quarter after eight. Are you ready? You've got too much powder on.

Helen—I know it.

Mr. Halycon—Well, look me up when you come down; I want to see you before the rush. I'll be in the library with your uncle.

Mrs. Halycon—And don't forget the powder.

Mr. and Mrs. Halycon go out.

Helen—Hook up my belt, will you, Cecilia?

Cecilia—Yes. (*She sets at it, Helen in the meanwhile regarding herself in the mirror.*) What are you looking at yourself all the time for?

Helen—(*Calmly*) Oh, just because I like myself.

Cecilia—I am all twittered! I feel as if I were coming out myself. It is rotten of them not to let me come to the dance.

Helen—Why, you've just only put your hair up. You'd look ridiculous.

Cecilia—(*Quietly*) I know where you keep your cigarettes and your little silver bottle.

Helen—(*Starting so as to unloosen several hooks, which Cecilia patiently does over again*) Why, you horrible child! Do you go prying around among all my things?

Cecilia—All right, tell Mother.

Helen—What do you do, just go through my drawers like a common little sneak-thief?

Cecilia—No, I don't. I wanted a handkerchief, and I went to looking and I couldn't help seeing them.

Helen—That's what comes of letting you children fool around with no chaperons, read anything you want to, and dance until two every Saturday night all summer. If it comes to that, I'll tell something I saw that I didn't say anything about. Just before we came into town, that night you asked me if you could take Blaine MacDonough home in the electric, I happened to be passing at the end of the drive by the club, and I saw him kiss you.

Cecilia—(*Unmoved*) We were engaged.

Helen—(*Frantically*) Engaged! You silly little fool! If any older people heard that you two were talking like that, you wouldn't be allowed to go with the rest of your crowd.

CECILIA—That's all right, but you know why you didn't tell, because what were *you* doing there by the drive with John Cannel?

HELEN—Hush! You little devil.

CECILIA—All right. We'll call it square. I just started by wanting to tell you that Narry knows where those cigarettes are too.

HELEN—(*Losing her head*) You and Narry have probably been smoking them.

CECILIA—(*Amused*) Imagine Narry smoking.

HELEN—Well, *you* have been anyway.

CECILIA—You had better put them somewhere else.

HELEN—I'll put them where you can't find them, and if you weren't going back to school this week, I would go to Mother and tell her the whole thing.

CECILIA—Oh, no you wouldn't. You wouldn't even do it for my good. You're too selfish.

Helen, still very superior, marches into the next room. Cecilia goes softly to the door, slams it without going out, and disappears behind the bureau. She emerges tip-toe, takes a cushion from an arm chair, and retires again to her refuge. Helen again reappears. Almost immediately a whistle sounds outside, twice repeated. She looks annoyed and goes to the window.

HELEN—John!

JOHN—(*From below*) Helen, can I see you a moment?

HELEN—No, indeed. There are people all over the house. Mother would think I had gone mad if she saw us talking out of the window.

JOHN—(*Hopefully*) I'll climb up.

HELEN—John, don't. You'll tear your dress clothes. (*He is evidently making good, as deduced from a few muttered fragments, barely audible.*) Look out for the spike by the ledge. (*A moment later he appears in the window, a young man of twenty-two, good-looking, but at present not particularly cheerful.*)

HELEN—(*Sitting down*) You simple boy! Do you want the family to kill me? Do you realize how conspicuous you are?

JOHN—(*Hopefully*) I'd better come in.

HELEN—No, you had better not. Mother may be up at any moment.

JOHN—Better turn out the lights. I make a good movie standing like this on this ledge.

Helen hesitates and then turns out all the lights except an electric lamp on the dresser.

HELEN—(*Assuming an effective pose in the arm chair*) What on earth do you want?

JOHN—I want you. I want to know that you are mine when I see you dancing around with this crowd tonight.

HELEN—Well, I am not. I belong to myself tonight, or rather to the crowd.

JOHN—You've been rotten to me this week.

HELEN—Have I?

JOHN—You're tired of me.

HELEN—No, not that. The family. (*They have evidently been over this ground before.*)

JOHN—It isn't the family, and you know it.

HELEN—Well, to tell the truth, it isn't exactly the family.

JOHN—I know it isn't. It's me—and you, and I'm getting desperate. You've got to do something one way or the other. We are engaged, or—

HELEN—Well, we are not engaged.

JOHN—Then what are we? What do you think about me, or do you think about me? You never tell me anymore. We're drifting apart. Please, Helen—!

HELEN—It's a funny business, John, just how I do feel.

JOHN—It isn't funny to me.

HELEN—No, I don't suppose it is. You know, if you just weren't so in love with me—

JOHN—(*Gloomily*) Well, I am.

HELEN—You see, there is no novelty in that. I always know just what you are going to say.

JOHN—I wish *I* did. When you first met me, you used to tell me that you loved to hear me talk, because you never knew what I was going to say.

HELEN—Well, I've found out. I like to run things, but it gets monotonous to always know that I am the key to the situation. If we are together, and I feel high, we enjoy ourselves. If I feel unhappy, then we don't; or anyway you don't. How you're feeling never has anything to do with it.

JOHN—Wouldn't it be that way with most couples?

HELEN—Oh, I suppose so. It would be if I were the girl.

JOHN—Well, what do you want?

HELEN—I want—Oh, I'll be frank for once. I like the feeling of going after them. I like the thrill when you meet them and notice that they've got black hair that's wavy, but awfully neat, or have dark lines under their eyes, and look charmingly dissipated, or have funny smiles that come and go and leave you wondering whether they smiled at all. Then I like the way they begin to follow you with their eyes. They're interested. Good! Then I begin to place him. Try to get his type, find what he likes; right then the romance begins to lessen for me and increase for him. Then come a few long talks.

JOHN—(*Bitterly*) I remember.

HELEN—Then, John, here's the worst of it. There's a point where everything changes.

JOHN—(*Mournfully interested*) What do you mean?

HELEN—Well, sometimes it's a kiss and sometimes it's long before anything like that. Now if it's a kiss, it can do one of three things.

JOHN—Three! It's done a thousand to me.

HELEN—It can make him get tired of you, but a clever girl can avoid this. It's only the young ones and the heroines of magazine epigrams that are kissed and deserted. Then there's the second possibility. It can make you tired of him. This is usual. He immediately thinks of nothing but being alone with the girl, and she, rather touchy about the whole thing, gets snappy, and he's first lovesick, then discouraged, and finally lost.

JOHN—(*More grimly*) Go on.

HELEN—Then the third state is where the kiss really means something, where the girl lets go of herself and the man is in deadly earnest.

JOHN—Then they're engaged?

HELEN—Exactly.

JOHN—Weren't we?

HELEN—(*Emphatically*) No, we distinctly were not. I knew what I was doing every blessed second, John Cannel.

JOHN—Very well, don't be angry. I feel mean enough already.

HELEN—(*Coldly*) Do you?

JOHN—Where do I come in? This is all a very clever system of yours, and you've played through it. You go along your way looking for another movie hero with black hair, or light hair, or red hair, and I am left with the same pair of eyes looking at me, the same lips moving in the same words to another poor fool, the next—

HELEN—For Heaven sakes don't cry!

JOHN—Oh, I don't give a damn what I do!

HELEN—(*Her eyes cast down to where her toe traces a pattern on the carpet*) You are very young. You would think from the way you talk that it was my fault, that I tried not to like you.

JOHN—Young! Oh, I'm in the discard, I know.

HELEN—Oh, you'll find someone else.

JOHN—I don't want anyone else.

HELEN—(*Scornfully*) You're making a perfect fool of yourself.

There is a silence. She idly kicks the heel of her slipper against the rung of the chair.

JOHN—(*Slowly*) It's this damn Charlie Wordsworth.

HELEN—(*Raising her eyes quickly*) If you want to talk like that you'd better go. Please go now.

She rises. John watches her a moment and then admits his defeat.

JOHN—Helen, don't let's do like this. Let's be friends. Good God, I never thought I would have to ask you for just that.

She runs over and takes his hand, affecting a hopeful cheerfulness which immediately revolts him. He drops her hand and disappears from the window. She leans out and watches him.

HELEN—Watch for that spike. Oh, John, I warned you. You've torn your clothes.

JOHN—(*Drearily from below*) Yes, I've torn my clothes. I certainly play in wonderful luck. Such an effective exit.

HELEN—Are you coming to the dance?

JOHN—No, of course I am not. Do you think I'd come just to see you and Charlie—

HELEN—(*Gently*) Good-night, John.

She closes the window. Outside a clock strikes nine. The clatter of a few people on the stairway comes muffled through the door. She turns on the lights and, going up to the glass, looks long and with an intense interest at herself. A powder puff comes into use for an instant. An errant wisp of hair is tucked into position, and a necklace from somewhere slides into place.

MRS. HALYCON—(*Outside*) Oh, Helen!

HELEN—Coming, Mother.

She opens the top bureau drawer, takes out a silver cigarette case, and a miniature silver flask, and places them in a side drawer of the writing desk. Then she turns out all the lights and opens the door. The tuning of violins comes in nervous twangs and discord up the stairs. She turns once more and stands by the window. From below, there is a sudden burst of sound, as the orchestra swings into "Poor Butterfly." The violins and faint drums and a confused chord from a piano, the rich odor of powder and new silk, a blend of laughters all surge together into the room. She dances toward the mirror, kisses the vague reflection of her face, and runs out the door.

Silence for a moment. Bundled figures pass along the hall, silhouetted against the lighted door. The laughter heard from below becomes doubled and multiplied. Suddenly a moving blur takes shape behind the bureau. It resolves itself into a human figure, which arises, tip-toes over and shuts the door. It crosses the room, and the lights go on again. Cecilia looks about her and, with the light of definite purpose in her rich green eyes, goes to the desk drawer, takes out the minature flask and the cigarette case. She lights a cigarette and, puffing and coughing, walks to the pier-glass.

CECILIA—(*Addressing her future self*) Oh, yes! Really, coming out is such a farce nowadays, y'know. We really play around so much before we are seventeen, that it's positive anticlimax. (*Shaking hands with a visionary middle-aged man of the world*) Yes, I b'lieve I've heard m' sister speak of you. Have a puff. They're very good. They're Coronas. You don't smoke? What a pity.

She crosses to the desk and picks up the flask. From downstairs the rain of clapping between encores rises. She raises the flask, uncorks it, smells it, tastes a little, and then drinks about the equivalent of two cocktails. She replaces the flask, makes a wry face and, as the music starts again, fox-trots slowly around the room, waving the cigarette with intense seriousness, and watching herself in the long mirror.

CURTAIN

"PENROD AND SAM"

"Penrod and Sam," by Booth Tarkington, '93, another collection of "Penrod" stories, is the typical second book of a series. At times it maintains the rather high level of humor set by its predecessor, "Penrod," but certain of the stories seem to have been turned out solely to fill a contract with the "Cosmopolitan" magazine.

The same set of characters figures once more. Mr. Tarkington has done what so many authors of juvenile books fail to do: he has admitted the unequaled snobbishness of boyhood and has traced the neighborhood social system which, with Penrod and Sam at the top, makes possible more than half the stories. Herman and Verman, the colored brethren, may be socially eligible, but Maurice Levy, barely a "regular fellow," is never quite admitted as an equal. Georgie Basset, "the best boy in town," and Roddy Bitts, the hothouse plant, are clearly outside the pale; although we claim that there is still hope for Roddy, there is a certain disagreeableness about him which is too sure to be despised. It is to be regretted that Carlie Chitten, a future Machiavelli, figures in only one story. He and Penrod are truer types of success than are to be found in the intricacies of a dozen psychological novels.

The first two stories, "The Bonded Prisoner" and "Bingism," belong distinctly in the filler class, although both have Tarkington touches. The third story, "The In-or-In," the history of an ill-fated secret society, is really funny, and so is the next one, "The Story of Whitey," the horse that was rescued in spite of himself. "Conscience" and "Gipsy" are not so good, but the following tale, "Wednesday Madness," is uproariously funny. It is as good as the best parts of "Seventeen." Penrod tries to pass off a rather sentimental letter of his sister's as his own composition, in answer to a demand made at school for a model letter to a friend. This leads to a wild Wednesday of fights, flights, and fatalities, the last of which is the spanking which awaits him as he trudges home at seven-thirty.

"Penrod's Busy Day" and "On Account of the Weather" are both amusing; the "Horn of Fame" is rather poor. The book ends with "The Party," easily the best story. From the sleek advent of Carlie Chitten to Marjorie's confession that she loves Penrod because of his capabilities for evil, it is extremely well done, and brings back a dozen like experiences to the reader's memory. Where Mr. Tarkington gets his knowledge of child psychology, I am unable to understand. It has become a tradition to mention Tom Brown as an ideal boy's story, but as a matter of fact, the heroes of Owen Johnson, Compton Mackenzie, and Booth Tarkington are far more interesting and far truer to facts.

("Penrod and Sam," *by Booth Tarkington. Doubleday Page &
Co., New York. $1.35 net.)*

"BOY KILLS SELF . . ."

BOY KILLS SELF RATHER THAN PET.

—New York Journal.

Nice fellow!!

***

THINGS THAT NEVER CHANGE. NO. 3982

Is it $\left\{ \begin{array}{l} \text{hot} \\ \text{cold} \end{array} \right\}$ enough for you?

PRECAUTION PRIMARILY

*The scene is a paint box. Large greens and whites form the back,
a blue leans against the side and many small greens edged with
orange are scattered around artistically. As the curtain rises music
is falling gently from the strange melancholy individuals who sit in
front dressed in their blacks and whites. They all look sadly at the
stage which is now filled with people dressed in purple splotched
with mauve sitting on pale violets.*

*The chorus can be heard to remark vaguely in the old English in
which all opening choruses are written.*

Oh gleeumph wax wash ich
Vil na wan in bun oh
Bun-gi-wow
Il bur lee burly. Oh Gish Bush!

*They accompany this by the appropriate dance. The audience
lean back wearily and wait for the play to begin.*

*Enter the football team disguised as chorus men and the Prom
Committee in pink tights.*

Cue: "Look back in your score books; look at Hank O'Day."

Song.
Henry O'Day, Henry O'Day,
King of the neutrals were you;
Kaisers or Kings, Hughie Jenn*ings*
All were impartially blue.
Called a ball
When you meant a strike;
Heard them call
"For the love of Mike," etc.

(*Pause.*)

(*Enter two mere striplings, stripped, boiled in grease paint and decorated in Hawaiian straw.*)

Song.

Junior, shave your mustache, you're souring all the milk.

(*At the back of the Casino the long-haired authors walk up and down feeling about as comfortable as the Kaiser's own before another offensive.*)

FIRST AUTHOR—How do you think the thing's going?

SECOND DITTO—Fine! Not two minutes ago I heard a laugh in the eighteenth row. It was my joke about the—

FIRST AUTHOR—Your joke, Ha-Ha! you make me laugh—Did my line about—, etc.

FIRST MUSIC WRITER (*aside*)—As if anyone listened to the dialogue.

SECOND MUSIC WRITER—How my songs do stand out.

LYRICIST—Remarkable how a good lyric redeems a bad tune. (*Listens to the silent audience and wishes the senior in the front row would control his whooping-cough until the dialogue begins again.*)

(*Behind the scenes.*)

CORINNE—Knockout girl in the front row.

CHLORINE—No dope.

CORINNE—She likes my eyes.

CHLORINE—Wait till she sees your legs in the next chorus.

FLUORINE (the leading lady)—Don't spoil my entrance.

BROMINE—Grab on, freshman—one—two—pull! (Blankety-blank! dash! dash!)

IODINE—All right, everybody—Hurry up! Get your pink silk overcoats.

THE WHOLE HALOGEN FAMILY (*simultaneously*)—

> À bas with the pony ballet,
> Ha-Ha to the pony ballet,
>   Their faces are phoney,
>   On places they're bony,
> Scorn chases the pony ballet.

ENTHUSIASTIC YOUNG PRECEPTOR—Progressive! Ah! After the true Washington Square manner.

AVERAGE STUDENT (*who doesn't know what he wants and kicks when he gets it*)—Where's the plot?

Moral of the show: You can't please all of the people all of the time.

CURTAIN

THE SPIRE AND THE GARGOYLE

The night mist fell. From beyond the moon it rolled, clustered about the spires and towers, and then settled below them so that the dreaming peaks seemed still in lofty aspiration toward the stars. Figures that dotted the daytime like ants now brushed along as ghosts in and out of the night. Even the buildings seemed infinitely more mysterious as they loomed suddenly out of the darkness, outlined each by a hundred faint squares of yellow light. Indefinitely from somewhere a bell boomed the quarter hour and one of the squares of light in an east campus recitation hall was blotted out for an instant as a figure emerged. It paused and resolved itself into a boy who stretched his arms wearily and, advancing, threw himself down full length on the damp grass by the sun-dial. The cool bathed his eyes and helped to force away the tiresome picture of what he had just left, a picture that, in the two strenuous weeks of examinations now just over, had become indelibly impressed upon his memory—a room with the air fairly vibrating with nervous tension, silent with the presence of twenty boys working desperately against time, searching every corner of tired brains for words and figures which seemed forever lost. The boy out on the grass opened his eyes and looked back at the three pale blurs which marked the windows of the examination room. Again he heard:

"There will be fifteen minutes more allowed for this examination." There had followed silence broken by the snapping of verifying watches and the sharp frantic race of pencils. One by one the seats had been left vacant and the little preceptor with the tired look had piled the booklets higher. Then the boy had left the room to the music of three last scratching pencils.

In his case it all depended on this examination. If he passed it he would become a sophomore the following fall; if he failed, it meant that his college days faded out with the last splendors of June. Fifty cut recitations in his first wild term had made necessary the extra course of which he had just taken the examination. Winter muses, unacademic and cloistered by 42nd Street and Broadway, had stolen hours from the dreary stretches of February and March. Later, time had crept insidiously through the lazy April afternoons and seemed so intangible in the long spring twilights. So June found him unprepared. Evening after evening the senior singing, drifting over the campus and up to his window, drew his mind for an instant to the unconscious poetry of it and he, goading on his spoiled and over-indulged faculties, bent to the revengeful books again. Through the careless shell that covered his undergraduate consciousness had broken a deep and almost reverent liking for the grey walls and Gothic peaks and all they symbolized in the store of the ages of antiquity.

In view of his window a tower sprang upward, grew into a spire, yearning higher till its uppermost end was half invisible against the morning skies. The transiency and relative unimportance of the campus figures except as holders of a sort of apostolic succession had first impressed themselves on him in contrast with this spire. In a lecture or in an article or in conversation, he had learned that Gothic architecture with its upward trend was peculiarly adapted to colleges, and the symbolism of this idea had become personal to him. Once he had associated the beauty of the campus night with the parades and singing crowds that streamed through it, but in the last month the more silent stretches of sward and the quiet halls with an occasional late-burning scholastic light held his imagination with a stronger grasp—and this tower in full view of his window became the symbol of his perception. There was something terribly pure in the slope of the chaste stone, something which led and directed and called. To him the spire became an ideal. He had suddenly begun trying desperately to stay in college.

"Well, it's over," he whispered aloud to himself, wetting his hands in the damp and running them through his hair. "All over."

He felt an enormous sense of relief. The last pledge had been duly indited in the last book, and his destiny lay no longer in his own hands, but in those of the little preceptor, whoever he was: the boy had never seen him before—and the face,—he looked like one of the gargoyles that nested in dozens of niches in some of the buildings. His glasses, his eyes, or his mouth gave a certain grotesque upward slant to his whole cast of feature that branded him as of gargoyle origin, or at least gargoyle kinship. He was probably marking the papers. Perhaps, mused the boy, a bit of an interview, an arrangement for a rereading in case of the ever possible failure would be—to interrupt his thought the light went out in the examination room and a moment later three figures edged along the path beside him while a fourth struck off south toward the town. The boy jumped to his feet and, shaking himself like a wet spaniel, started after the preceptor. The man turned to him sharply as he murmured a good evening and started trudging along beside.

"Awful night," said the boy.

The gargoyle only grunted.

"Gosh, that was a terrible examination." This topic died as unfruitfully as that of the weather, so he decided to come directly to the point.

"Are you marking these papers, sir?"

The preceptor stopped and faced him. Perhaps he didn't want to be reminded of the papers, perhaps he was in the habit of being exasperated by anything of this sort, but most probably he was tired and damp and wanted to get home.

"This isn't doing you any good. I know what you're going to say—that this is the crucial examination for you and that you'd like me to go over your paper with you, and so on. I've heard the same thing a hundred times from a hundred students in the course of this last two weeks. My answer is 'No, No,' do you understand? I don't care to know your identity and I won't be followed home by a nagging boy."

Simultaneously each turned and walked quickly away, and the boy suddenly realized with an instinct as certain as divination that he was not going to pass the examination.

"Damned gargoyle," he muttered.

But he knew that the gargoyle had nothing to do with it.

II

Regularly every two weeks he had been drifting out Fifth Avenue. On crisp autumn afternoons the tops of the shining auto buses were particularly alluring. From the roofs of other passing buses a face barely seen, an interested glance, a flash of color assumed the proportion of an intrigue. He had left college five years before and the buses and the art gallery and a few books were his intellectual relaxation. Freshman year Carlyle's "Heroes and Hero-Worship," in the hands of an impassioned young instructor, had interested him particularly. He had read practically nothing. He had neither the leisure to browse thoughtfully on much nor the education to cram thoughtfully on little, so his philosophy of life was molded of two elements: one the skeptical office philosophy of his associate, with a girl, a ten-thousand-dollar position, and a Utopian flat in some transfigured Bronx at the end of it; and the other, the three or four big ideas which he found in the plain-speaking Scotsman, Carlyle. But he felt, and truly, that his whole range was pitifully small. He was not naturally bookish; his taste could be stimulated as in the case of "Heroes and Hero-Worship" but he was still and now always would be in the stage where every work and every author had to be introduced and sometimes interpreted to him. "Sartor Resartus" meant nothing to him nor ever could.

So Fifth Avenue and the top of the buses had really grown to stand for a lot. They meant relief from the painted, pagan crowds of Broadway, the crowded atmosphere of the blue serge suits and grated windows that he met downtown and the dingy middle-class cloud that hovered on his boarding house. Fifth Avenue had a certain respectability which he would have once despised; the people on the buses looked better fed, their mouths came together in better lines. Always a symbolist, and an idealist, whether his model had been a profligate but magnetic sophomore or a Carlylized Napoleon, he sought around him in his common life for something to cling to, to stand for what religions and families and philosophies of life had stood for. He had a certain sense of fitness which convinced him that his old epicureanism, romantic as it might have been in the youth of his year at college, would have been exotic and rather disgusting in the city itself. It was much too easy; it lacked the penance of the five o'clock morning train back to college that had faced himself and his fellow student revelers; it lacked the penance of the long morning in classes and the poverty of weeks. It had been something to have, a reputation, even such a reputation as this crowd had had, but dissipation from the New York standpoint seemed a matter of spats and disgustingly rich Hebrews, and shoddy Bohemianism had no attraction for him.

Yet he was happy this afternoon. Perhaps because the bus on which he rode was resplendent in its shining new coat of green paint, and the stick-of-candy glamor of it had gone into his disposition. He lit a cigarette and made himself rather comfortable until he arrived at his destination. There were only certain sections of the museum that he visited. Statuary never attracted him, and the Italian madonnas and Dutch gentlemen with inconsequent gloves and books in the foreground rather bored him. It was only here and there in an old picture tucked away in the corner that his eye caught the glare of light on snow in a simple landscape or the bright colors and multiple figures of a battle painting, and he was drawn into long and detailed fits of contemplation and frequent revisits.

On this particular afternoon he was wandering rather aimlessly from one room to another when he suddenly noticed a small man in overshoes, his face latticed with enormous spectacles, thumbing a catalogue in front of a Flemish group. He started, and with a sense of recollection walked by him several times. Suddenly he realized that here was that one-time instrument of his fate, the gargoyle, the little preceptor who had flunked him in his crucial examination.

Oddly enough his first sensation was one of pleased reminiscence and a desire for conversation. Following that he had a curious feeling of shyness, untinged by any bitterness. He paused, staring heavily, and instantly the huge glasses glimmered suspiciously in his eyes.

"Pardon me, sir, but do you remember me?" he asked eagerly.

The preceptor blinked feverishly.

"Ah—no."

He mentioned the college and the blinks became more optimistic. He wisely decided to let the connection rest there. The preceptor couldn't, couldn't possibly remember all the men who had passed before his two "Mirrors of Shalott" so why bring up old, accusing facts—besides—he felt a great desire to chat.

"Yes—no doubt—your face is familiar, you'll pardon my—my chilliness a moment since—a public place." He looked around depreciatingly. "You see, I've left the university myself."

"So you've gone up in the game?" He instantly regretted this remark for the little man answered rather quickly:

"I'm teaching in a high school in Brooklyn." Rather embarrassed, the younger man tried to change the subject by looking at the painting before them, but the gargoyle grimly continued:

"I have—a—rather a large family, and much as I regretted leaving the university, the salary was unfortunately very much of a factor."

There was a pause during which both regarded the picture steadily. Then the gargoyle asked a question:

"How long since you've graduated?"

"Oh, I never graduated. I was there for only a short while." He was sure now that the gargoyle had not the slightest conception of his identity; he might rather enjoy this, however, and he had a pleasant notion that the other was not averse to his company.

"Are you staying here much longer?" The gargoyle was not, and together they moved to a restaurant two blocks down where they indulged in milk, tea and jam and discussed the university. When six o'clock pushed itself into the crowded hours it was with real regret that they shook hands, and the little man, manipulating his short legs in mad expostulation, raced after a Brooklyn car. Yes, it had been distinctly exhilarating. They had talked of academic atmospheres, of hopes that lay in the ivied walls, of little things that could only have counted after the mystic hand of the separation had made them akin. The gargoyle had touched lightly upon his own story, of the work he was doing, of his own tepid, stuffy environment. It was his hope some day to get back, but now there were young appetites to satisfy (the other thought grotesquely of the young gargoyles)—if he could see his way clear in the next few years,—so it went, but through all his hopeful talk there was a kind of inevitability that he would teach in a Brooklyn high school till the last bell called him to his last class. Yes, he went back occasionally. He had a younger brother who was an instructor there.

So they had talked, knit together by the toast and the sense of exile. That night the shrivelled spinster on his left at table asked him what college he thought would be worthy of ushering her promising nephew into the outer world. He became voluble and discoursive. He spoke of ties that bind, of old associations, and remarked carelessly, as he left her, that he was running back himself for a day the next week. But afterwards he lay awake and thought until the chairs and bedposts of his room became grey ghosts in the dawn.

III

The car was hot and stuffy with most of the smells of the state's alien population. The red plush seats radiated dust in layers and strata. The smoking car had been even more impossible with filthy floor and heavy air. So the man sat next to a partly open window in the coach and shivered against the cutting cloud of fog that streamed in over him. Lights sped by, vaguely blurred and spreading, marking towns and farmhouses with the democratic indiscrimination of the mist. As the conductor heralded each station the man felt a certain thrill at the familiarity of the names. The times and conditions under which he had heard them revolved in a medley of memories of his one year. One station particularly near the university had a peculiar significance for him because of the different ways it had affected him while he had been in college. He had noted it at the time. September of his entrance year, it had been the point where he grew acutely nervous and fidgety. Returning that November from a football defeat, it had stood for all that seemed gloomy in the gloomy college he was then going back to. In February it had meant the place to wake and pull oneself together, and as he had passed it for the last time that June, he had wondered with a sudden sinking of his heart if it was to be the last time. Now as the train shook and trembled there for a moment, he stared out the window and tried to get an impression. Oddly enough his first one came back to him; he felt rather nervous and uncertain.

He had discovered a few minutes ago that the little preceptor sat ahead of him three seats, but the younger man had not joined him or even addressed him. He wanted to draw to himself every impression he could from this ride.

They drew in. Grip in hand, he swung off the train, and from force of habit turned toward the broad steps that led to the campus. Then he stopped and, dropping his suitcase, looked before him. The night was typical of the place. It was very like the night on which he had taken his last examination, yet somehow less full and less poignant. Inevitability became a reality and assumed an atmosphere of compelling and wearing down. Where before the spirit of spires and towers had thrilled him and had made him dreamily content and acquiescent, it now overawed him. Where before he had realized only his own inconsequence, he now realized his own impotence and insufficiency. The towers in faint outlines and the battlemented walls of vague buildings fronted him. The engine from the train he had just left wheezed and clanged and backed; a hack drove off; a few pale self-effacing town boys strode away voicelessly, swallowed up in the night. And in front of him the college dreamed on—awake. He felt a nervous excitement that might have been the very throb of its slow heart.

A figure brushed violently into him, almost knocking him off his feet. He turned and his eyes pierced the trembling darkness of the arc-light to find the little preceptor blinking apprehensively at him from his gargoyle's eyes.

"Good evening."

He was hesitatingly recognized.

"Ah—how do you do? How do you do? Foggy evening, hope I didn't jar you."

"Not at all. I was just admiring the serenity." He paused and almost felt presumptuous.

"Are you—ah—pretending to be a student again?"

"I just ran out to see the place. Stay a night perhaps." Somehow this sounded far-fetched to him. He wondered if it did to the other.

"Yes?—I'm doing the same thing. My brother is an instructor here now you know. He's putting me up for a space." For an instant the other longed fiercely that he too might be invited to be "put up for a space."

"Are you walking up my way?"

"No—not quite yet."

The gargoyle smiled awkwardly. "Well, good-night."

There was nothing more to say. Eyes staring, he watched the little figure walking off, propelled jerkily by his ridiculous legs.

Minutes passed. The train was silent. The several blurs on the station platform became impersonal and melted into the background. He was alone face to face with the spirit that should have dominated his life, the mother that he had renounced. It was a stream where he had once thrown a stone, but the faint ripple had long since vanished. Here he had taken nothing, he had given nothing: nothing?—his eyes wandered slowly upward—up—up—until by straining them he could see where the spire began—and with his eyes went his soul. But the mist was upon both. He could not climb with the spire.

A belated freshman, his slicker rasping loudly, slushed along the soft path. A voice from somewhere called the inevitable formula toward an unknown window. A hundred little sounds of the current drifting on under the fog pressed in finally on his consciousness.

"Oh God!" he cried suddenly, and started at the sound of his own voice in the stillness. He had cried out from a complete overwhelming sense of failure. He realized how outside of it all he was. The gargoyle, poor tired little hack, was bound up in the fabric of the whole system much more than he was or ever could be. Hot tears of anger and helplessness rushed to his eyes. He felt no injustice, only a deep mute longing. The very words that would have purged his soul were waiting for him in the depths of the unknown before him— waiting for him where he could never come to claim them. About him the rain dripped on. A minute longer he stood without moving, his head bent dejectedly, his hands clenched. Then he turned and, picking up his suitcase, walked over to the train.

The engine gave a tentative pant, and the conductor, dozing in a corner, nodded sleepily at him from the end of the deserted car. Wearily he sank onto a red plush seat and pressed his hot forehead against the damp window pane.

RAIN BEFORE DAWN

The dull, faint patter in the drooping hours
   Drifts in upon my sleep and fills my hair
   With damp; the burden of the heavy air
Is strewn upon me where my tired soul cowers,
Shrinking like some lone queen in empty towers
   Dying. Blind with unrest I grow aware:
   The pounding of broad wings drifts down the stair
And sates me like the heavy scent of flowers.

I lie upon my heart. My eyes like hands
Grip at the soggy pillow. *Now the dawn*
Tears from her wetted breast the splattered blouse
Of night; lead-eyed and moist she straggles o'er the lawn,
Between the curtains brooding stares and stands
Like some drenched swimmer—Death's within the house!

"DAVID BLAIZE"

Of late years there have been really good boys' stories, with the boy treated from a subjective point of view, neither cynically nor sentimentally. In the class belong "The Varmint," "Youth's Encounter," "Seventeen," and perhaps a new book, "David Blaize," by E. F. Benson, author of "Dodo." Benson, by the way, is one of the famous Benson trilogy with Arthur C. Benson and the late Monsignor Robert Hugh Benson. The book carries the English hero through his last year at a "private" school and through three forms at an English public school, presumably Eton under the name of Marchester.

Frank Maddox, David's first and last hero, is the strongest personality in the book, David being rather a peg on which the author hangs virtues and adventures. The book starts well and until three-quarters of the way through is very interesting. Then follows a long and, to an American, dry and unintelligible account of a cricket match in which, by careful sounding, we fathom that the hero and his idol, Frank Maddox, in the orthodox Ralph Henry Barbour manner, win the day for the school.

Mr. Benson's indebtedness to Compton Mackenzie and Kipling is very great. Swinburne introduces David to literature as he did Michael in "Youth's Encounter," and the disagreement of David with the prefects is very like certain chapters in Stalky's career. The one incident which forms the background of the book is foreign to anything in our preparatory schools and, although handled with an overemphasized delicacy, seems rather unnecessary and unhealthy from our point of view.

One of the great charms of the book lies in the chapters where Frank first lights upon David near the old cathedral and where David is visiting Frank at the seashore. The chapter on David's love affair is poorly written and seems a half-hearted attempt to make him seem well-rounded. The last melodramatic incident, the injury and recovery of the hero, is well done, but does not go for unity. The first two-thirds of the book is immensely entertaining, the last third disappointing.

("David Blaize," *by E. F. Benson. The George Doran Company, New York. $1.35 net*).

"McCAULAY MISSION"

McCaulay Mission—Water Street.
Service at five. Drunkards especially invited.

—*N. Y. Sun.*

If we send a delegation to Northfield, we should certainly be represented here.

* * *

POPULAR PARODIES—NO. 1

I'm off to the Math. School
    To pass it or bust.
If Conics don't get me
    Then Politics must.

Chorus.
Professor how long
    Do I have to wait?
Do you debar me now
    Or will you hesitate?

THE DIARY OF A SOPHOMORE

Sunday—March 18th.

Felt nervous all day—temperature 99 8/10. Jim and Heck and Joe came in after dinner. We are going to stick together. Everybody says "stick to your friends"—I'm sticking like a leech—they can't shake me off. Hope I get a *Seaweed* bid.

Monday—

No mail—Jim, Heck and Joe not in rooms, college in anarchy—shall not leave room until I get a bid. Temperature 89.7.

Tuesday—

No mail—except a bill from Sinclair's. Sophomores wanted me to join commons club—Told them I'd like to but I'd promised to stick with my friends. Got Jim, Heck and Joe bids to commons club. Why don't they come to see me.

Wednesday—

Joe came over and said he and Heck were in the *Pillbox* section—Jim is going *Star and Garter*. I have a good chance for *Pillbox*—Turned down commons again.

Thursday—

We are all going *Star and Garter*. I'm glad I waited. We shook hands on it and Jim and Heck wept. Emotion is in the air. Temperature, 100.

Friday—

Peter Hype told me to hold off for *Lung and Coatcheck*. I told him I was going to stick with my friends. Hope he didn't think I meant it.

Saturday—

Bid for *Lung and Coatcheck*. I hate to leave Joe and Heck. Shook hands with all the "Lungs." Was introduced to several fellows in my class.

Sunday—

Awful excitement. Temperature 102.

Monday—

Signed up *Seaweed*. Jim was foolish to throw away his chances. It's every man's business to look out for himself. Heck and Joe were a drag on me. They'll be very happy in *Star and Garter*. Wrote Doris about it. Temperature, normal.

UNDULATIONS OF AN UNDERGRADUATE

I've been for North Edwards selected,
    I've roomed in a cupboard in Blair.
In Witherspoon dark and dejected,
    I've slept without sunshine or air.
My janitress kept me from study,
    And awfully long-winded she were,
Her mouth didn't shut so I overcut,
    And I learned about college from her.

A senior who came from our city
    And practically lived for the glass,
Would tell me in epigrams witty
    The way to be big in my class.
He took me to hatters and tailors
    And coached me on how to look slim;
He taught me to drink but forbade me to think,
    And I learned about college from him.

A girl that I met at the seashore
    And took for a summer-day sail
Told stories of brothers at Princeton
    Of friends and fiancées at Yale.
She knew all the men who played hockey,
    She knew when the promenades were,
She thought me a bore till I asked her to four,
    And I learned about college from her.

The dean, since my marks were pathetic,
    Had sent me a summons to call,
He greeted me, apologetic,
    And smiled, "This is social, that's all."
He said if I chanced to the city
    I might be remembering him
To Babbie Larove at the Cocoanut Grove,
    And I learned about college from him.

TARQUIN OF CHEAPSIDE

Running footsteps.—Light, soft-soled shoes, made of queer leathery cloth brought from Ceylon, setting the pace; thick flowing boots, two pairs, dark blue and gilt, reflecting the moonlight in blunt gleams and flashes, following a hundred yards behind. Soft Shoes cleaves the moonlight for a haggard second, then darts into a blind labyrinth of alleys and becomes merely an unsteady scuffle in the darkness ahead. In go Flowing Boots with swords lurching and with clumsy stumbling, cursing the black lanes of London. Soft Shoes leaps a gate and straggles through a hedge-row. Flowing Boots leaps the gate and straggles through a hedge-row;—and there is the watch ahead—two murderous pikemen with ferocious expressions acquired in Calais and the Spanish marches. But there is no cry for help. The pursued does not fall panting and clutching his purse at their feet nor do the pursuers raise a hue and cry—Soft Shoes goes by like a rush of air. The watch curse and hesitate, look behind and then spread their pikes grimly across the road and wait. A cloud scurries across the sky and blackens the narrow street.

Again the pale sheen skims the eaves and roofs; the chase is on once more, but one of Flowing Boots leaves a little black trail until he binds himself clumsily as he runs, with fine lace caught from his throat.

It was no case for the watch tonight. There had been devil's work and the devil seemed to be he who appeared faintly in front, heel over gate, knee over fence. Moreover, the adversary was evidently traveling near home, or at any rate in that part of London consecrated to him, for the streets were narrowing and the houses hung over more and more, furnishing natural ambushes often utilized for battle, murder and sudden death. So they twisted, down long sinuous lanes where the moonlight was shut away, except for tiny patches and glints. Ahead the quarry was running blindly, minus his leather jerkin, dripping with sweat and scanning his ground carefully on both sides. Suddenly he slowed down and, retracing his steps, darted down an alley darker and narrower and longer than any he had yet explored. Two hundred yards down he stopped short and crammed himself into a niche in the wall where he huddled and panted silently like a grotesque god, very faintly outlined in the gloom.

Twenty yards beyond him the others stopped and he heard a whispered colloquy.

"Within thirty yards now."

"Yes, I was atune to that scuffle; it stopped!"

"He's hid."

"Stay together and, by the Virgin, we'll split him!"

Their voices lowered and Soft Shoes could hear no more, nor did he wait to, for at a stealthy step in his direction, he sprang in three paces across the alley, where he bounded up, flapped for a moment on the edge of the wall like a huge bird, and disappeared, gulped down by the hungry night at a mouthful.

* * *

Peter Caxter read late, too late, he had recently discovered. His eyes were getting particularly dim for his young time of life; his stomach was swelling to portliness. Tall and misbuilt, lazy too, he was spurred on in his studies by conscience got in heartfuls at Cambridge, and ambition carefully distilled through her subjects by Elizabeth, by the grace of Luther, Queen of England. Peter having completed a rather painful sea-voyage, and stored up great hunks of Elizabethan anecdote for his future grandchildren, was now flitting cumbrously back to his neglected books—and what a book he had this night! "The Faerie Queene," by one Edmund Spenser, lay before him under the wavering candlelight.

THE LEGEND OF BRITOMARTIS OR OF CHASTITY
It falles me here to write of Chastity,
That fayrest vertue, farre above the rest—

A sudden rush of feet on the stairs, and a man darted into the room, a man panting and gasping and on the verge of a collapse.

"Peter," he blurted out, "I must be hidden—I'm in a scrape—it's death if the two men who will come here after me find me!"

Peter showed little surprise. His guest had been in various difficulties before and had entrusted him with his extrication. And the visitor, when his gasps gave way to quick precise breathing, lost his culprit's air and looked very much at his ease. Indeed a casual observer might have said that he was proud of some recent exploit.

"Two fools with long swords and short wits harrying me over half of London like a terrified rabbit!"

"There were three fools in the chase then," said Peter ironically, as he took a pole from a corner and dislodged a trap door which led to a sort of garret above. He pointed upward. The other crouched, jumped, caught at the edge of the aperture and, struggling for a moment, swung himself up and was lost in the darkness above. The hatch was replaced; there was a scurry like the exodus of rats, an oath muffled by the floor, then silence. Peter picked up the "Legend of Britomartis, or of Chastity" and settling himself—waited.

Five minutes later a scramble on the stairs was followed by a prolonged hammering on the door. He sighed, put down the book, and, picking up the candle, rose.

"Who is there?"

"Open—Or we will burst in the door!"

Peter opened it a bare eight inches and held the candle high. He pitched his voice so that it sounded timorous and querulous.

"May not a peaceable citizen of London rest undisturbed from marauders for one small hour of the night?"

"Open, gossip, and quick, or we'll pitch a yard of steel through the crack there!"

The shadows of the two gallants fell in huge wavering outlines over the moonlit stairs, and by the light Peter characterized his opponents in a quick glance. They were gentlemen, hastily but richly attired. One was a man of thirty, greatly distraught and nervous from intense excitement and anxiety. The other, the one with the bloody hand, was younger, and though he was quiet and restrained, his lips were set with grim purpose. Peter let them in.

"Is there a man hidden here?" said the elder fiercely.

"No."

"Has there been anyone on the stairs?"

Peter replied that ten minutes ago there had been someone on the landing below trying to get into a room, but that whoever he had been, he had failed and gone away. Would they be so kind as to inform him for whom they were searching and why.

"There has been violence done—to a woman," said the younger man slowly. "My sister—and his wife. Who we are does not matter. If you are hiding this man it may cost you your life."

"Do you know who he—this man—is?" asked Peter quickly.

The elder man sank onto a chair and dropped his face in his hands.

"God's Word—We do not know even that."

Peter rather winced. This was more tragedy than he had bargained for.

The younger man had been searching about Peter's two rooms, poking his sword into anything that looked at all suspicious. He noticed the trap door.

"What's that?"

"It is not used," said Peter. "It is an attic—the trap is nailed down." Suddenly he thought of the pole and drew in his breath sharply, but the other turned away with an air of finality.

"It would take ten minutes to get up there without a ladder unless the man were a tumbler."

"A tumbler," repeated the elder dully.

"Let us go."

They went silently, sad and impotent, and Peter closed and barred the door after them. After a safe ten minutes he took the pole and poked the trap door open. When the other stood before him he began:

"There has been deviltry in your life, and much of it—there have been drinking and women and blood, but when I face two men with a tale even half told like this—————."

His guest stopped him.

"Peter—you'd never understand. You've helped me before. You've got to, got to help me now. Do you hear? I shall not argue. I want pen and paper and your bedroom, Peter." He grew angry. "Peter are you trying to interfere—what right have you? I am responsible only to myself for what I do."

He took a pen and ink and a sheaf of paper from the table and without another word walked into the other room and shut the door. Peter grunted, started after him and then, reconsidering, went back and picking up "The Faerie Queene" sank into his chair.

Three o'clock went into four. The room paled and the dark outside became damp and chill—and Peter bent low over his table, tracing through the pattern of "The Faerie Queene." Dragons chortled along the narrow streets outside; when the sleepy armourer's boy began his work at five, the heavy clink and clank of plate and linked mail swelled to the significance of marching cavalcades.

The fog shut down at the first streak of dawn and the room was greyish yellow at six when Peter tiptoed to his cupboard bedroom and opened the door. His guest turned to him red-eyed, death-pale, unseeing. He had been writing hard and the prie-dieu on which he wrote was piled with a stack of paper, while around on the floor were littered scraps of almost virgin pages. Peter softly closed the door and returned to his syren. Outside, the clump of boots, the croaking of old beldames from attic to attic, the dull murmur of morning unnerved him and, half dozing, he slumped in his chair and his dreaming brain worked chaotically on the imagery that stacked it. He was on a cloud and the way to heaven lay over groaning bodies crushed near the sun. He shuddered and trod the way. He was in a wood where he killed a bird of paradise for its plumage. Someone was trying to barter his soul for the world, and the soul was bartered. When a hot hand touched his shoulder he awoke with a start. The fog was thick in the room and his guest seemed a grey ghost, made of some like misty stuff where he stood beside him, the sheaf of paper in his hand.

"Read this, Peter, and lock it away and let me sleep until tomorrow."

Peter took the pile and looked at it curiously. The other threw himself down full length on the couch and sank almost immediately into a deep slumber, with breathing regular, but brow wrinkled in queer corners.

Peter yawned sleepily and glanced at the scrawled first page—
then he began reading aloud softly:

> *The Rape of Lucrece.*
> *From the besieged Ardea all in post,*
> *Borne by the trustless wings of false desire,*
> *Lust-breathed Tarquin leaves the Roman host,—*

THE PRINCE OF PESTS
A Story of the War

It was night in July, 1914. A man and his board of directors sat around a table in a palace at Berlin. The man was tall, with a moustache and a short arm. Who was he?—oh, reader, can you guess? He wore a military uniform, green with grey facings; his pants were blue with red facings.

"Your Highness," Von Boodlewaden was saying, "everything is ready."

The Kaiser shook his head sadly and folded his arms; at least he tucked the short one in with the other. Then he took his short leg and crossed it over his long one, and having scratched his long ear came to business.

"Nietzsche," he said, and waited for his words to have effect. Von Nicklebottom immediately sprang upon the table and led the customary cheer for Nietzsche—three locomotives with three seidels of beer on the end.

"Nietzsche," continued the Kaiser, "has said it. We will conquer by the sword." As he said this he ran his hand lovingly along his sword, then trying its edge on a bit of celery which he munched tentatively.

"Your Highness," cried Von Munchennoodle. "Belgium must be sacrificed."

The Kaiser bit his lip until the blood ran slowly down to the table where it spread into little livid pools of red and yellow liquid. His councillors dipped their fingers in it and reverently crossed themselves. Deeply affected the Kaiser pledged them.

"And what of America?" asked Pistachio, Chancellor of the Domino Club.

"America?" said the Kaiser, rising to his full height. "Charles II had his Cromwell, Caesar had his Brutus, and Wilson—"

There were cries of "plagiarism" and the Kaiser paused.

"Daniel Webster was a German," he continued, rather abashed. Turning to the man on his center, Baron Badenuf, Chancellor of the Shakespearegoetheteutonic League, he commanded him.

"Look him up, Baddy."

There was an hour while Badenuf looked up Webster, during which an absolute silence was maintained, broken only by the Kaiser as he ran his sword rapidly up and down his neck, where he had caught prickly heat the summer before playing leap-frog on the beach at Ostend with Czar Nicholas. Badenuf finally returned.

"I find in the life of Webster," he announced, "the relevant news that he once stopped at the Sauerkraut Inn while passing through Pennsylvania. This proves the case, for no one but a German would stop at a German inn unless he has to, and Daniel didn't."

There were three wild cheers at this and according to the ancient German custom they prepared to pledge each other in the royal blood. The Kaiser tried his lip again but all the blood had gone out of it long ago. So he opened an artery in his leg with an olive fork.

They all gulped it down heartily while a German band played "Ach du lieber Augustin" and the Kaiser's valet strapped his paralyzed arm to his sword so he could have his picture taken.

"THESE RIFLES . . ."

"These rifles *** will probably not be used for shooting, although they are of a powerful type capable of before commencing actual firing reaching a distance of two miles."

—*The Daily Princetonian*

Some rifles! Lord help Germany!

* * *

"IT IS ASSUMED . . ."

"It is assumed that the absence of submarines from the Pacific will not necessitate American naval activities in that ocean."

—*New York Evening Post*

Will it not not?

* * *

ETHEL HAD HER SHOT OF BRANDY . . .

Ethel had her shot of brandy while she powdered for the ball,
If a quart of wine was handy she was sure to drink it all;
People thought she was a dandy—called her Ethyl Alcohol.

* * *

"YALE'S SWIMMING TEAM . . ."

Yale's swimming team will take its maiden plunge tonight.

—*New York Sun*

How perfectly darling!

BABES IN THE WOODS

I

At the top of the stairs she paused. The emotions of divers on spring-boards, leading ladies on opening nights, and lumpy, bestriped young men on the day of the Big Game crowded through her. She felt as if she should have descended to a burst of drums or to a discordant blend of gems from "Thaïs" and "Carmen." She had never been so worried about her appearance, she had never been so satisfied with it. She had been sixteen years old for two months.

"Isabelle!" called Elaine from her doorway.

"I'm ready." She caught a slight lump of nervousness in her throat.

"I've got on the wrong slippers and stockings—you'll have to wait a minute."

Isabelle started toward Elaine's door for a last peek at a mirror, but something decided her to stand there and gaze down the stairs. They curved tantalizingly and she could just catch a glimpse of two pairs of masculine feet in the hall below. Pump-shod in uniform black they gave no hint of identity, but eagerly she wondered if one pair were attached to Kenneth Powers. This young man, as yet unmet, had taken up a considerable part of her day—the first day of her arrival. Going up in the machine from the station Elaine had volunteered, amid a rain of questions and comment, revelation and exaggeration—

"Kenneth Powers is simply *mad* to meet you. He's stayed over a day from college and he's coming tonight. He's heard so much about you—"

It had pleased her to know this. It put them on more equal terms, although she was accustomed to stage her own romances with or without a send-off. But following her delighted tremble of anticipation came a sinking sensation which made her ask:

"How do you mean he's heard about me? What sort of things?"

Elaine smiled—she felt more or less in the capacity of a showman with her more exotic guest.

"He knows you're good-looking and all that." She paused— "I guess he knows you've been kissed."

Isabelle had shuddered a bit under the fur robe. She was accustomed to being followed by this, but it never failed to arouse in her the same feeling of resentment; yet—in a strange town it was an advantage. She was a speed, was she? Well? Let them find out. She wasn't quite old enough to be sorry nor nearly old enough to be glad.

"Anne (this was another schoolmate) told him, I didn't— I knew you wouldn't like it," Elaine had gone on naively. "She's coming over tonight to the dinner."

Out the window Isabelle watched the high-piled snow glide by in the frosty morning. It was ever so much colder here than in Pittsburg: the glass of the side door was iced and the windows were shirred with snow in the corners. Her mind played still with the one subject. Did he dress like that boy there who walked calmly down what was evidently a bustling business street in moccasins and winter-carnival costume? How very *western!* Of course he wasn't that way: he went to college, was a freshman or something. Really she had no distinct idea of him. A two-year-back picture had not impressed her except by the big eyes, which he had probably grown up to by now. However in the last two weeks at school, when her Christmas visit to Elaine had been decided on, he had assumed the proportions of a worthy adversary. Children, the most astute of matchmakers, plot and plan quickly; and Elaine had cleverly played a word sonata to Isabelle's excitable temperament. Isabelle was and had been for some time capable of very strong, if very transient emotions.

They drew up at a spreading red stone building, set back from the snowy street. Mrs. Terrell greeted her rather impersonally and Elaine's various younger brothers were produced from the corners where they skulked politely. Isabelle shook hands most tactfully. At her best she allied all with whom she came in contact, except older girls and some women. All the impressions that she made were conscious. The half dozen girls she met that morning were all rather impressed—and as much by her direct personality as by her reputation. Kenneth Powers seemed an unembarrassing subject of conversation. Evidently he was a bit light of love. He was neither popular nor unpopular. Every girl there seemed to have had an affair with him at some time or other, but no one volunteered any really useful information. He was going to fall for her. Elaine had issued that statement to her young set and they were retailing it back to Elaine as fast as they set eyes on Isabelle. Isabelle resolved mentally that if necessary she would force herself to like him—she owed it to Elaine. What if she were terribly disappointed? Elaine had painted him in such glowing colors—he was good-looking, had a "line" and was properly inconstant. In fact he summed up all the romance that her age and environment led her to desire. Were those his dancing shoes that fox-trotted tentatively around the soft rug below?

All impressions and in fact all ideas were terribly kaleido-scopic to Isabelle. She had that curious mixture of the social and artistic temperaments, found often in two classes—society women and actors. Her education, or rather her sophistication, had been absorbed from the boys who had dangled upon her favor; her tact was instinctive, and her capacity for love affairs was limited only by the number of boys she met. Flirt smiled from her large, black-brown eyes and figured in her intense physical magnetism.

So she waited at the head of the stairs that evening while slippers and stockings were changed. Just as she was getting impatient Elaine came out beaming with her accustomed good nature and high spirits. Together they descended the broad stairs while the nervous searchlight of Isabelle's mind flashed on two ideas. She was glad she had high color tonight and she wondered if he danced well.

Downstairs the girls she had met in the afternoon surrounded her for a moment, looking unbelievably changed by the soft yellow light; then she heard Elaine's voice repeating a cycle of names, and she found herself bowing to a sextet of black and white and terribly stiff figures. The name Powers figured somewhere, but she did not place him at first. A confused and very juvenile moment of awkward backings and bumpings, and everyone found themselves arranged talking to the very persons they least desired to. Isabelle maneuvered herself and Peter Carroll, a sixth-former from Hotchkiss whom she had met that afternoon, to a seat at the piano. A reference, supposedly humorous, to the afternoon was all she needed. What Isabelle could do socially with one idea was remarkable. First she repeated it rapturously in an enthusiastic contralto; then she held it off at a distance and smiled at it—her wonderful smile; then she delivered it in variations and played a sort of mental catch with it, all this in the nominal form of dialogue. Peter was fascinated and totally unconscious that this was being done not for him but for the black eyes that glistened under the shining, carefully watered hair a little to her left. As an actor even in the fullest flush of his own conscious magnetism gets a lasting impression of most of the people in the front row, so Isabelle sized up Kenneth Powers. First, he was of middle height, and from her feeling of disappointment she knew that she had expected him to be tall and of Vernon Castle-ish slenderness. His hair and eyes were his most noticeable possessions—they were black and they fairly glittered. For the rest, he had rather dark skin with a faint flush and a straight romantic profile, the effect set off by a close-fitting dress suit and a silk ruffled shirt of the kind that women still delight in on men, but men were just beginning to get tired of.

Kenneth was just quietly smiling.

"Don't *you* think so?" she said suddenly, turning to him innocent-eyed.

There was a stir near the door and Elaine led the way to dinner. Kenneth struggled to her side and whispered:

"You're my dinner partner—Isabelle."

Isabelle gasped—this was rather quick work. Of course it made it more interesting, but really she felt as if a good line had been taken from the star and given to a minor character. She musn't lose the leadership a bit. The dinner table glittered with laughter at the confusion of getting places, and then curious eyes were turned on her, sitting near the head. She was enjoying this immensely, and Peter Carroll was so engrossed with the added sparkle of her rising color that he forgot to pull out Elaine's chair and fell into a dim confusion. Kenneth was on the other side, full of confidence and vanity, looking at her most consciously. He started directly and so did Peter.

"I've heard a lot about you—"

"Wasn't it funny this afternoon—"

Both stopped. Isabelle turned to Kenneth shyly. Her face was always enough answer for anyone, but she decided to speak.

"How—who from?"

"From everybody—for years." She blushed appropriately. On her right Peter was hors-de-combat already, although he hadn't quite realized it.

"I'll tell you what I thought about you when I first saw you," Kenneth continued. She leaned slightly toward him and looked modestly at the celery before her. Peter sighed—he knew Kenneth and the situations that Kenneth was born to handle. He turned to Elaine and asked her when she was going back to school.

II

Isabelle and Kenneth were distinctly not innocent, nor were they particularly hardened. Moreover, amateur standing had very little value in the game they were beginning to play. They were simply very sophisticated, very calculating and finished young actors, each playing a part that they had played for years. They had both started with good looks and excitable temperaments and the rest was the result of certain accessible popular novels, and dressing-room conversation culled from a slightly older set. When Isabelle's eyes, wide and innocent, proclaimed the ingénue most, Kenneth was proportionately less deceived. He waited for the mask to drop off, but at the same time he did not question her right to wear it. She, on her part, was not impressed by his studied air of blasé sophistication. She came from a larger city and had slightly an advantage in range. But she accepted his pose. It was one of the dozen little conventions of this kind of affair. He was aware that he was getting this particular favor now because she had been coached. He knew that he stood for merely the best thing in sight, and that he would have to improve his opportunity before he lost his advantage. So they proceeded, with an infinite guile that would have horrified the parents of both.

After dinner the party swelled to forty and there was dancing in a large ex-playroom downstairs. Everything went smoothly—boys cut in on Isabelle every few feet and then squabbled in the corners with: "You might let me get more than an *inch*," and "She didn't like it either—she told me so next time I cut in." It was true—she told everyone so, and gave every hand a parting pressure that said "You know that your dances are *making* my evening."

But time passed, two hours of it, and the less subtle beaux had better learned to focus their pseudo-passionate glances elsewhere, for eleven o'clock found Isabelle and Kenneth on a leather lounge in a little den off the music room. She was conscious that they were a handsome pair and seemed to belong distinctively on this leather lounge while lesser lights fluttered and chattered downstairs. Boys who passed the door looked in enviously—girls who passed only laughed and frowned and grew wise within themselves.

They had now reached a very definite stage. They had traded ages, eighteen and sixteen. She had listened to much that she had heard before. He was a freshman at college, sang in the glee club and expected to make the freshman hockey-team. He had learned that some of the boys she went with in Pittsburg were "terrible speeds" and came to parties intoxicated—most of them were nineteen or so, and drove alluring Stutzes. A good half of them seemed to have already flunked out of various boarding schools and colleges, but some of them bore good collegiate names that made him feel rather young. As a matter of fact Isabelle's acquaintance with college boys was mostly through older cousins. She had bowing acquaintance with a lot of young men who thought she was "a pretty kid" and "worth keeping an eye on." But Isabelle strung the names into a fabrication of gaiety that would have dazzled a Viennese nobleman. Such is the power of young contralto voices on leather sofas.

I have said that they had reached a very definite stage—nay more—a very critical stage. Kenneth had stayed over a day to meet her and his train left at twelve-eighteen that night. His trunk and suitcase awaited him at the station and his watch was already beginning to worry him and hang heavy in his pocket.

"Isabelle," he said suddenly. "I want to tell you something."
They had been talking lightly about "that funny look in her eyes,"
and on the relative merits of dancing and sitting out, and Isabelle
knew from the change in his manner exactly what was coming—
indeed she had been wondering how soon it would come. Kenneth
reached above their heads and turned out the electric light so that
they were in the dark except for the glow from the red lamps that
fell through the door from the music room. Then he began:

"I don't know—I don't know whether or not you know what
you—what I'm going to say. Lordy Isabelle—this sounds like a line,
but it isn't."

"I know," said Isabelle softly.

"I may never see you again—I have darned hard luck sometimes."
He was leaning away from her on the other arm of the lounge, but
she could see his black eyes plainly in the dark.

"You'll see me again—silly." There was just the slightest emphasis on the last word—so that it became almost a term of endearment.
He continued a bit huskily:

"I've fallen for a lot of people—girls—and I guess you have
too—boys, I mean, but honestly you—" he broke off suddenly and
leaned forward, chin on his hands, a favorite and studied gesture.
"Oh what's the use, you'll go your way and I suppose I'll go
mine."

Silence for a moment. Isabelle was quite stirred—she wound her
handkerchief into a tight ball and, by the faint light that streamed
over her, dropped it deliberately on the floor. Their hands touched
for an instant but neither spoke. Silences were becoming more
frequent and more delicious. Outside another stray couple had come
up and were experimenting on the piano. After the usual preliminary of "Chopsticks," one of them started "Babes in the Woods"
and a light tenor carried the words into the den—

> Give me your hand
> I'll understand
> We're off to slumberland.

Isabelle hummed it softly and trembled as she felt Kenneth's hand
close over hers.

"Isabelle," he whispered. "You know I'm mad about you. You *do* give a darn about me."

"Yes."

"How much do you care—do you like anyone better?"

"No." He could scarcely hear her, although he bent so near that he felt her breath against his cheek.

"Isabelle, we're going back to school for six long months and why shouldn't we—if I could only just have one thing to remember you by—"

"Close the door." Her voice had just stirred so that he half wondered whether she had spoken at all. As he swung the door softly shut, the music seemed quivering just outside.

> Moonlight is bright
> Kiss me good-night.

What a wonderful song, she thought—everything was wonderful tonight, most of all this romantic scene in the den with their hands clinging and the inevitable looming charmingly close. The future vista of her life seemed an unended succession of scenes like this, under moonlight and pale starlight, and in the backs of warm limousines and in low cosy roadsters stopped under sheltering trees—only the boy might change, and this one was so nice.

"Isabelle!" His whisper blended in the music and they seemed to float nearer together. Her breath came faster. "Can't I kiss you Isabelle—Isabelle?" Lips half parted, she turned her head to him in the dark. Suddenly the ring of voices, the sound of running footsteps surged toward them. Like a flash Kenneth reached up and turned on the light, and when the door opened and three boys, the wrathy and dance-craving Peter among them, rushed in, he was turning over the magazines on the table, while she sat, without moving, serene and unembarrassed, and even greeted them with a welcoming smile. But her heart was beating wildly and she felt somehow as if she had been deprived.

It was evidently over. There was a clamour for a dance; there was a glance that passed between them, on his side, despair, on hers, regret, and then the evening went on, with the reassured beaux and the eternal cutting-in.

At quarter to twelve Kenneth shook hands with her gravely, in a crowd assembled to wish him good-speed. For an instant he lost his poise, and she felt slightly foolish when a satirical voice from a concealed wit on the edge of the company cried:

"Take her outside, Kenneth!" As he took her hand he pressed it a little and she returned the pressure as she had done to twenty hands that evening—that was all.

At two o'clock upstairs Elaine asked her if she and Kenneth had had a "time" in the den. Isabelle turned to her quietly. In her eyes was the light of the idealist, the inviolate dreamer of Joan-like dreams.

"No!" she answered. "I don't do that sort of thing anymore—he asked me to but I said 'No.'"

As she crept into bed she wondered what he'd say in his special delivery tomorrow. He had such a good-looking mouth—would she ever—?

"Fourteen angels were watching over them," sang Elaine sleepily from the next room.

"Damn!" muttered Isabelle and punched the pillow into a luxurious lump—"Damn!"

PRINCETON—THE LAST DAY

The last light wanes and drifts across the land,
The low, long land, the sunny land of spires.
The ghosts of evening tune again their lyres
And wander singing, in a plaintive band
Down the long corridors of trees. Pale fires
Echo the night from tower top to tower.
Oh sleep that dreams and dream that never tires,
Press from the petals of the lotus-flower
Something of this to keep, the essence of an hour!

No more to wait the twilight of the moon
In this sequestered vale of star and spire;
For one eternal morning of desire
Passes to time and earthy afternoon.
Here, Heraclitus, did you build of fire
And changing stuffs your prophecy far hurled
Down the dead years; this midnight I aspire
To see, mirrored among the embers, curled
In flame, the splendor and the sadness of the world.

"THE CELT AND THE WORLD"

After his most entertaining "End of a Chapter," Mr. Leslie has written what I think will be a more lasting book. "The Celt and the World" is a sort of bible of Irish patriotism. Mr. Leslie has endeavored to trace a race, the Breton, Scotch, Welsh, and Irish Celt, through its spiritual crises and he emphasizes most strongly the trait that Synge, Yeats and Lady Gregory have made so much of in their plays, the Celt's inveterate mysticism. The theme is worked out in an era-long contrast between Celt and Teuton, and the book becomes ever ironical when it deals with the ethical values of the latter race. "Great is the Teuton indeed," it says. "Luther in religion, Bessemer in steel, Nietzsche in philosophy, Rockefeller in oil—Cromwell and Bismarck in war." What a wonderful list of names! Could anyone but an Irishman have linked them in such damning significance?

In the chapter on the conversion of the Celt to Christianity are traced the great missionary achievements of the Celtic priests and philosophers Dungal, Fergal, Abelard, Duns Scotus and Eriugena. At the end of the book that no less passionate and mystical, although unfortunate, incident of Pearse, Plunkett and the Irish Republic, is given sympathetic but just treatment.

To an Irishman the whole book is fascinating. It gives one an intense desire to see Ireland free at last to work out her own destiny under Home Rule. It gives one the idea that she would do it directly under the eyes of God and with so much purity and so many mistakes. It arouses a fascination with the mystical lore and legend of the island which "can save others, but herself she cannot save." The whole book is colored with an unworldliness, and an atmosphere of the futility of man's ambitions. As Mr. Leslie says in the foreword to "The End of a Chapter" (I quote inexactly) we have seen the suicide of the Aryan race, "the end of one era and the beginning of another to which no Gods have as yet been rash enough to give their names."

"The Celt and the World" is a rather pessimistic book: not with the dreary pessimism of Strindberg and Sudermann, but with the pessimism which might have inspired "What doth it profit a man if he gaineth the whole world and loseth his own soul." It is worth remarking that it ends with a foreboding prophecy of a Japanese-American war in the future. The book should be especially interesting to anyone who has enjoyed "Riders to the Sea," or "The Hour-Glass." He will read an engrossing view of a much discussed race and decide that the Irishman has used heaven as a continued referendum for his ideals, as he has used earth as a perennial recall for his ambitions.

("The Celt and the World," *by Shane Leslie. New York: Charles Scribner's Sons.*)

SENTIMENT—AND THE USE OF ROUGE

This story has no moral value. It is about a man who had fought for two years and how he came back to England for two days, and then how he went away again. It is unfortunately one of those stories which must start at the beginning, and the beginning consists merely of a few details. There were two brothers (two sons of Lord Blachford) who sailed to Europe with the first hundred thousand. Lieutenant Richard Harrington Syneforth, the elder, was killed in some forgotten raid; the younger, Lieutenant Clayton Harrington Syneforth, is the hero of this story. He was now a Captain in the Seventeenth Sussex and the immoral thing in the story happens to him. The important part to remember is that when his father met him at Paddington Station and drove him uptown in his motor, he hadn't been in England for two years—and this was in the early spring of 1917. Various circumstances had brought this about, wounds, advancement, meeting his family in Paris, and mostly being twenty-two and anxious to show his company an example of indefatigable energy. Besides, most of his friends were dead and he had rather a horror of seeing the gaps they'd leave in his England. And here is the story.

He sat at dinner and thought himself rather stupid and unnecessarily moody as his sister's light chatter amused the table. Lord and Lady Blachford, himself and two unsullied aunts. In the first place he was rather doubtful about his sister's new manner. She seemed, well, perhaps a bit loud and theatrical; and she was certainly pretty enough not to need so much paint. She couldn't be more than eighteen, and paint—it seemed so useless. Of course he was used to it in his mother, would have been shocked had she appeared in her unrouged furrowedness, but on Clara it merely accentuated her youth. Altogether he had never seen such obvious paint, and, as they had always been a shockingly frank family, he told her so.

"You've got too much stuff on your face." He tried to speak casually and his sister, nothing wroth, jumped up and ran to a mirror.

"No, I haven't," she said, calmly returning.

"I thought," he continued, rather annoyed, "that the criterion of how much paint to put on was whether men were sure you'd used any or not."

His sister and mother exchanged glances and both spoke at once.

"Not now, Clay, you know—" began Clara.

"Really, Clay," interrupted his mother, "you don't know exactly what the standards are, so you can't quite criticize. It happens to be a fad to paint a little more."

Clayton was now rather angry.

"Will all the women at Mrs. Severance's dance tonight be striped like this?"

Clara's eyes flashed.

"Yes!"

"Then I don't believe I care to go."

Clara, about to flare up, caught her mother's eye and was silent.

"Clay, I want you to go," said Lady Blachford hastily. "People want to see you before they forget what you look like. And for tonight let's not talk about war or paint."

In the end Clay went. A navy subaltern called for his sister at ten and he followed in lonesome state at half-past. After half an hour he had had all he wanted. Frankly, the dance seemed all wrong. He remembered Mrs. Severance's ante-bellum affairs—staid, correct occasions they were, with only a mere scattering from the faster set, just those people who couldn't possibly be left out. Now it all was blent, somehow, in one set. His sister had not exaggerated, practically every girl there was painted, over-painted; girls whom he remembered as curate-hunters, holders of long conversations with earnest young men on incense and the validity of orders, girls who had been terrifyingly masculine and had talked about dances as if they were the amusement of the feeble-minded—all were there, trotting through the most extreme steps from over the water. He danced stiffly with many who had delighted his youth, and he found that he wasn't enjoying himself at all. He found that he had come to picture England as a land of sorrow and asceticism, and while there was little extravagance displayed tonight, he thought that the atmosphere had fallen to that of artificial gaiety rather than risen to a stern calmness. Even under the carved, gilt ceiling of the Severances there was strangely an impression of dance-hall rather than dance. People arrived and departed most informally and, oddly enough, there was a dearth of older people rather than of younger. But there was something in the very faces of the girls, something which was half enthusiasm and half recklessness, that depressed him more than any concrete thing.

When he had decided this and had about made up his mind to go, Eleanor Marbrooke came in. He looked at her keenly. She had not lost, not a bit. He fancied that she had not quite so much paint on as the others, and when he and she talked he felt a social refuge in her cool beauty. Even then he felt that the difference between her and the others was in degree rather than in kind. He stayed, of course, and one o'clock found them sitting apart, watching. There had been a drifting away and now there seemed to be nothing but officers and girls; the Severances themselves seemed out of place as they chattered volubly in a corner to a young couple who looked as if they would rather be left alone.

"Eleanor," he demanded, "why is it that everyone looks so—well, so loose—so socially slovenly?"

"It's terribly obvious, isn't it?" she agreed, following his eyes around the room.

"And no one seems to care," he continued.

"No one does," she responded, "but, my dear man, we can't sit here and criticize our hosts. What about me? How do I look?"

He regarded her critically.

"I'd say on the whole that you've kept your looks."

"Well, I like that." She raised her brows at him in reproof. "You talk as if I were some shelved, old play-about, just over some domestic catastrophe."

There was a pause; then he asked her directly.

"How about Dick?"

She grew serious at once.

"Poor Dick—I suppose we were engaged."

"Suppose!" he said, astonished. "Why it was understood by everyone. Both our families knew. I know I used to lie awake and envy my lucky brother."

She laughed.

"Well, we certainly thought ourselves engaged. If war hadn't come we'd be comfortably married now, but if he were still alive under these circumstances, I doubt if we'd be even engaged."

"You weren't in love with him?"

"Well, you see, perhaps that wouldn't be the question, perhaps he wouldn't marry me and perhaps I *couldn't* marry him."

He jumped to his feet, astounded, and her warning hush just prevented him from exclaiming aloud. Before he could control his voice enough to speak she had whisked off with a staff officer. What could she mean?—except that in some moment of emotional excitement she had—but he couldn't bear to think of Eleanor in that light. He must have misunderstood—he must talk more with her. No, surely—if it had been true she wouldn't have said it so casually. He watched her—how close she danced. Her bright brown hair lay against the staff officer's shoulder, and her vivacious face was only two or three inches from his when she talked. All things considered Clay was becoming more angry every minute with things in general.

Next time he danced with her she seized his arm, and before he knew her intention, they had said good-byes to the Severances and were speeding away in Eleanor's limousine.

"It's a nineteen-thirteen car—imagine having a four-year-old limousine before the war."

"Terrific privation," he said ironically. "Eleanor, I want to speak to you—"

"And I to you. That's why I took you away. Where are you living?"

"At home."

"Well then we'll go to your old rooms in Grove Street. You've still got them, haven't you?"

Before he could answer she had spoken to the chauffeur and was leaning back in the corner smiling at him.

"Why Eleanor, we can't do that—talk there—"

"Are the rooms cleaned?" she interrupted.

"About once a month I think, but—"

"That's all that's necessary. In fact it'll be wonderfully proper, won't be clothes lying around the room as there usually are at bachelor teas. At Colonel Hotesane's farewell party, Gertrude Evarts and I saw—in the middle of the floor, well, my dear, a series of garments and—as we were the first to arrive we—"

"Eleanor," said Clay firmly. "I don't like this."

"I know you don't, and that's why we're going to your rooms to talk it over. Good heavens, do you think people worry these days about where conversations take place, unless they're in wireless towers, or shoreways in coast towns?"

The machine had stopped and before he could bring further argument to bear she had stepped out and scurried up the steps, where she announced that she would wait until he came and opened the door. He had no alternative. He followed, and as they mounted the stairs inside he could hear her laughing softly at him in the darkness.

He threw open the door and groped for the electric light, and in the glow that followed both stood without moving. There on the table sat a picture of Dick. Dick almost as they had last seen him, worldly wise and sophisticated, in his civilian clothes. Eleanor was the first to move. She crossed swiftly over, the dust rising with the swish of her silk, and elbows on the table said softly:

"Poor old handsome, with your beautiful self all smashed." She turned to Clay: "Dick didn't have much of a soul, such a small soul. He never bothered about eternity and I doubt if he knows any—but he had a way with him, and oh, that magnificent body of his, red gold hair, brown eyes—" her voice trailed off and she sank lazily onto the sofa in front of the hearth.

"Build a fire and then come and put your arm around me and we'll talk." Obediently he searched for wood while she sat and chatted. "I won't pretend to busybody around and try to help—I'm far too tired. I'm sure I can give the impression of home much better by just sitting here and talking, can't I?"

He looked up from where he knelt at her feet, manipulating the kerosene can, and realized that his voice was husky as he spoke.

"Just talk about England—about the country a little and about Scotland and tell me things that have happened, amusing provincial things and things with women in them— Put yourself in," he finished rather abruptly.

Eleanor smiled and kneeling down beside him lit the match and ran it along the edge of the paper that undermined the logs. She twisted her head to read it as it curled up in black at the corners. "August 14th, 1915. Zeppelin raid in—there it goes," as it disappeared in little licking flames. "My little sister—you remember Katherine: Kitty, the one with the yellow hair and the little lisp— she was killed by one of those things—she and a governess, that summer."

"Little Kitty," he said sadly. "A lot of children were killed I know, a lot. I didn't know she was gone." He was far away now and a set look had come into his eyes. She hastened to change the subject.

"Lots—but we're not on death tonight. We're going to pretend we're happy. Do you see?" She patted his knee reprovingly. "We *are* happy. We *are!* Why you were almost whimsical a while ago. I believe you're a sentimentalist. Are you?"

He was still gazing absently at the fire but he looked up at this.

"Tonight, I am—almost—for the first time in my life. Are you, Eleanor?"

"No. I'm romantic. There's a huge difference. A sentimental person thinks things will last; a romantic person hopes they won't."

He was in a reverie again and she knew that he had hardly heard her.

"Excuse please," she pleaded, slipping close to him. "Do be a nice boy and put your arm around me." He put his arm gingerly about her until she began to laugh quietly. Then he hastily withdrew it and, bending forward, talked quickly at the fire.

"Will you tell me why in the name of this mad world we're here tonight? Do you realize that this is—was a bachelor apartment before the bachelors all married the red widow over the channel— and you'll be compromised?"

She seized the straps of his shoulder belt and tugged at him until his grey eyes looked into hers.

"Clay, Clay, don't—you musn't use small petty words like that at this time. Compromise! What's that to words like Life and Love and Death and England. Compromise! Clay I don't believe anyone uses that word except servants." She laughed. "Clay, you and our butler are the only men in England who use the word compromise. My maid and I have been warned within a week— How odd—Clay, look at me."

He looked at her and saw what she intended, beauty heightened by enthusiasm. Her lips were half parted in a smile, her hair just so slightly disarranged.

"Damned witch," he muttered. "You used to read Tolstoy, and believe him."

"Did I?" Her gaze wandered to the fire. "So I did, so I did." Then her eyes came back to him and the present. "Really, Clay, we must stop gazing at the fire. It puts our minds on the past and tonight there's got to be no past or future, no time, just tonight, you and I sitting here and I most tired for a military shoulder to rest my head upon." But he was off on an old tack, thinking of Dick, and he spoke his thoughts aloud.

"You used to talk Tolstoy to Dick and I thought it was scandalous for such a good-looking girl to be intellectual."

"I wasn't, really," she admitted. "It was to impress Dick."

"I was shocked, too, when I read something of Tolstoy's. I struck the something Sonata."

"'Kreutzer Sonata,'" she suggested.

"That's it. I thought it was immoral for young girls to read Tolstoy and told Dick so. He used to nag me about that. I was nineteen."

"Yes, we thought you quite the young prig. We considered ourselves advanced."

"You're only twenty, aren't you?" asked Clay suddenly.

She nodded.

"Don't you believe in Tolstoy anymore?" he asked, almost fiercely.

She shook her head and then looked up at him almost wistfully.

"Won't you let me lean against your shoulder just the smallest bit?"

He put his arm around her, never once taking his eyes from her face, and suddenly the whole strength of her appeal burst upon him. Clay was no saint, but he had always been rather decent about women. Perhaps that's why he felt so helpless now. His emotions were not complex. He knew what was wrong, but he knew also that he wanted this woman, this warm creature of silk and life who crept so close to him. There were reasons why he oughtn't to have her, but he had suddenly seen how love was a big word like Life and Death, and she knew that he realized and was glad. Still they sat without moving for a long while and watched the fire.

II

At two-twenty next day Clay shook hands gravely with his father and stepped into the train for Dover. Eleanor, comfortable with a novel, was nestled into a corner of his compartment, and as he entered she smiled a welcome and closed the book.

"Well," she began. "I felt like a minion of the almighty secret service as I slid by your inspiring and impeccable father, swathed in yards and yards of veiling."

"He wouldn't have noticed you without your veil," answered Clayton, sitting down. "He was really most emotional under all that brusqueness. Really, you know, he's quite a nice chap. Wish I knew him better."

The train was in motion; the last uniforms had drifted in like brown, blown leaves, and now it seemed as if one tremendous wind was carrying them shoreward.

"How far are you going with me?" asked Clayton.

"Just to Rochester, an hour and a half. I absolutely had to see you before you left, which isn't very Spartan of me. But really, you see, I feel that you don't quite understand about last night, and look at me as" she paused "well—as rather exceptional."

"Wouldn't I be rather an awful cad if I thought about it in those terms at all?"

"No," she said cheerily. "I, for instance, am both a romanticist and a psychologist. It does take the romance out of anything to analyze it, but I'm going to do it if only to clear myself in your eyes."

"You don't have to—" he began.

"I know I don't," she interrupted, "but I'm going to, and when I've finished you'll see where weakness and inevitability shade off. No, I don't believe in Zola."

"I don't know him."

"Well, my dear, Zola said that environment is environment, but he referred to families and races, and this is the story of a class."

"What class?"

"Our class."

"Please," he said, "I've been wanting to hear."

She settled herself against his shoulder and, gazing out at the vanishing country, began to talk very deliberately.

"It was said, before the war, that England was the only country in the world where women weren't safe from men of their own class."

"One particular fast set," he broke in.

"A set, my dear man, who were fast but who kept every bit of their standing and position. You see even that was reaction. The idea of physical fitness came in with the end of the Victorians. Drinking died down in the universities. Why you yourself once told me that the really bad men never drank, rather kept themselves fit for moral or intellectual crimes."

"It *was* rather Victorian to drink much," he agreed. "Chaps who drank were usually young fellows about to become curates, sowing the conventional wild oats by the most orthodox tippling."

"Well," she continued, "there had to be an outlet—and there was, and you know the form it took in what you called the fast set. Next enter Mr. Mars. You see as long as there was moral pressure exerted, the rotten side of society was localized. I won't say it wasn't spreading, but it was spreading slowly, some people even thought rather normally, but when men began to go away and not come back, when marriage became a hurried thing and widows filled London, and all traditions seemed broken, why then things were different."

"How did it start?"

"It started in cases where men were called away hurriedly and girls lost their nerve. Then the men didn't come back—and there were the girls—"

He gasped.

"That was going on at the beginning?—I didn't know at all."

"Oh it was very quiet at first. Very little leaked out into daylight, but the thing spread in the dark. The next thing, you see, was to weave a sentimental mantle to throw over it. It was there and it had to be excused. Most girls either put on trousers and drove cars all day or painted their faces and danced with officers all night."

"And what mighty principle had the honor of being a cloak for all that?" he asked sarcastically.

"Now here, you see, is the paradox. I can talk like this and pretend to analyze, and even sneer at the principle. Yet I'm as much under the spell as the most wishy-washy typist who spends a week-end at Brighton with her young man before he sails with the conscripts."

"I'm waiting to hear what the spell is."

"It's this—self sacrifice with a capital S. Young men going to get killed for us—we would have been their wives—we can't be— therefore we'll be as much as we can. And that's the story."

"Good God!"

"Young officer comes back," she went on; "must amuse him, must amuse him; must give him the impression that people here are with him, that it's a big home he's coming to, that he's appreciated. Now you know, of course, in the lower classes that sort of thing means children. Whether that will ever spread to us will depend on the duration of the war."

"How about old ideas, and standards of woman and that sort of thing?" he asked, rather sheepishly.

"Sky-high, my dear—dead and gone. It might be said for utility that it's better and safer for the race that officers stay with women of their own class. Think of the next generation in France."

To Clay the whole compartment had suddenly become smothering. Bubbles of conventional ethics seemed to have burst and the long stagnant gas was reaching him. He was forced to seize his mind and make it cling to whatever shreds of the old still floated on the moral air. Eleanor's voice came to him like the grey creed of a new materialistic world; the contrast was the more vivid because of the remains of erotic honor and sentimental religiosity that she flung out with the rest.

"So you see, my dear, utility, heroism and sentiment all combine and *le voici*. And we're pulling into Rochester." She turned to him pathetically. "I see that in trying to clear myself I've only indicted my whole sex," and with tears in their eyes they kissed.

On the platform they talked for half a minute more. There was no emotion. She was trying to analyze again, and her smooth brow was wrinkled in the effort. He was endeavoring to digest what she had said, but his brain was in a whirl.

"Do you remember," he asked, "what you said last night about love being a big word like Life and Death?"

"A regular phrase; part of the technique of—of the game; a catch word." The train moved off and as Clay swung himself on the last car she raised her voice so that he could hear her to the last—"*Love is a big word, but I was flattering us. Real Love's as big as Life and Death, but not that love—not that—*" Her voice failed and mingled with the sound of the rails, and to Clay she seemed to fade out like a grey ghost on the platform.

III

When the charge broke and the remnants lapped back like spent waves, Sergeant O'Flaherty, a bullet through the left side, dropped beside him, and as weary castaways fight half listlessly for shore, they crawled and pushed and edged themselves into a shell crater. Clay's shoulder and back were bleeding profusely and he searched heavily and clumsily for his first-aid package.

"That'll be that until the Seventeenth Sussex gets reorganized," remarked O'Flaherty, sagely. "Two weeks in the rear and two weeks home."

"Damn good regiment it was, O'Flaherty," said Clay. They would have seemed like two philosophic majors commenting from safe behind the lines had it not been that Clay was flat on his back, his face in a drawn ecstasy of pain, and that the Irishman was most evidently bleeding to death. The latter was twining an improvised tourniquet on his thigh, watching it with the careless casual interest a bashful suitor bestows upon his hat.

"I can't get up no emotion over a regiment these nights," he commented disgustedly. "This'll be the fifth I was in that I seen smashed to hell. I joined these Sussex byes so I needn't see more o' me own go."

"I think you know everyone in Ireland, Sergeant."

"All Ireland's me friend, Captain, though I niver knew it 'till I left. So I left the Irish, what was left of them. You see when an English bye dies he does some play actin' before. Blood on an Englishman always calls rouge to me mind. It's a game with him. The Irish take death damn serious."

Clayton rolled painfully over and watched the night come softly down and blend with the drifting smoke. They were certainly between the devil and the deep sea and the slang of the next generation will use "no man's land" for that. O'Flaherty was still talking.

"You see you has to do somethin'. You haven't any God worth remarkin' on. So you pass from life in the names of your holy principles, and hope to meet in Westminster."

"We're not mystics, O'Flaherty," muttered Clay, "but we've got a firm grip on God and reality."

"Mystics, my eye, beggin' your pardon, Captain," cried the Irishman. "A mystic ain't no race, it's a saint. You got the most airy way o' thinkin' in the wurruld an yit you talk about plain faith as if it was cloud gazin'. There was a lecture last week behind Vimy Y.M.C.A., an' I stuck my head in the door; 'Tan-gi-ble,' the fellow was sayin', 'we must be Tan-gi-ble in our religion, we must be practical' an' he starts off on Christian brotherhood an' honorable death—so I stuck me head out again. An' you got lots a good men dyin' for that every day—tryin' to be tan-gi-ble, dyin' because their father's a duke or because he ain't. But that ain't what I got to think of. An' right here let's light a pipe before it gets dark enough for the damn burgomasters to see the match and practice on it."

Pipes, as indispensible as the hard ration, were going in no time, and the sergeant continued as he blew a huge lungful of smoke towards the earth with incongruous supercaution.

"I fight because I like it, an' God ain't to blame for that, but when it's death you're talkin' about I'll tell you what I get an' you don't. Père Dupont gets in front of the Frenchies an' he says:

'*Allons, mes enfants!*' fine! an' Father O'Brien, he says: 'Go on in byes and bate the Luther out o' them'—great stuff! But can you see the Reverent Updike—Updike just out o' Oxford, yellin' 'mix it up, chappies,' or 'soak 'em blokes'?—No, Captain, the best leader you ever get is a six-foot rowin' man that thinks God's got a seat in the House o' Commons. All sportin' men have to have a bunch o' cheerin' when they die. Give an Englishman four inches in the sportin' page this side of the whistle an' he'll die happy—but not O'Flaherty."

But Clay's thoughts were far away. Half delirious, his mind wandered to Eleanor. He had thought of nothing else for a week, ever since their parting at Rochester, and so many new sides of what he had learned were opening up. He had suddenly realized about Dick and Eleanor; they must have been married to all intents and purposes. Of course Clay had written to Eleanor from Paris, asking her to marry him on his return, and just yesterday he had gotten a very short, very kind, but definite refusal. And he couldn't understand at all.

Then there was his sister—Eleanor's words still rang in his ear. "They either put on trousers and act as chauffeurs all day or put on paint and dance with officers all night." He felt perfectly sure that Clara was still, well—virtuous. Virtuous—what a ridiculous word it seemed, and how odd to be using it about his sister. Clara had always been so painfully good. At fourteen she had sent to Boston for a souvenir picture of Louisa M. Alcott to hang over her bed. His favorite amusement had been to replace it by some startling soubrette in tights, culled from the pages of the "Pink Un." Well Clara, Eleanor, Dick, he himself, were all in the same boat, no matter what the actuality of their innocence or guilt. If he ever got back—

The Irishman, evidently sinking fast, was talking rapidly.

"Put your wishy-washy pretty clothes on everythin', but it ain't no disguise. If I get drunk it's the flesh and the devil; if you get drunk it's your wild oats. But you ain't disguisin' death, not to me you ain't. It's a damn serious affair. I may get killed for me flag, but I'm goin' to die for meself. 'I die for England' he says. 'Settle up with God, you're through with England' I says."

He raised himself on his elbow and shook his fist toward the German trenches.

"It's you an' your damn Luther!" he shouted. "You been protestin' and analyzin' until you're makin' my body ache and burn like hell; you been evolvin' like Mister Darwin, an' you stretched yourself so far that you've split. Everythin's in-tan-gi-ble except your God. Honor an' Fatherland an' Westminster Abbey, they're all in-tan-gi-ble except God an' sure you got him tan-gi-ble. You got him on the flag an' in the constitution. Next you'll be writin' your bibles with Christ sowin' wild oats to make him human. You say he's on your side. Onc't, just onc't, he had a favorite nation and they hung Him up by the hands and feet and his body hurt him and burn't him," his voice grew fainter. "Hail Mary, full of grace, the Lord is wit' thee—" His voice trailed off; he shuddered and was dead.

The hours went on. Clayton lit another pipe, heedless of what German sharpshooters might see. A heavy March mist had come down and the damp was eating into him. His whole left side was paralyzed and he felt chill creep slowly over him. He spoke aloud.

"Damned old mist—damned lucky old Irishman—Damnation." He felt a dim wonder that he was to know death but his thoughts turned as ever to England, and three faces came in sequence before him. Clara's, Dick's and Eleanor's. It was all such a mess. He'd like to have gone back and finished that conversation. It had stopped at Rochester—he had stopped living in the station at Rochester. How queer to have stopped there—Rochester had no significance. Wasn't there a play where a man was born in a station, or a handbag in a station, and he'd stopped living at—what did the Irishman say about cloaks, Eleanor said something about cloaks, too, he couldn't see any cloaks, didn't feel sentimental—only cold and dim and mixed up. He didn't know about God—God was a good thing for curates—then there was the Y.M.C.A. God—and he always wore short sleeves, and bumpy Oxfords—but that wasn't God—that was just the man who talked about God to soldiers. And then there was O'Flaherty's God. He felt as if he knew him, but then he'd never called him God—he was fear and love, and it wasn't dignified to fear God—or even to love him except in a calm respectable way. There were so many Gods it seemed—he had thought that Christianity was monotheistic, and it seemed pagan to have so many Gods.

Well, he'd find out the whole muddled business in about three minutes, and a lot of good it'd do anybody else left in the muddle. Damned muddle—everything a muddle, everybody offside, and the referee gotten rid of—everybody trying to say that if the referee were there he'd have been on their side. He was going to go and find that old referee—find him—get hold of him, get a good hold—cling to him—cling to him—ask him—

ON A PLAY TWICE SEEN

Here in the figured dark I watch once more;
　　There with the curtain rolls a year away,
　　A year of years—There was an idle day
Of ours, when happy endings didn't bore
Our unfermented souls, and rocks held ore:
　　Your little face beside me, wide-eyed, gay,
　　Smiled its own repertoire, while the poor play
Reached me as a faint ripple reaches shore.

Yawning and wondering an evening through
　　I watch alone—and chatterings of course
　　　Spoil the one scene which somehow *did* have charms;
You wept a bit, and I grew sad for you
　　Right there, where Mr. X defends divorce
　　　And What's-Her-Name falls fainting in his arms.

"VERSES IN PEACE AND WAR"

Mr. Leslie, after starting out as a sort of Irish Chesterton, now produces a diminutive volume of poetry under the title of "Verses in Peace and War". In this poetical era of titles like "Men, Women, and Ghosts," and "Sword Blades and Poppy Seed," Mr. Leslie is liable to be out-advertised by that dashing soubrette of American rhyming, Miss Amy Lowell, but if one desires poetry instead of the more popular antics of the School of Boston Bards and Hearst Reviewers, let him sit down for an hour with Mr. Leslie's little book. At first, one gets the impression of rather light verse, but soon finds that it is the touch rather than the verse which is light. The same undercurrent of sadness which runs through Mr. Leslie's prose is evident in his poetry, and gives it a most rare and haunting depth. In the series, "Epitaphs for Aviators," two are particularly apt. The one on Lieutenant Hamel:

> Nor rugged earth nor untamed sky
> Gave him his death to die,
> But gentlest of the Holy Three—
> The long grey liquid Sea.

And the one on Lieutenant Chavez:

> One flying past the Alps to see
>   What lay beyond their crest—
> Behind the snows found Italy
>   Beyond the mountains—rest.

There is a savor of the Greek in his poem "The Hurdlers," dedicated to two of England's representatives in the last Olympian games, since killed in Flanders. The lines:

> Oh, how are the beautiful broken,
> And how are the swiftest made slow—

sound as if they'd scan as well in Greek as in English. The lighter poems such as "Nightmare" and "Rubies" are immensely well done as are the Irish poems "The Two Mothers" and "A Ballad of China Tea," but the brightest gem of the coffer is the poem "The Dead Friend," beginning:

> I drew him then unto my knees,
> My friend who was dead,
> And I set my live lips over his,
> And my heart to his head.

Mr. Leslie has a most distinct gift, and the only pity is that his book is so small. Poets are really so very rare that it seems almost unfair for them to become essayists. Despite Mr. Taine, in the whole range from Homer's "Odyssey" to Master's idiocy, there has been but one Shakespeare, and every lost name leaves a gap that it, and it only, could have filled.

("Verses in Peace and War," *by Shane Leslie; Scribner's.*)

"GOD, THE INVISIBLE KING"

The fad of rediscovering God has reached Mr. Wells. Started by Tolstoi (who has since backed his case by fathering a brand new revolution) it has reached most of the Clever People, including Bernard Shaw, who tried to startle us last year with his preface to "Androcles and the Lion." But Mr. Wells has added very little. Like Victor Hugo, he has nothing but genius and is not of the slightest practical help. Neither a pacifist nor a crusader, he has been wise enough to keep God out of the war, which is only what the sanest people have been doing all along; if any war was ever made on earth it is this one.

If there is anything older than the old story it is the new twist. Mr. Wells supplies this by neatly dividing God into a creator and a Redeemer. On the whole we should welcome "God, the Invisible King" as an entertaining addition to our supply of fiction for light summer reading.

("God, the Invisible King," *by H. G. Wells; Macmillan Co.*)

THE CAMEO FRAME

Golden, golden is the air,
Golden is the air,
Golden frets of golden mandolins,
Golden notes of golden violins,
Fair . . . Oh wearily fair;
Skeins from woven basket
Mortal may not hold,
Oh what young extravagant god,
Who would know or ask it . . .
Who could give such gold . . .

Oh the proud page
In the gold gloaming,
When the light whispers
And the souls roaming,
Ports the grey train,
Sees the gold hair
In the gay
The golden air

She posed that day by the marble pool
    At half after five, so her fancy led;
Her slim grey pages, her lord, her fool
    Clacked various clacks as they watched the head
Acomba was doing . . . his own request . . .
    Her head—just from swirling hair to throat,
With clinging silk for a shoulder sheath
    And half the curve of a breast beneath.

"Head to the left...so...Can you stand
   A little more sun on hair and face?"
Then as he lightly touched her hand
   She whispered to him a time, a place
Then he aloud: "Here's the very light,
   My Lord, for the gold and rose effect...
Such a light over pool and sky
As cameo never was graven by."

Over her grey and velvet dress
   Under her molten, beaten hair
Color of rose in mock distress
   Flushes and fades and makes her fair
Fills the air from her to him
   With light and languor and little sighs
Just so subtly he scarcely knows
Laughing lightning, color of rose.

And grey to rose, and rose to gold
   The color of day is twain, is one;
And he blinds his eyes that his heart may hold
   This cameo on the setting sun,
And lip and fingers as lip and lip
   Burn together and chill apart
And he turns his head as he sees her go,
Beautiful, pitiful, cameo.

        Oh the proud page
        In the green gloaming,
        When the grass whispers
        And the souls roaming,
        Ports the grey train,
        Sees the gold hair
        In the gay
        The golden air.

II

The night was another fragile frame
    Tall and quiet and fair to fill;
It made for Acomba when he came
    A silver setting . . . He watched until
She fluttered down from the guarded hall
    A weary leaf from a dreary tree,
Fluttered to him where the breezes cool
Made pale love to the marble pool.

Then the moon and his heart sank low . . .
    All that he knew of a sudden there
Was just that the light on the cameo
    Was not the light that had made it fair . . .
Not the grey and not the rose,
    Not the gold of the afternoon,
So he kissed it sadly and spoke a name
And he pressed it back in its silver frame.

And youth in anger, and time in tears
    Sat at his feet and bade him take . . .
"Once a day for a thousand years
    Think of the gold her hair will make . . .
Shaper of lips you may not kiss
    Scorn you the soul where colors touch
Kept for you in a golden sleep! . . . ."
But he could never say why . . . or weep.

So ice by day and ghost by night
    The cameo lay till its moment came
And blushed for the sunset bold and bright
    Gold and rose in its velvet frame,
And he who made it would stand and smile,
    Pause and pity and count the years,
Watch and watch till the frame turned blue
Knower of things was he . . . . he knew . . .

Golden, golden is the air,
Golden is the air,
Golden frets of golden mandolins,
Golden notes from golden violins,
Fair, oh wearily fair;
Skeins from woven basket
Mortal may not hold
Oh what young extravagant god
Who would know or ask it
Who could give such gold!

THE PIERIAN SPRINGS AND THE LAST STRAW

My Uncle George assumed, during my childhood, almost legendary proportions. His name was never mentioned except in verbal italics. His published works lay in bright, interesting bindings on the library table—forbidden to my whetted curiousity until I should reach the age of corruption. When one day I broke the orange lamp into a hundred shivers and glints of glass, it was in search of closer information concerning a late arrival among the books. I spent the afternoon in bed and for weeks could not play under the table because of maternal horror of severed arteries in hands and knees. But I had gotten my first idea of Uncle George—he was a tall, angular man with crooked arms. His opinion was founded upon the shape of the handwriting in which he had written, "To you, my brother, with heartiest of futile hopes that you will enjoy and approve of this: George Rombert." After this unintelligible beginning, whatever interest I had in the matter waned, as would have all my ideas of the author, had he not been a constant family topic.

When I was eleven I unwillingly listened to the first comprehensible discussion of him. I was fidgeting on a chair in barbarous punishment when a letter arrived and I noticed my father growing stern and formidable as he read it. Instinctively I knew it concerned Uncle George—and I was right.

"What's the matter Tom?—Someone sick?" asked my mother rather anxiously.

For answer Father rose and handed her the letter and some newspaper clippings it had enclosed. When she had read it twice (for her naive curiosity could never resist a preliminary skim) she plunged—

"Why should she write to you and not to me?"

Father threw himself wearily on the sofa and arranged his long limbs decoratively.

"It's getting tiresome, isn't it? This is the third time he's become—involved." I started, for I distinctively heard him add under his breath, "Poor damn fool!"

"It's much more than tiresome," began my mother. "It's disgusting; a great strong man with money and talent and every reason to behave and get married (she implied that these words were synonymous) playing around with serious women like a silly, conceited college boy. You'd think it was a harmless game!"

Here I put in my word. I thought that perhaps my being *de trop* in the conversation might lead to an early release.

"I'm here," I volunteered.

"So I see," said Father in the tones he used to intimidate other young lawyers downtown; so I sat there and listened respectfully while they plumbed the iniquitous depths.

"It is a game to him," said my father. "That's all part of his theory."

My mother sighed. "Mr. Sedgewick told me yesterday that his books had done inestimable harm to the spirit in which love is held in this country."

"Mr. Sedgewick wrote him a letter," remarked my father rather dryly, "and George sent him the book of Solomon by return post—"

"Don't joke, Thomas," said Mother, crowding her face with eyes. "George is treacherous, his mind is unhealthy—"

"And so would mine be, had you not snatched me passionately from his clutches—and your son here will be George the second, if he feeds on this sort of conversation at his age." So the curtain fell upon my Uncle George for the first time.

Scrappy and rough-pieced information on this increasingly engrossing topic fitted gradually into my consciousness in the next five years, like the parts of a picture puzzle. Here is the finished portrait from the angle of seventeen years—Uncle George was a Romeo and a misogamist, a combination of Byron, Don Juan, and Bernard Shaw, with a touch of Havelock Ellis for good measure. He was about thirty, had been engaged seven times and drank ever so much more than was good for him. His attitude toward women was the *pièce-de-résistance* of his character. To put it mildly he was not an idealist. He had written a series of novels, all of them bitter, each of them with some woman as the principal character. Some of the women were bad. None of them were quite good. He picked a rather weird selection of Lauras to play muse to his whimsical Petrarch; for he could write, write well.

He was the type of author who gets dozens of letters a week from solicitors, aged men and enthusiastic young women who tell him that he is "prostituting his art" and "wasting golden literary opportunities." As a matter of fact he wasn't. It was very conceivable that he might have written better despite his unpleasant range of subject, but what he had written had a huge vogue that, strangely enough, consisted not of the usual devotees of prostitute art, the eager shopgirls and sentimental salesmen to whom he was accused of pandering, but of the academic and literary circles of the country. His shrewd tenderness with nature (that is, everything but the white race), his well-drawn men and the particularly cynical sting to his wit gave him many adherents. He was ranked in the most staid and severe of reviews as a coming man. Long psychopathic stories and dull germanized novels were predicted of him by optimistic critics. At one time he was the Thomas Hardy of America, and he was several times heralded as the Balzac of his century. He was accused of having the great American novel in his coat pocket, trying to peddle it from publisher to publisher. But somehow neither matter nor style had improved; people accused him of not "living." His unmarried sister and he had an apartment where she sat greying year by year with one furtive hand on the bromo-seltzer and the other on the telephone receiver of frantic feminine telephone calls. For George Rombert grew violently involved at least once a year. He filled columns in the journals of society gossip. Oddly enough most of his affairs were with debutantes—a fact which was considered particularly annoying by sheltering mothers. It seemed as though he had the most serious way of talking the most outrageous nonsense, and as he was most desirable from an economic point of view, many essayed the perilous quest.

Though we had lived in the East since I had been a baby, it was always understood that home meant the prosperous Western city that still supported the roots of our family tree. When I was twenty

I went back for the first time and made my only acquaintance with Uncle George.

I had dinner in the apartment with my aunt, a very brave, gentle old lady who told me, rather proudly, I thought, that I looked like George. I was shown his pictures from babyhood, in every attitude: George at Andover, on the Y.M.C.A. committee, strange anatomy; George at Williams in the center of the Literary Magazine Picture; George as head of his fraternity. Then she handed me a scrapbook containing accounts of his exploits and all favorable criticism of his work.

"He cares nothing at all about all this," she explained. I admired and questioned, and remember thinking, as I left the apartment to seek Uncle George at his club, that between my family's depressed opinion of him and my aunt's elated one my idea of him was muddled to say the least. At the Iroquois Club I was directed to the grill, and there, standing in the doorway, I picked one out of the crowd, who, I was immediately sure, was he. Here is the way he looked at the time. He was tall with magnificent iron grey hair and the pale soft skin of a boy, most remarkable in a man of his mode of life. Drooping green eyes and a sneering mouth complete my picture of his physical self. He was rather drunk, for he had been at the club all afternoon and for dinner, but he was perfectly conscious of himself, and the dulling of faculties was only perceivable in a very cautious walk and a crack in his voice that sank it occasionally to a hoarse whisper. He was talking to a table of men, all in various stages of inebriation, and holding them by a most peculiar and magnetic series of gestures. Right here I want to remark that this influence was not dependent so much upon a vivid physical personality but on a series of perfectly artificial mental tricks, his gestures, the peculiar range of his speaking voice, the suddenness and terseness of his remarks.

I watched him intently while my hall boy whispered to him, and he walked slowly and consciously over to me to shake hands gravely and escort me to a small table. For an hour we talked of family things, of healths and deaths and births. I could not take my eyes off him. The blood-shot streakedness of his green eyes made me think of weird color combinations in a child's paint-box. He had been looking bored for about ten minutes, and my talk had been dwindling despondently down, when suddenly he waved his hand as if to brush away a veil, and began to question me.

"Is that damn father of yours still defending me against your mother's tongue?"

I started, but, strangely, felt no resentment.

"Because," he went on, "it's the only thing he ever did for me all his life. He's a terrible prig. I'd think it would drive you wild to have him in the house."

"Father feels very kindly toward you, sir," I said rather stiffly.

"Don't," he protested smiling. "Stick to veracity in your own family and don't bother to lie to me. I'm a totally black figure in your mind, I'm well aware. Am I not?"

"Well—you've—you've had a twenty years' history."

"Twenty years—hell—" said Uncle George. "Three years' history and fifteen years' aftermath."

"But your books—and all."

"Just aftermath, nothing but aftermath. My life stopped at twenty-one one night in October at sixteen minutes after ten. Do you want to hear about it? First I'll show you the heifer and then I'll take you upstairs and present you to the altar."

"I, you—if you—" I demurred feebly, for I was on fire to hear the story.

"Oh,—no trouble. I've done the story several times in books and life and around many a littered table. I have no delicacy anymore—I lost that in the first smoke. This is the totally blackened heifer whom you're talking to now."

So he told me the story.

"You see it began sophomore year—began most directly and most vividly in Christmas vacation of sophomore year. Before that she'd always gone with a younger crowd—set, you young people call it now,"—he paused and clutched with mental fingers for tangible figures to express himself. "Her dancing, I guess, and beauty and the most direct, unprincipled personality I've ever come in contact with. When she wanted a boy there was no preliminary scouting among other girls for information, no sending out of tentative approaches meant to be retailed to him. There was the most direct attack by every faculty and gift that she possessed. She had no divergence of method—she just made you conscious to the highest degree that she was a girl"—he turned his eyes on me suddenly and asked:

"Is that enough—do you want a description of her eyes and hair and what she said?"

"No," I answered, "go on."

"Well, I went back to college an idealist. I built up a system of psychology in which dark ladies with alto voices and infinite possibilities floated through my days and nights. Of course we had the most frantic correspondence—each wrote ridiculous letters and sent ridiculous telegrams, told all our acquaintances about our flaming affair and—well you've been to college. All this is banal, I know. Here's an odd thing. All the time I was idealizing her to the last possibility, I was perfectly conscious that she was about the faultiest girl I'd ever met. She was selfish, conceited and uncontrolled and since these were my own faults I was doubly aware of them. Yet I never wanted to change her. Each fault was knit up with a sort of passionate energy that transcended it. Her selfishness made her play the game harder, her lack of control put me rather in awe of her, and her conceit was punctuated by such delicious moments of remorse and self-denunciation that it was almost—almost dear to me— Isn't this getting ridiculous? She had the strongest effect on me. She made me want to do something for her, to get something to show her. Every honor in college took on the semblance of a presentable trophy."

He beckoned to a waiter to my infinite misgiving, for though he seemed rather more sober than when I had arrived, he had been drinking steadily, and I knew my own position would be embarrassing if he became altogether drunk.

"Then"—between sips—"we saw each other at sporadic intervals, quarreled, kissed and quarreled again. We were equals; neither was the leader. She was as interested in me as I was fascinated by her. We were both terrifically jealous, but there was little occasion to show it. Each of us had small affairs on the side but merely as relaxations when the other was away. I didn't realize it but my idealism was slowly waning—or increasing into love—and rather a gentle sort of love." His face tightened. "This isn't cup sentiment."

I nodded and he went on: "Well, we broke off in two hours, and I was the weak one."

"Senior year I went to her school dance in New York, and there was a man there from another college of whom I became very jealous and not without cause. She and I had a few words about it, and half an hour later I walked out on the street in my coat and hat, leaving behind the melancholy statement that I was through for good. So far so good. If I'd gone back to college that night or if I'd gone and gotten drunk or done almost anything wild or resentful, the break would never have occurred—she'd have written next day. Here's what did happen. I walked along Fifth Avenue letting my imagination play on my sorrow, really luxuriating in it. She'd never looked better than she had that night, never; and I had never been so much in love. I worked myself up to the highest pitch of emotional imagination and moods grew real on me and then—Oh poor damn fool that I was—am—will always be—I went back. Went back! Couldn't I have known or seen—I knew her and myself—I could have plotted out for anyone else or, in a cool mood, for myself just what I should have done, but my imagination made me go back, drove me. Half a thought in my brain would have sent me to Williamstown or the Manhattan bar. Another half thought sent me back to her school. When I crossed the threshold it was sixteen minutes after ten. At that minute I stopped living."

"You can imagine the rest. She was angry at me for leaving, hadn't had time to brood, and when she saw me come in she resolved to punish me. I swallowed it hook and bait and temporarily lost confidence, temper, poise, every single jot of individuality or attractiveness I had. I wandered around that ballroom like a wild man trying to get a word with her, and when I did I finished the job. I begged, pled, almost wept. She had no use for me from that hour. At two o'clock I walked out of that school a beaten man."

"Why the rest—it's a long nightmare—letters with all the nerve gone out of them, wild imploring letters; long silences hoping she'd care; rumors of her other affairs. At first I used to be sad when people still linked me up with her, asked me for news of her, but finally when it got around that she'd thrown me over people didn't ask me about her anymore, they told me of her—crumbs to a dog. I wasn't the authority anymore on my own work, for that's what she was—just what I'd read into her and brought out in her. That's the story—" He broke off suddenly and rose; tottering to his feet, his voice rose and rang through the deserted grill.

"I read history with a new viewpoint since I had known Cleopatra and Messalina and Montespan,"—he started toward the door.

"Where are you going?" I asked in alarm.

"We're going upstairs to meet the lady. She's a widow now for awhile, so you must say Mrs.—see—Mrs."

We went upstairs, I carefully behind with hands ready to be outstretched should he fall. I felt particularly unhappy. The hardest man in the world to handle is one who is too sober to be vacillating and too drunk to be persuaded; and I had, strange to say, an idea that my uncle was eminently a person to be followed.

We entered a large room. I couldn't describe it if my life depended on it. Uncle George nodded and beckoned to a woman at a bridge four across the room. She nodded and, rising from the table, walked slowly over. I started—naturally—

Here is my impression—a woman of thirty or a little under, dark, with intense physical magnetism and a most expressive mouth capable as I soon found out of the most remarkable change of expression by the slightest variance in facial geography. It was a mouth to be written to, but, though it could never have been called large, it could never have been crowded into a sonnet—I confess I have tried. Sonnet indeed! It contained the emotions of a drama and the history, I presume, of an epic. It was, as near as I can fathom, the eternal mouth. There were eyes also, brown, and a high warm coloring; but oh the mouth . . . .

I felt like a character in a Victorian romance. The little living groups scattered around seemed to move in small spotlights around us, acting out a comedy "down stage." I was self-conscious about myself but purely physically so; I was merely a property; but I was very self-conscious for my uncle. I dreaded the moment when he should lift his voice or overturn the table or kiss Mrs. Fulham bent dramatically back over his arm while the groups would start and stare. It was enormously unreal. I was introduced in a mumble and then forgotten.

"Tight again," remarked Mrs. Fulham.

My uncle made no answer.

"Well, I'm having a heavy bridge game, and we're ever so much behind. You can just have my dummy time. Aren't you flattered?" She turned to me. "Your uncle probably told you all about himself and me. He's behaving so badly this year. He used to be such a pathetic, innocent little boy and such a devil with the debutantes."

My uncle broke in quickly with a rather grandiose air:

"That's sufficient I think, Myra, for you."

"You're going to blame me again?" she asked in feigned astonishment. "As if I—"

"Don't—Don't," said my uncle thickly. "Let one poor damn fool alone."

Here I found myself suddenly appreciating a sudden contrast. My uncle's personality had dropped off him like a cloak. He was not the romantic figure of the grill, but a less sure, less attractive and somewhat contemptible individual. I had never seen personalities act like that before. Usually you either had one or you didn't. I wonder if I mean personality or temperament or perhaps that brunette alto tenor mood that lies on the borderland.... At any rate my uncle's mood was now that of a naughty boy to a stern aunt, almost that of a dog to his master.

"You know," said Mrs. Fulham, "your uncle is the only interesting thing in town. He's such a perfect fool."

Uncle George bowed his head and regarded the floor in a speculative manner. He smiled politely, if unhappily.

"That's your idea."

"He takes all his spite out on me."

My uncle nodded. Mrs. Fulham's partners called over to her that they had lost again and that the game was breaking up. She got rather angry.

"You know," she said coldly to Uncle George, "you stand there like a trained spaniel letting me say anything I want to you— Do you know what a pitiful thing you are?"

My uncle had gone a dark red. Mrs. Fulham turned again to me.

"I've been talking to him like this for ten years—like this or not at all. He's my little lap dog. Here George, bring me my tea, write a book about me; you're snippy, Georgie, but interesting." Mrs. Fulham was rather carried away by the dramatic intensity of her own words and angered by George's unmovable acceptance. So she lost her head.

"You know," she said tensely, "my husband often wanted to horsewhip you, but I've begged you off. He was very handy in the kennels and always said he could handle any kind of dog!"

Something had snapped. My uncle rose, his eyes blazing. The shift of burden from her to her husband had lifted a weight from his shoulders. His eyes flashed, but the words stored up for ten years came slow and measured.

"Your husband—Do you mean that crooked broker who kept you for five years? Horsewhip me! That was the prattle he may have used around the fireside to keep you under his dirty thumb. By God, I'll horsewhip your next husband myself." His voice had risen, and the people were beginning to look up. A hush had fallen on the room, and his words echoed from fireplace to fireplace.

"He's the damn thief that robbed me of everything in this hellish world!"

He was shouting now. A few men drew near. Women shrank to the corners. Mrs. Fulham stood perfectly still. Her face had gone white, but she was still sneering openly at him.

"What's this?" He picked up her hand. She tried to snatch it away but he tightened his grip and, twisting the wedding ring off her finger, he threw it on the floor and stamped it into a beaten button of gold.

In a minute I had his arms held. She screamed and held up her broken finger. The crowd closed around us.

In five minutes Uncle George and I were speeding homeward in a taxi. Neither of us spoke; he sat staring straight before him, his green eyes glittering in the dark. I left next morning after breakfast.

* * *

The story ought to end here. My Uncle George should remain with Marc Antony and De Musset as a rather tragic semi-genius, ruined by a woman. Unfortunately the play continues into an inartistic sixth act where it topples over and descends like Uncle George himself in one of his more inebriated states, contrary to all the rules of dramatic literature. One month afterward Uncle George and Mrs. Fulham eloped in the most childish and romantic manner the night before her marriage to the Honorable Howard Bixby was to have taken place. Uncle George never drank again, nor did he ever write or in fact do anything except play a middling amount of golf and get comfortably bored with his wife.

Mother still doubts and predicts gruesome fates for his wife, Father is frankly astonished and not too pleased. In fact I rather believe he enjoyed having an author in the family, even if his books did look a bit decadent on the library table. From time to time I receive subscription lists and invitations from Uncle George. I keep them for use in my new book, "Theories of Genius." You see, I claim that if Dante had ever won—but a hypothetical sixth act is just as untechnical as a real one.

THE STAYING UP ALL NIGHT

The warm fire.
The comfortable chairs.
The merry companions.
The stroke of twelve.
The wild suggestion.
The good sports.
The man who hasn't slept for weeks.
The people who have done it before.
The long anecdotes.
The best looking girl yawns.
The forced raillery.
The stroke of one.
The best looking girl goes to bed.
The stroke of two.
The empty pantry.
The lack of firewood.
The second best looking girl goes to bed.
The weather-beaten ones who don't.
The stroke of four.
The dozing off.
The amateur "life of the party."
The burglar scare.
The scornful cat.
The trying to impress the milkman.
The scorn of the milkman.
The lunatic feeling.
The chilly sun.
The stroke of six.
The walk in the garden.
The sneezing.
The early risers.

The volley of wit at you.
The feeble come-back.
The tasteless breakfast.
The miserable day.
8 P. M.—Between the sheets.

INTERCOLLEGIATE PETTING-CUES

2. "You really don't look comfortable there."

OUR AMERICAN POETS

I

Robert Service.

The red blood throbs
And forms in gobs
　　On the nose of Hank McPhee.
With a wild "Ha-Ha!" he shoots his pa
　　Through the frozen arctic lea.

II

Robert Frost.

A rugged young rhymer named Frost,
Once tried to be strong at all cost
　　The mote in his eye
　　May be barley or rye,
But his right in that beauty is lost.

Though the meek shall inherit the land,
He prefers a tough bird in the hand,
　　He puts him in inns,
　　And feeds him on gins,
And the highbrows say, "Isn't he grand?"

CEDRIC THE STOKER
(The true story of the Battle of the Baltic)

The grimy coal-hole of the battleship of the line was hot, and Cedric felt the loss of his parasol keenly. It was his duty to feed the huge furnace that sent the ship rolling over and over in the sea, heated the sailors' bedrooms, and ran the washing machine. Cedric was hard at work. He would fill his hat with a heap of the black coals, carry them to the huge furnace, and throw them in. His hat was now soiled beyond recognition, and try as he might he could not keep his hands clean.

He was interrupted in his work by the jingle of the telephone bell. "Captain wishes to speak to you, Mr. Cedric," said the girl at the exchange. Cedric rushed to the phone.

"How's your mother," asked the Captain.

"Very well, thank you, sir," answered Cedric.

"Is it hot enough for you, down there?" said the Captain.

"Quite," replied Cedric, courteously.

The Captain's voice changed. He would change it every now and then. "Come to my office at once," he said. "We are about to go into action and I wish your advice."

Cedric rushed to the elevator, and getting off at the fourth floor, ran to the office. He found the Captain rubbing his face with cold cream to remove sunburn.

"Cedric," said the Captain, sticking a lump of the greasy stuff into his month, and chewing it while he talked, "you are a bright child. Rattle off the binomial theorem."

Cedric repeated it forwards, backwards, and from the middle to both ends.

"Now name all the salts of phosphoric acid!"

Cedric named them all, and four or five extra.

"Now the Iliad!"

Here Cedric did his most difficult task. He repeated the Iliad backwards leaving out alternately every seventh and fourth word.

"You *are* efficient," said the Captain smilingly. He took from his mouth the cold cream, which he had chewed into a hard porous lump, and dropped it back into the jar. "I shall trust you with all our lives." He drew Cedric closer to him.

"Listen," he whispered; "the enemy are attacking in force. They are far stronger than we. We outnumber them only five to one: nevertheless we shall fight with the utmost bravery. As commander of the fleet, I have ordered the crews of all my ships to struggle to the last shell and powder roll, and then to flee for their lives. This ship is not so fast as the others so I guess it had better begin fleeing now!"

"Sir—" began Cedric, but he was interrupted by the staccato noise of the huge forward turret pop-guns as the two fleets joined in battle. They could hear the sharp raps of the paddles as the bosuns spanked their crews to make them work faster. Their ears were deafened by the cursing of the pilots as the ships fouled one another. All the hideous sounds of battle rose and assailed them. Cedric rushed to the window and threw it open. He shrank back, aghast. Bearing down upon them, and only ten miles away, was the huge *Hoboken*, the biggest of all ferry-boats, captured by the enemy from the Erie Railroad in the fall of '92. So close she was that Cedric could read her route sign "Bronx West to Toid Avenoo." The very words struck him numb. On she came, and on, throwing mountains of spray a mile in front of her and several miles to her rear.

"Is she coming fast, boy?" asked the Captain.

"Sir, she's making every bit of a knot an hour," answered Cedric, trembling.

The Captain seized him roughly by the shoulders. "We'll fight to the end," he said, "even though she is faster than we are. Quick! To the cellars, and stoke, stoke, STOKE!!"

Cedric, unable to take his eyes from the terrible sight, ran backwards down the passageway, fell down the elevator shaft, and rushed to the furnace. Madly he carried coal back and forth, from the bin to the furnace door, and then back to the bin. Already the speed of the ship had increased. It tore through the water in twenty-foot jumps. But it was not enough. Cedric worked more madly, and still more madly. At last he had thrown the last lump of coal into the furnace. There was nothing more to be done. He rested his tired body against the glowing side of the furnace.

Again the telephone bell rang. Cedric answered it himself, not wishing to take the exchange girl away from her knitting. It was the Captain. "We must have more speed," he shouted. "We must have more speed. Throw on more coal—more coal!"

For a moment Cedric was wrapped in thought, his face twitching with horror. Then he realized his duty, and rushed forward *****

Late that evening, when they were safe in port, the Captain, smoking his after-dinner cigar, came down to the stoke-hole. He called for Cedric. There was not a sound. Again he called. Still there was silence. Suddenly the horror of the truth rushed upon him. He tore open the furnace door and, convulsed with sobs, drew forth a Brooks-Livingstone Collar, a half-melted piece of Spearmint gum, and a suit of Yerger asbestos underwear. For a moment he held them in his arms, and then fell howling upon the floor. The truth had turned out to be the truth.

Cedric had turned himself into calories.

CITY DUSK

Come out ... out
To this inevitable night of mine
Oh you drinker of new wine,
Here's pageantry.... Here's carnival,
Rich dusk, dim streets and all
The whisperings of city night....

I have closed my book of fading harmonies
(The shadows fell across me in the park),
And my soul was sad with violins and trees,
And I was sick for dark,
When suddenly it hastened by me, bringing
Thousands of lights, a haunting breeze,
And a night of streets and singing....

I shall know you by your eager feet
And by your pale, pale hair;
I'll whisper happy incoherent things
While I'm waiting for you there....

All the faces unforgettable in dusk
Will blend to yours,
And the footsteps like a thousand overtures
Will blend to yours,
And there will be more drunkenness than wine
In the softness of your eyes on mine....

Faint violins where lovely ladies dine,
The brushing of skirts, the voices of the night
And all the lure of friendly eyes.... Ah there
We'll drift like summer sounds upon the summer air....

MY FIRST LOVE

All my ways she wove of light
   Wove them half alive,
Made them warm and beauty-bright...
   So the shining, ambient air
   Clothes the golden waters where
     The pearl fishers dive.

When she wept and begged a kiss
   Very close I'd hold her,
Oh I know so well in this
   Fine, fierce joy of memory
   She was very young like me
     Tho half an aeon older.

Once she kissed me very long,
   Tip-toed out the door,
Left me, took her light along,
   Faded as a music fades...
   Then I saw the changing shades,
   Color-blind no more.

MARCHING STREETS

Death slays the moon and the long dark deepens,
  Hastens to the city, to the drear stone-heaps,
Films all eyes and whispers on the corners,
  Whispers to the corners that the last soul sleeps.

Gay grow the streets now torched by yellow lamplight,
  March all directions with a long sure tread.
East, west they wander through the blinded city,
  Rattle on the windows like the wan-faced dead.

Ears full of throbbing, a babe awakens startled,
  Sends a tiny whimper to the still gaunt room.
Arms of the mother tighten round it gently,
  Deaf to the patter in the far-flung gloom.

Old streets hoary with dear, dead foot-steps
  Loud with the tumbrils of a gold old age
Young streets sand-white still unheeled and soulless,
  Virgin with the pallor of the fresh-cut page.

Black streets and alleys, evil girl and tearless,
  Creeping leaden-footed each in thin, torn coat,
Wine-stained and miry, mire-choked and winding,
  Wind like choking fingers on a white, full throat.

White lanes and pink lanes, strung with purpled roses,
  Dance along the distance weaving o'er the hills,
Beckoning the dull streets with stray smiles wanton,
  Strung with purpled roses that the stray dawn chills.

Here now they meet tiptoe on the corner,
  Kiss behind the silence of the curtained dark;
Then half unwilling run between the houses,
  Tracing through the pattern that the dim lamps mark.

Steps break steps and murmur into running,
  Death upon the corner spills the edge of dawn
Dull the torches waver and the streets stand breathless;
  Silent fades the marching and the night-noon's gone.

THE POPE AT CONFESSION

The gorgeous Vatican was steeped in night,
  The organs trembled to my heart no more,
But with the blend of colors on my sight
  I loitered through a sombre corridor
And suddenly I heard behind a screen
  The faintest whisper, as from one in prayer,
I glanced around, then passed, for I had seen
  A hushed and lonely room . . . and two were there—

A ragged friar, half in a dream's embrace
  Leaned sideways, soul intent, as if to seize
    The last grey ice of sin that ached to melt
    And faltered from the lips of him who knelt—
  A little bent old man upon his knees
With pain and sorrow in his holy face.

RECORD OF VARIANTS

The tables below record emendations, all editorial, in the original texts from the *Now and Then*, the *Newman News*, the *Daily Princetonian*, the *Princeton Tiger*, the *Nassau Literary Magazine*, and the volumes of Triangle Club music and lyrics. The reading to the left of the bracket is the emended reading; the reading to the right is the original reading. Substantives are intermixed with accidentals. The following symbols are used:

~   the same word
∧   absence of punctuation
stet   refusal to emend where an emendation might be called for

"The Mystery of the Raymond Mortgage"

4.6	outside] outside of	8.31	den dey] den day
4.23	of the house,] ~~~∧	8.32	street. I'll] street, ~
5.16	before,] ~∧	8.37	she!] ~,
6.20	look?] ~,	9.4	stairs!] ~,
7.12	fired and,] ~~∧	9.9	do it,] ~~∧
7.30	all this!] ~~,	9.16	forgot Mrs. Raymond!]
7.30	exclaimed I,] ~~~∧		~~~∧
7.32	said,] ~∧	9.22	around;] ~,
7.35	who] whom		

"Reade, Substitute Right Half"

10.2	battered Crimson] ~, crimson	10.12	knees,] ~∧
		10.16	head] hear
10.3	Blues'] blues	10.25	Come on,] ~~∧
10.5	three!] ~,	11.8	Mirdle] Mridle
10.7	Crimson] crimson *two readings*	11.15	himself. Even] ~∧ even
		11.16	Blues'] blue
10.8	and, shaking] ~∧~	11.18	lineman] line man

"A Debt of Honor"

13.10	Sanderson] ~,	14.26	says,] ~∧
13.19	morning,] ~∧	14.28	it by] it-by
13.23	life,] ~∧	14.31	general] General
13.28	on Jan.] ~~,	14.32	orderly,] ~∧
14.18	answered Jack,] ~~∧	14.32	horse,] ~∧
14.19	the Confederate] The Conferderate	15.5	Federal fire] federal ~
14.20	shot." And] ~;" and	15.14	of he] of him

"S.P.A. Men in College Athletics"

16.7	hockey] hocky	16.29	Williams] ~'
16.11	football] foot-fall	17.2	awhile] a while

"The Room with the Green Blinds"

18.2	ominous-looking] ~∧~	21.6	revolver. "] ~.∧
18.7–8	hospitable-looking] ~∧~	21.7	manor;] ~∧
18.20	Georgia,] Ga.,	21.7	I,] ~∧
18.24	until Carmatle] When ~	21.27	Abraham] Albraham
18.28	second floor] third ~	21.29	"Mr. Carmatle] ∧~~
19.4	flicker,] ~∧	21.31	Forrest's] Forest's
19.19	bloodstain] blood stain	21.33	Appomattox] Appomatox
19.21	clean-shaven] ~∧~	21.34	Pike] pike
19.35	right] left	22.6	western] Western
20.11	explanation. The] ~, the	22.11	clothes,] ~∧
20.17	that. Who] ~, who		

"'Football'"

25.18	straight-arm] ~∧~

"Election Night"

27.5	bonfire,] ~∧

"A Luckless Santa Claus"

28.6	Package-laden] ~∧~	32.1	shoes] shoe
28.16–17	stood laughing] ~-~	32.6	mocking] mockingly
28.22	hard-earned] ~∧~ *two readings*	32.10	perceived,] ~∧
		32.13	ugly-looking] ~∧~
29.8	can!] ~.	32.29	light,] ~;
30.25	his] has	32.32	knees,] ~∧

"Pain and the Scientist"

34.4	for,] ~∧	37.3	pillow,] ~∧
34.17	pitch,] ~∧	37.17	slippery-looking] ~∧~
35.2	conical-shaped] ~∧~	38.2	'mind] ∧~
35.9	night-cap] ~∧~ *three*	38.2	everything.'] ~.∧
	readings	38.3	Mr.] '~.
36.15	lie!] ~,	38.18	hour's] hours'
36.17	cannot] can not		

"The Trail of the Duke"

39.1	door,] ~∧	42.3	café] cafe *two readings*
39.7	grumbling,] ~∧	42.10	still,] ~;
39.10	sweating] sweatting	42.22	position,] ~∧
39.11	winter,] ~∧	42.36	East-Side] east-side
40.4	roof garden] ~-~	43.1	sideburns] side burns
40.7	fiancée] fiancee	43.9	door,] ~∧
40.31	it's] it	43.10	Doddy!] ~,
41.5	do?"] ~.∧	43.12	mailman] mail man
41.35	searching,] ~;	43.17	I'm] Im

Fie! Fie! Fi-Fi!

47.10	us] no	54.25	Pete,] ~∧
47.21	À] A *two readings*	56.5	*Sady*] ~.
47.23	Tommy,] ~∧	59.25	*All*] ~ H.
50.3	so:] so.	61.10	forget] forgot
50.14	in∧] ~,	61.27	*Quartet*] *Quartette*
51.7	deuce] duce	62.9	Fi-fi] Fifi *six readings*
52.34	music.] ~∧	63.12	too] to

The Evil Eye

68.31	Garden] garden	72.21	Hellos";] Hellos;"
70.5	me";] ~;"	73.8	lose] loose
70.17	borne] born	74.21	multi-millionaires] ~∧~
70.21	Honolulu] Honolula	76.6	Fades] Fade
70.32	Maine,] ~∧	76.27	Its] ~'
71.5	Orient] orient	78.11	you";] you;"
72.10	you're] your	81.8	one";] one;"

Safety First!

82.26	*Students*] *Studends*	84.17	domes,] ~∧
83.27	liver. They] ~∧~	84.21	Hochs,"] Hochs",
84.5	Belgians] Belgiums	85.15	Percy,] ~∧
84.7	cure,] ~∧	85.29	couldn't] could'nt

86.8	beautiful] beautifull	93.9	Little] little
86.22	dipperful] dipper full	93.11	true.] ~,
88.1	beautiful] beautifull	93.13	joyful] joyfull
88.21	Robespierre] Robespiere	93.14	out,] ~∧
91.1	We'll] we'll	93.24	Gleaming] gleaming
91.1	night,] ~∧	94.27	We'd] we'd
91.13	isn't] is'nt	95.10	liberty.] ~,
91.14	forgetful] forgetfull	95.33	eukalali] euralali
91.17	thunderstorms] thunder storms	97.1	fistful,] fistfull ∧
91.19	Safety] safety	97.6	seven-reel] ~∧~
91.23	doesn't] does'nt	97.9	aren't] are'nt
92.4	Temptation's] temptation's	97.12	I've] Ive
92.6	kid∧] ~,	97.27	wouldn't] would'nt
92.10	Pretty] pretty	97.29	feelin'] feeling'
92.12	Pavlova] Pavlowa	98.17	blues, melodious] ~∧~
92.17	shouldn't] should'nt	98.27	angling,] ~∧
93.3	maid.] ~,	98.30	clinging,] ~∧
93.7	Of] of	99.9	Gazing] gazing
		100.20	outdid] out did

"'Shadow Laurels'"

102.15	Jacques] Jaques	107.26	he] you
102.16	penetrating;] ~,	108.1	*down)*] ~.)
102.17	clean-shaven] ~∧~	108.3	uneducated] educated
103.16	Here,] ~∧	108.5	write?] ~.
103.17	States] states	108.15	*François'*] *François*
104.2	know,] ~∧	108.18	*Chandelle, who*] ~∧*who*
104.21	years.] ~∧	109.13	sit] sat
104.21	*head)*] ~.)	109.13	black-eyed] ~∧~
105.9	rotter] rotler	109.13	sleepy-looking] ~∧~
105.13	best friends?] ~~.	109.18	well,] ~∧
105.26	Meridien,] ~∧	109.19	drunk?] ~.
105.34	me] ~,	109.29	*Gallic*] *gallic*
106.25	*more)*] ~.)	109.35	*even François,*] ~~∧
107.10	he] we	110.12	hand,] ~∧

"May Small Talk"

111.8	thing";] ~;"	111.17	trancendental,
111.17	trancendental,] ~∧		consequental] *stet*
			deliberate misspellings

"The Ordeal"

112.11	lay brother] lay-brother	112.24	prayer book] prayer-book
	four readings	112.30	kindly,] ~∧

113.10	delirious] delirous,	116.5	other's eye,] ~~∧
113.18	self-sacrifice] ~∧~	116.7	his eye,] ~~∧
113.27	psychical] physical	116.10	hot,] ~:
113.27	ego,] ~∧	116.15	was there;] ~~,
114.22	fireflies] fire-flys	116.21	rose,] ~∧
114.23	negro quarters] ~-~	116.26	out,] ~∧
114.31	incoherent music] ~, ~	116.28	God-sense;] ~,
115.3	Wycliffe;] ~,	116.33	realm,] ~∧
115.6	Inquisition] inquisition	116.33	expression,] ~∧
115.8	crystal] chrystal	117.7	body,] ~∧
115.29	sacrament] Sacrament	117.32	glow,] ~∧
115.32	Magnificat] magnificat		

"A Cheer for Princeton"

120.3	Glory] "~

"The Conquest of America"

121.3	gentilissimo] gentlissimo	121.24	invested;] ~,
121.9	had] has	122.17	guns,] ~∧
121.12	city;] ~,	122.21	meringue] marangue
121.21	entrenched] intrenched	122.24	P-rade] p-rade

"To My Unused Greek Book"

123.7	syllabi] syllibi	123.22	happy] ~,

"Our Next Issue"

124.10	inimitable] inimatable

"Jemina"

126.16	pailful] pail full	128.10	but,] ~∧
127.9	inborn] unborn	128.11	windows] window
127.21	bass] base	128.35	loophole,] ~∧

"The Usual Thing"

131.27	peccadillos] peccadillo's	134.14	Elizabethan] Elizabethian
132.13	Rembrandt's] Rembrant's	134.22	breathe] breath
133.6	friends?] ~.	134.26	Greenwich] ~,
133.26	Jules:] ~,	135.29	intelligent-looking] ~∧~
133.30	forever?] ~.	136.2	plebeian] plebian
133.33	captain] Captain	136.7	willfully] wilfully,
134.12	batting] batton		

"Little Minnie McCloskey"

137.15	Sangfroid,] ~∧	137.30	knew.)] ~.∧
137.15	hostess;] ~,	137.31	Red,] ~∧
137.16	pajamas,] ~∧	138.1	Boils,] ~∧
137.17	Yaeger] yaeger	138.15	wove] weaved
137.29	McCloskey. (All] ~∧ (all		

"The Old Frontiersman"

142.8	1776).] ~.)	143.18	pain,] ~∧
142.18	muzzle-loading] ~∧~	143.19	and, taking] ~∧~
143.17	and, frantic] ~∧~	143.20	frontiersman,] ~∧

"The Debutante"

144.13	*time,*] ~;	147.34	*room.*] ~∧
144.14	*herself,*] ~∧	148.10	*mirror.*] ~∧
144.20	*eyes,*] ~∧	148.15	Why,] ~∧
145.5	*mirror*∧] ~.	148.19	*hooks,*] ~∧
145.9	"old lady,"] ∧Old Lady,∧	149.25	indeed. There] ~, there
145.11	Because] because	149.29	don't. You'll] ~, you'll
145.13	*mold*] *mould*	150.34	*I*] I
145.17	"old lady."] ∧Old Lady.∧	151.4	anyway] anyways
145.18	*herself.*] ~∧	151.7	so. It] ~, it
145.22	*feet,*] ~∧	151.11	wavy] wavey
145.32	know,] ~∧	151.13	smiles∧] ~,
145.32	Mother. Tight] mother, tight	151.19	John,] ~∧
		152.9	it. You] ~, you
146.4	*slang nor*] ~, ~	153.6	*and, going*] ~∧~
146.6	Now, Narry.] ~∧~,	153.6	*to the glass,*] *to glass*∧
146.6	Now, Helen.] now∧ Helen∧	153.19	*powder*∧] ~,
		153.27	*her and*] ~,~
146.7	quiet.] ~∧	153.27	*and, with*] ~∧~
146.9	*pier-glass,*] ~∧	153.28	*eyes,*] ~∧
146.10	Now, I've] ~∧~	153.30	*cigarette*∧] ~,
146.17	father's,] ~∧	153.30	*and, puffing*] ~∧~
146.36	*chair.*] ~∧	153.30	*coughing,*] ~∧
147.1	cut-in dance] cut-in-dance	153.32	Really,] ~∧
147.19	tired-looking] ~∧~	154.4-5	*and, as*] ~∧~
147.28	*and, besides*] ~∧~	154.5	*again,*] ~∧ *she*

"'Penrod and Sam'"

155.3	predecessor,] ~∧	155.26	Madness,"] ~",
155.6	figures] figure	155.26	uproariously] uproarously
155.24	Whitey,"] ~",		

| 156.3 | Party,"] ~", | 156.9 | Johnson] Johnston |
| 156.4 | confession] ~, | 156.10 | Mackenzie] McKenzie |

"The Spire and the Gargoyle"

161.12	wearily and,] ~, ~∧	165.26	one-time] ~∧~
161.12	advancing,] ~∧	165.32	me,] ~∧
162.7	spring] Spring	166.5	university] University
162.14	Gothic] gothic	167.5	discoursive] *stet (coinage)*
162.34	damp] ~,	167.6	carelessly,] ~∧
163.5	feature] ~,	167.12	strata] stratas
163.27	you'd] you'ld	167.16	by, vaguely] ~∧~∧
164.3	buses] busses *four readings*	167.25	fidgety] figidity
		167.28	oneself] one's self
164.8	Carlyle's] Carlisle's	167.31	window] ~,
164.9	instructor,] ~∧	168.5	and, dropping] ~∧~∧
164.14	ten-thousand-dollar] ~∧~∧~	169.9	stone,] ~∧
		169.26	waiting for him] waiting him
164.16	Scotsman] Scotchman		
164.20–21	every author] very ~	169.29	turned] ~,
164.34	had a certain] had certain	169.29–30	and, picking] ~∧~∧
165.3	revelers;] ~,	169.30	suitcase,] suit case∧
165.4	classes] ~,	169.33	seat∧] ~,
165.7	Bohemianism] Bohemeanism		

"Rain Before Dawn"

| 170.12 | *and moist*] (~~) |

"'David Blaize'"

171.2	view,] ~∧	171.20	Encounter,] ~∧
171.13	of the way] the way	171.21	Stalky's] Stalkey's
171.16	idol,] ~∧	171.23	and, although] ~∧~∧
171.18	Mackenzie] MacKenzie	172.1	hero,] ~∧

"The Diary of a Sophomore"

| 175.9 | every man's] everyman's |

"Undulations of an Undergraduate"

| 176.20 | fiancées] fiancees |

"Tarquin of Cheapside"

178.–	Cheapside] Cheepside	180.17	Britomartis,] ~∧
178.4	following] ~,	180.20	and, picking] ~∧~
178.10	straggles] straggle	180.27	Open,] ~∧
178.12	marches] marshes	181.2	someone] some one
178.26	or at any] ~ in ~	182.5	then, reconsidering] ~∧~
179.2	and, retracing] ~∧~	182.6	Faerie Queen] Faery
179.5	niche] nitch		Queene *two readings*
179.21	life;] ~,	182.17	prie-dieu] Prie-dieu
179.28	cumbrously] cumberously	182.22	morning∧] ~,
179.29	Faerie Queen] Faery	182.22	him and] ~, ~
	Queene	182.22	dozing,] ~∧
179.32	falles] palls	182.23	chaotically] chaoticly
179.33	That fayrest] The ~	182.25	trod] tread
179.33	farre] far	182.27	Someone] Some one
179.33	rest—] ~"—	182.30	stuff] ~,
180.10	ironically] ironicly	183.6	*breathed*] *breathing*
180.15	replaced;] ~,	183.6	*host,—*∧] *host,—* "

"The Prince of Pests"

184.12	came] come	185.22	Augustin] Augustine

"Babes in the Woods"

187.3	leading ladies] ~-~	189.22	instinctive,] ~∧
187.4	Game] ~,	189.34	names,] ~∧
187.14	peek] peak	189.35	sextet] sextette
188.4	good-looking] ~∧~	190.2	maneuvered] manouvered
188.7	being] be	190.4	afternoon,] ~,
188.17	Pittsburg] *stet An*	190.16	disappointment] ~,
	acceptable spelling at the	190.20	flush] ~,
	time of publication.	190.26	innocent-eyed] ~∧~
188.20	street] ~,	190.34	places,] ~∧
188.23	two-year-back] ~∧~∧~	191.21	finished∧] ~,
188.28	quickly;] ~∧	191.24	accessible] accesable
188.30	if very] ~ not ~	191.27	proportionately]
189.3	unembarrassing]		proportionally
	unembarrased	192.4	playroom] play-room
189.10	mentally] ~,	192.10	it, and] ~∧~
189.10	necessary] ~,	192.11	elsewhere,] ~∧
189.11	disappointed?] ~.	192.14	distinctively] distinctivly
189.12	good-looking] ~∧~	192.15	downstairs] down stairs
189.19	classes—society] ~, ~	192.17	frowned] ~,
189.21	favor;] ~,	193.20	mean,] ~∧

193.25	and, by] ~∧~	194.33	dance;] ~,
193.30	Chopsticks] chospticks	194.36	cutting-in] ~∧~
193.32	Give] "~	195.3	poise,] ~∧
193.34	slumberland.] ~."	195.3	foolish] ~,
194.13	Moonlight] "~	195.5	Kenneth!] ~.
194.14	good-night.] ~."	195.12	anymore] any more
194.15	song,] ~∧	195.15	good-looking] ~∧~
194.27	light,] ~∧	195.17	them,] ~∧

"Princeton — The Last Day"

196.12	one∧] ~,	196.14	Heraclitus] Heracletus

"'The Celt and the World'"

197.4	Breton] Bretton	197.14–15	are traced] is ~
197.10	says.] ~,	198.2	Strindberg] Strinberg
197.14	Christianity] christianity,		

"Sentiment — and the Use of Rouge"

199.9	Clayton] Clay	202.36	chauffeur] chauffer
199.13	Station] station	203.1	there—"] ~—."
199.15	1917] nineteen seventeen	203.3	but—"] ~—."
200.4	sister,] ~∧	203.8	we—"] ~—."
200.7	continued,] ~∧	203.28	Clay:] ~∧
200.8	put on∧] ~~,	204.1	feet,] ~∧
200.25	subaltern] subaltran	204.5	Put] put
200.31	somehow] some how	204.5	in,] ~∧
200.34	incense] incence	204.9	corners.] ~,
201.3	asceticism,] acetisism∧	204.10	goes,] ~∧
201.6	Severances∧] ~'	204.15	sadly.] ~,
201.7–8	dance. People] ~, people	204.15	"A] "a
201.17–18	between her] ~ she	204.16	He was] he ~
201.28	care,] ~∧	204.23	fire∧] ~,
201.29	but, my] ~∧~	204.26	difference. A] ~∧ a
201.32	whole] ~,	204.27	last;] ~,
201.34	shelved,] ~∧	204.27	won't] wont
202.3	Suppose!] ~.	204.32	about her] about
202.3	said, astonished] ~∧~	204.32	Then] When
202.4	everyone. Both] ~∧ both	204.33	it and, bending] ~, ~∧~
202.13	feet, astounded,] ~∧ ~∧	205.15	Her gaze] her ~
202.21	shoulder,] ~∧	205.20	tack,] ~∧
202.25	Severances] ~'	205.20	Dick,] ~∧
202.27	four-year-old] ~∧~∧~	206.20	impeccable] impecable

206.24	know,] ~∧			*original reading, is meant*
206.33	me∧] ~,			*to be confused, though he*
207.1	romanticist] romantiscist			*uses "Captain" again later*
207.13	hear."] ~.∧			*in the story.*
207.14	shoulder and,] ~, ~∧	210.28	sayin',] ~∧
207.23	universities] Universities	210.29	practical] practicle
207.33	thought] ~,	210.33	duke] Duke
208.4	girls—"] ~.—."	210.37	lungful] lung full
208.17	week-end] ~∧~	211.4	*Allons*] *Allon*
208.20	capital] capitol	211.6	Reverent] reverent
208.21	us—we] us.—We	211.17	Eleanor; they] ~, ~
209.4	erotic] errotic	211.23	chauffeurs] chauffers
209.11	again,] ~∧	211.33	back—] ~—.
209.29	first-aid] ~∧~	212.5	Luther!] ~,
209.30	that until] that	212.7	Mister] mister
209.33	regiment] ~,	212.16	thee—"] ~—."
210.24	Captain] lieutenant	213.3	Gods] God's
	It is possible that the	213.12	ask him—∧] ~~—.
	wounded soldier, in the		

"'Verses in Peace and War'"

215.2	diminutive] diminitive	216.13	Odyssey] Oddysey
216.2	Rubies] ~,		

"The Cameo Frame"

219.5	aloud:] ~∧	219.16	lightning] lightening

"The Pierian Springs and the Last Straw"

222.3	bindings] binding	224.11	that, strangely] ~∧~
222.12	written,] ~∧	224.20	America,] ~∧
222.14	beginning,] ~∧	224.22	pocket,] ~∧
222.18	fidgeting] figeting	224.24	improved;] ~,
222.22	Someone] Some one	224.32	nonsense,] ~∧
223.2	started,] ~∧	225.9	scrapbook] scrap-book
223.3	breath,] ~∧	225.12	thinking,] ~∧
223.23	Mother,] mother∧	225.14	aunt's] aunts
223.31	years,] ~∧	225.16	there,] ~∧
223.33	misogamist] mesogamist	225.22	club] Club
223.37	*pièce-de-résistance*]	225.23	himself,] ~∧
	piece-de-resistance	225.26	men,] ~∧
224.6	author who] ~ that	225.32–33	him, and] ~∧~

226.1	minutes,] ~∧		229.6	Messalina] Messaline
226.2	down,] ~∧		229.9	awhile,] ~∧
226.15	hell—"] ~—,"		229.17	and, rising] ~∧~
226.18	aftermath. My] ~, my		229.17	table,] ~∧
226.22	you—"] ~—,"		229.25	tried.] ~,
226.25	anymore] any more		229.31	us, acting] ~∧ who were
226.29	sophomore] Sophmore			acting
	two readings		230.3	game,] ~∧
227.7	idealist.] ~,		230.9	think,] ~∧
227.19–20	awe of her,] ~~~∧		230.29	nodded.] ~,
227.28	steadily,] ~∧		230.29	partners] pardners
227.31	equals;] ~,		231.1	snippy, Georgie,] ~∧ ~∧
227.33	jealous,] ~∧		231.6	horsewhip you,] ~~~∧
228.1	went on:] ~~;		231.10	flashed,] ~∧
228.1	hours,] ~∧		231.13	years?] ~.
228.5–6	it, and] ~∧~		231.16	risen,] ~∧
228.10	resentful,] ~∧		231.17	room,] ~∧
228.15	grew] grow		231.19	world!] ~.
228.18	or,] ~∧		231.22	white,] ~∧
228.25	brood,] ~∧		231.24	and, twisting] ~∧~
228.29	her,] ~∧		231.25	finger,] ~∧
228.35	her, asked] ~; ~		232.13	book,] ~∧ on
228.35	her, but] ~∧~		232.13	see,] ~∧

"The Pope at Confession"

244.1	Vatican] vatican

Hyphenated Compounds

The compound words in the table below are hyphenated at the ends of lines in the Cambridge texts. The hyphens should be preserved when quoting these words. Any other compound word hyphenated at the end of a line in this edition should be quoted as a single word.

10.19	light-haired		155.22	ill-fated
18.7	hospitable-looking		191.24	dressing-room
114.33	world-passion			

EXPLANATORY NOTES

Annotated here are references to public figures, literary and dramatic works, educational institutions, movie and stage performers, military heroes, sports stars, Broadway shows, commercial products, public reformers, composers, philosophers, religious leaders, and New York restaurants and nightclubs of the period.

"A Debt of Honor"

14.22–25 Lee's army . . .
Chancellorsville . . . Fredericksburg . . . General Jackson

The Confederate general Robert E. Lee (1807–70) was commander of the Army of Northern Virginia during the American Civil War; Thomas J. "Stonewall" Jackson (1824–63) was one of the South's most prominent generals. Chancellorsville and Fredericksburg were the sites of major battles during the Civil War. Jackson was accidentally killed by one of his own men at Chancellorsville.

"S.P.A. Men in College Athletics"

16.7 received his A

That is to say, Brooks received the monogram letter "A"—signifying "Academy"— for playing on the St. Paul Academy football and hockey teams. Only the regular players (as opposed to the substitutes who sat on the bench during contests) received these letters, made of heavy felt or chenille. The letters were sewn onto sweaters or jackets and worn as marks of athletic achievement. A student who had been awarded a monogram was said to have "lettered" or to be a "letterman." The "H" won in hockey, four lines on, stands for Harvard.

16.15 Yale Sheffield

Schunneman is enrolled in Sheffield Scientific School at Yale University, an under-graduate college which offered a three-year degree and did not require students to study Latin or Greek, both of which were required for a regular bachelor's degree from Yale. Such students, known as "Sheffies," were thought to be academically suspect.

"The Room with the Green Blinds"

18.21 on the Pullman

George Pullman (1831–97) invented his popular sleeping car for trains in 1857 but did not put it into commercial manufacture until 1865, the final year of the American Civil War. Sleeper cars had been in use on American railroads since the 1830s.

21.31 Forrest's cavalry

Nathan Bedford Forrest (1821–77) rose from the enlisted ranks to become a lieutenant-general in the Confederate army. He commanded cavalry units at Shiloh and Chickamauga and won fame for his raids on Union forces late in the war. Forrest was among the most romanticized of the Southern commanders: according to popular lore he had twenty-nine horses shot from under him in battle.

21.34 Cumberland Pike

This national road, the first built in the US, extended from Cumberland, Maryland, to Vandalia, Illinois. It was a major route for east–west migration and an important highway during the Civil War.

22.6–7 shot by some Union soldiers in a barn

John Wilkes Booth (b. 1838) assassinated Abraham Lincoln on 14 April 1865. He was found hiding in a tobacco barn on the Richard H. Garrett farm, near Bowling Green, Virginia, on 26 April. The barn was set on fire by the federal troops pursuing Booth, and he was shot in the neck (possibly he shot himself by accident) while still inside the barn. He was dragged to the porch of the Garrett farmhouse, where he died three hours later. Stories persisted for many years that Booth had not been killed, that the man shot at the Garrett farm was a double for Booth, and that Booth himself had escaped and was living in the American West under a false name. Fitzgerald might have been familiar with *Escape and Suicide of John Wilkes Booth* (1907), a book by Finis L. Bates which advances these suppositions.

"'Football'"

25.18–28 straight-arm ... pigskin

In American football it is legal for a player carrying the ball to fend off a would-be tackler by pushing him away with a straight-arm to the chest or forehead. The pigskin, ten lines on, is the football, made from the hide of a pig.

26.5 Newman, 1911

That is, a member of the graduating class of 1911 at the Newman School.

"A Luckless Santa Claus"

28.4 Salvation Army Santa Clauses

At Christmas it is traditional in the US for members of the Salvation Army, an organization devoted to helping the poor and indigent, to dress in Santa Claus costumes and solicit money on street corners.

30.28 street Arabs

Homeless urchins who roamed the streets of New York, scavenging for food and engaging in petty crime.

32.2 the Bowery

This street in lower Manhattan stretches for approximately a mile, from Cooper Square to Chatham Square. At the time in which the story is set, the Bowery was populated by beggars and derelicts and was lined with missions and flophouses.

"Pain and the Scientist"

34.9 Christian Scientist

Members of the Church of Christ, Scientist, established by Mary Baker Eddy in 1879, believe that man is spiritual, not material. The popular conception of Christian Scientists is that they reject conventional medical treatment and try to overcome sickness by love and prayer. During Fitzgerald's teenage years, Christian Science leaders were often accused of fraudulence and quackery.

"The Trail of the Duke"

39.17 mint juleps

A quintessential Southern drink for the hot months, concocted from bourbon, sugar, cracked ice, and sprigs of fresh mint.

39.19 breaking the Second Commandment

In the ordering of the Ten Commandments used by the Catholic Church, Dodson is taking the name of the Lord in vain.

40.14–15 up Fifth Avenue to Broadway

Dodson lives on "upper Fifth Avenue." At this point in his writing career, Fitzgerald might not have been entirely clear about the street layout of New York City. To stay on Fifth Avenue and reach Broadway, the character would have to walk down to the vicinity of Union Square, or leave Fifth Avenue and travel in a westerly direction, perhaps through Central Park. The story doesn't disclose whether Mirabel lives on upper or lower Broadway.

41.15 Sherry's

This fashionably ornate restaurant was located not on Broadway but at the southwest corner of Fifth Avenue and 45th Street, one block up from Delmonico's, its chief competitor, which is mentioned several paragraphs on and is glossed immediately below.

41.30 Delmonico's, Martin's

Delmonico's, an elegant restaurant at Fifth and 44th, is the setting for the Gamma Psi dance in Fitzgerald's 1920 novella "May Day." Martin's was a popular "lobster palace" of the period—a restaurant and cabaret situated on 26th Street at an earlier location for Delmonico's, which had moved uptown in 1897. Martin's was famous for its Art Nouveau décor and its painted murals of lightly clad females afloat in space.

Fie! Fie! Fi-Fi!

50.30–31 Herpicide . . . LePage's glue

Newbro's Herpicide, a popular patent medicine meant to combat dandruff and prevent baldness, was first sold to the public in 1899. It was developed by D. M. Newbro of Butte, Montana, and was widely advertised in national magazines. LePage's was a common liquid glue, manufactured (beginning in 1879) in Gloucester, Massachusetts. The adhesive in LePage's was extracted from fish skins.

58.17 Mutt and Jeff

"Mutt and Jeff" was a nationally syndicated daily comic strip created by Bud Fisher in 1907 for the *San Francisco Chronicle*. The lead characters were Augustus Mutt, a tall racetrack gambler who was constantly on the lookout for get-rich-quick schemes, and Jeff (who has no last name), a diminutive inmate of an insane asylum who often became entangled in Mutt's machinations.

The Evil Eye

68.31–32 Winter Garden dollies... "Follies"
The Winter Garden Theatre at Broadway and 50th, owned by the impresario Louis Minsky, was famous for its variety show, which featured scantily clad chorines and mildly risqué burlesque acts. Minsky was frequently attacked by the vice crusader John S. Sumner. Ziegfeld's *Follies*, a review with leggy girls, glittering costumes, and elaborate sets, was staged by Florenz Ziegfeld at the New Amsterdam Theatre, 214 West 42nd Street. Such Broadway stars as Kay Laurell, Lilyan Tashman, and Gilda Gray began their careers as *Follies* girls.

74.32 Craig Kennedy

This fictional detective was featured in a series of mystery stories written by Arthur Benjamin Reeve (1880–1936), a member of the Princeton class of 1903. The first Craig Kennedy story, "The Golf Dream," appeared in the *Nassau Lit* in May 1901. Reeve's stories were turned into silent film serials in which the heroine, named Elaine, was rescued from villains and thieves by Kennedy, who was always wearing a white coat.

81.20 Miss Deslys

Gaby Deslys (1881–1920), a French dancer and actress, was famous for her jewel collection and her romantic connection with King Manuel II of Portugal. Her dancing at the Hyperion Theater in New Haven in November 1911 caused rioting by the Yale students. At the peak of her popularity she earned $4,000 for each of her performances.

Safety First!

83.19 Ding Ding

A reference to the New York State penitentiary at Ossining, called Sing Sing, where the most violent criminals in the system were imprisoned and where executions were carried out.

86.11–12 Meccas, Murads and Fatimas

Popular brands of Turkish cigarettes. Meccas, a product of the American Tobacco Co., were priced at a nickel for a box of ten; Murads, from the P. Lorillard Co., were more expensive—15 cents for ten cigarettes. Fatimas, manufactured by Liggett and Myers, were the favorite cigarette of the movie star Jean Harlow.

87.6 Mister Comstock

The reformer Anthony Comstock (1844–1915) waged numerous public crusades against indecency in American life—especially in literature and movies, art and publishing. He was a favorite target of ridicule for H. L. Mencken, who turned his name into a noun—"Comstockery." Anthony Comstock did his work through the New York Society for the Suppression of Vice and the Boston Watch and Ward Society. Anthony Comstock Patch, the protagonist of Fitzgerald's novel *The Beautiful and Damned* (1922), is named for Comstock.

87.25 Bruce McRae

A stage and silent-film star, McRae (1867–1927) appeared in Broadway productions with such actors as Douglas Fairbanks and William Garwood. His films include *Via Wireless* (1915), *The Chain Invisible* (1916), and *Hazel Kirke* (1916).

88.25 Charlotte Corday

The Girondist sympathizer Charlotte Corday (1768–93) stabbed the revolutionary leader Jean-Paul Marat in his bath on 13 July 1793. She died on the guillotine four days later. Her name appears later in this volume in "Shadow Laurels."

92.12 Pavlova

The tiny Russian ballerina Anna Pavlova (1881–1931), among the most famous dancers of her time, was known especially for her performances in *Swan Lake*. She is credited with helping to invent the modern *pointe* shoe.

92.30 my Chickering

A grand piano manufactured by Chickering and Sons of Boston, an innovative company which developed a cast-iron plate that afforded greater tension for the strings on a concert-grade instrument.

95.33 eukalali

Fitzgerald means the ukulele, a small, four-stringed guitar, easy to play and popular with undergraduates of his time.

96.8 Franz Lehár

This Austrian composer (1870–1948) was famous for the waltz "Gold and Silver" (1902) and for his operettas, especially *The Merry Widow* (1905), which opened in an English-language version on Broadway in 1907 and was frequently revived in the years that followed.

97.16–18 Theda Bara . . . Olga Petrova

The dark-eyed cinema vamp Theda Bara (1885–1955) was born Theodosia Burr Goodman in Cincinnati; her most famous film was *Cleopatra* (1917), in which she wore a costume so revealing that the movie was banned in Chicago. Olga Petrova (1884–1977) was the stage name of the English actress Muriel Harding, a vaudeville and silent-film star during Fitzgerald's years at Princeton. She often played *femme fatale* roles and enjoyed a parallel career as a screenwriter and playwright.

99.5 a pony in Triangle plays

A chorus line of Princeton boys in drag, known as the "pony ballet," was a feature of every Triangle production. For details and photographs, see Donald Marsden, *The Long Kickline: A History of the Princeton Triangle Club* (Princeton: Princeton Triangle Club, 1968).

"'Shadow Laurels'"

106.31–33 Charlotte Corday . . . François Villon

Charlotte Corday is glossed earlier in the notes for *Safety First!* Other figures mentioned in this passage are Jean Fouquet (1420–81), a court painter during the reign of Louis XI, known today for his manuscript illuminations and portrait miniatures, and John Law (1671–1729), a Scottish economist who was among the first to advocate the use of paper money. François Villon is identified immediately below; Madame du Barry is glossed in the first annotation for "The Debutante."

110.9 Où sont les neiges d'antan?

The refrain from "Ballade des dames du temps jadis" by the French vagabond poet François Villon (ca. 1431–63). The translation, by Dante Gabriel Rossetti, is "Where are the snows of yesteryear?"

"May Small Talk"

111.14 heeler . . . the Prince

The *Princetonian* (the student newspaper at Princeton) was known to the students as "the Prince." A heeler is a beginning reporter.

"The Ordeal"

115.3–4 John Wycliffe . . . Alexander VI

Wycliffe (ca. 1320–84), an English theologian who advocated reform in the Roman Catholic Church, is credited with producing the first complete translation of the Bible into English. Fitzgerald is under the impression that Wycliffe was burned at the stake. Wycliffe was indeed condemned as a heretic but was not executed for his beliefs. Pope Alexander VI (ca. 1431–1503) would have been known to Fitzgerald as one of the most worldly and licentious of the popes; he poisoned his enemies (some of them members of his own family) and confiscated their property and goods to enrich himself.

115.34 St. Francis Xavier

This Catholic priest (1506–62), one of the original members of the Society of Jesus, was known for his missionary work in Goa, Ceylon, Malacca, and Japan.

"How They Head the Chapters"

118.11 Chobert Rambers

Fitzgerald is referring to the middlebrow artist and fiction-writer Robert W. Chambers (1865–1933), who produced over seventy novels during his career and was an illustrator for such magazines as *Life* and *Vogue*. Chambers is satirized as "Robert W. Shameless" in "The Usual Thing," later in this volume.

"A Cheer for Princeton"

120.1–5 Black and Orange . . . the Tiger's turn . . . Eli, Eli

Black and orange are the school colors of Princeton; the tiger is the mascot for the athletic teams. Yale students are called Elis. The name derives from the original benefactor of the university, Elihu Yale (1649–1721), a wealthy English businessman and politician.

"The Conquest of America"

121.17 Mgr. McGraw

John McGraw (1873–1934), known as "Little Napoleon," was the manager of the New York Giants professional baseball team from 1902 until 1932. He was one of the most successful baseball managers of all time: his teams posted 2,763 victories and won ten National League pennants and three World Series titles.

121.27 Busty's

The Café des Beaux Arts, a cabaret at Sixth Avenue and 40th Street in New York, was known as "Bustanoby's" (or "Busty's") after its proprietor, Louis Bustanoby. Fitzgerald caroused there as an undergraduate.

122.19–21 the Nass...Joe's...the Jigger Shop

The Nassau Inn, Joe's Variety Shop, and the Jigger Shop were establishments in Princeton that catered to students. In *This Side of Paradise*, Amory meets Thomas Parke D'Invilliers at Joe's and eats bacon buns, a local delicacy, at the Jigger. Students sometimes imbibed strong waters at the Nassau Inn.

122.24 P-rade

On the Saturday before the Princeton spring commencement, alumni who had returned for the occasion marched through the campus in a procession known as a P-rade. They wore silly or fanciful costumes and marched with their classes. The tradition originated in the 1890s.

"Our Next Issue"

124.1–13 Chaopolitan...Harrison Flagg...Jack
Undone...Elinor Gyn...Maurice Matterhorn

Satire of *Cosmopolitan*, a popular American magazine, and of James Montgomery Flagg (1877–1960), a magazine illustrator who later drew portraits of the Fitzgeralds for their co-authored article "Looking Back Eight Years," published in *College Humor* for June 1928. "Jack Undone" is Jack London (1876–1916), author of *The Call of the Wild* (1903), *White Fang* (1906), and *The Valley of the Moon* (1913). "Elinor Gyn" is the British novelist and screenwriter Elinor Glyn (1864–1943), who wrote mildly erotic fiction for women. Her most famous novel was *Three Weeks* (1907). It was she who first used the word "It" as a euphemism for sex appeal; she christened the screen star Clara Bow "the It girl." "Maurice Matterhorn" is the Belgian poet Maurice Maeterlinck (1862–1949), who won the Nobel Prize for Literature in 1911 and whose work appeared in translation in American periodicals.

"Jemina"

125.2 John Phlox, Jr.

"Jemina" is a parody of the work of the popular writer John Fox, Jr. (1862–1919), who was famous for his romantic novels about the denizens of the Cumberland Mountains. Fox was best known for *The Little Shepherd of Kingdom Come* (1903) and *The Trail of the Lonesome Pine* (1908).

126.21 The Doldrums and the Tantrums

Fitzgerald's readers would have recognized these families as take-offs of the Hatfields and McCoys, two Appalachian clans who fought a bloody, protracted feud along the West Virginia – Kentucky border during the 1880s.

126.24 slapjack

A simple children's card game in which the object is to slap any jack card that appears
face-up in a turnover pile.

"The Vampiest of the Vampires"

130.1 Kneeda Baral

A play on the name of Theda Bara, the movie temptress annotated above in the
notes for *Safety First!* Bara is credited with adding the word "vamp" to the English
language, both as a noun and a verb. Her publicists claimed that she had been born
in the shadow of the Sphinx, that "Bara" was the word "Arab" spelled backward,
and that "Theda" was an anagram for "death."

"The Usual Thing"

131.1 Robert W. Shameless

Another jab at the writer Robert W. Chambers, glossed above in the notes for "How
They Head the Chapters."

131.32 Tuxedo Park

This gated enclave in Orange County—located near the New Jersey border, some
40 miles outside New York City—was created in 1886 by Pierre Lorillard, heir to
an American tobacco fortune. Some of the residents of Tuxedo Park were wealthy
enough to maintain strings of polo ponies. The black dinner jacket known as a
tuxedo takes its name from the community, where it was first worn as a substitute
for white tie and tailcoat.

133.7–8 Saxon... Pierce-Arrow

The Saxon Motor Car Company in Detroit was one of the largest US automobile
makers in 1917. Saxon offered a two-seat runabout and a four-seat sedan. Corporate
tycoons and Hollywood stars favored the Pierce-Arrow, a luxury car manufactured
in Buffalo, New York.

135.28 "buckwheats"

Pancakes or flapjacks made of buckwheat flour, reputedly beloved of the rural people
satirized in this story.

"Little Minnie McCloskey"

137.17–18 Yaeger flannel

The Yaeger Milling Company in St. Louis (establ. 1876) was the largest flour milling operation in the US. Minnie is wearing a flour sack.

"One from Penn's Neck"

139.1–2 Penn's Neck ... Baby Ben

Penn's Neck is a small community near Princeton. A Baby Ben was a popular wind-up alarm clock, used by college students during Fitzgerald's day.

"'Triangle Scenery by Bakst'"

139.22 Bakst

From approximately 1909 until 1922, Léon Bakst (1866–1924) was a costume and set designer for Serge Diaghilev's Ballets Russes. Bakst created the scenery for Diaghilev's productions of *Cleopatra* (1909), *Scheherazade* (1910), *Le Spectre de la rose* (1911), and *Daphnis et Chloé* (1912).

"The Old Frontiersman"

143.8–9 "The Last Rose of Summer"

This sentimental poem, written in 1805 by the Irish poet Thomas Moore (1779–1852), was set to music by Sir John Stevenson (1761–1833) and became a popular song in music halls and other places of entertainment: " 'Tis the last rose of summer / Left blooming alone; / All her lovely companions / Are faded and gone... / So soon may I follow, / When friendships decay, / From Love's shining circle / The gems drop away."

"The Debutante"

144.23 *Sapho, Venus, Madam Du—*

Temptresses all. Sapho (not the Greek lyric poet Sappho) is the eponymous heroine of Alphonse Daudet's *Sapho* (1884), a novel that examines the demi-monde of crime and prostitution in Paris. Venus, the Roman goddess of love, beauty, and fertility, numbered Mars and Vulcan among her romantic interests. Madame du Barry, born a commoner, was mistress to the French king Louis XV. Suspected of giving aid to fugitives during the French Revolution, she died on the guillotine in 1793.

145.5 "*Poor butterfly . . .*"

Helen is singing "Poor Butterfly," by John L. Golden and Raymond Hubbell, first performed on Broadway in *The Big Show* (1916) and popular with American troops during the First World War. In the song a Japanese maiden falls in love with an American sailor. The refrain, slightly misquoted here, runs: "Poor Butterfly! 'neath the blossoms waiting / Poor Butterfly! For she loved him so." The lyrics several lines onward (*"The moments pass into hours . . ."*) are also from the song.

153.37 Coronas

Expensive cigarettes smoked by women—though it would have been considered improper for a young lady of Cecilia's social class to be seen smoking in public.

"'Penrod and Sam'"

155.1 Booth Tarkington

Tarkington (1869–1946), an alumnus of Princeton, helped to found the Triangle Club at the university in 1891. He went on to become one of the most successful authors of his time. He is remembered today for his novels *The Gentleman from Indiana* (1899), *Seventeen* (1916), and *The Magnificent Ambersons* (1918) and for the Penrod stories, all first published in the *Saturday Evening Post* and later collected in three volumes: *Penrod* (1914), *Penrod and Sam* (1916)—the book Fitzgerald is reviewing here—and *Penrod Jashber* (1929). Fitzgerald's Basil Duke Lee stories, published in the *Post* in 1928 and 1929, were influenced by the Penrod stories.

156.8 Tom Brown

Fitzgerald is referring to *Tom Brown's Schooldays* (1857), a boys' novel by the English writer Thomas Hughes (1822–96). The story is set at Rugby School; the climactic event in the narrative is a cricket match. Hughes published a sequel, *Tom Brown at Oxford*, in 1861. Owen Johnson and Compton Mackenzie, mentioned later in the sentence, are glossed below in the notes for Fitzgerald's review of *David Blaize*.

"Precaution Primarily"

158.– Precaution Primarily

This piece, as its title suggests, is a spoof of *Safety First!*—the 1916 Triangle production, for which Fitzgerald had written the lyrics.

159.5 Casino

This large wooden theatre building was erected on the Princeton campus in 1895. Booth Tarkington raised money to finance the structure after he left Princeton. The Casino provided a venue for campus theatricals, including the Triangle Club productions. It burned down in 1924 and was not replaced.

"The Spire and the Gargoyle"

161.13 the sun-dial

Fitzgerald's protagonist is lying on the grass near the Mather Sun Dial, which today stands at the center of a quadrangle formed by McCosh Hall, Dickinson Hall, and the Princeton Chapel.

161.24–25 the snapping of verifying watches

Wrist watches were not yet commonly worn by men at the time of the story. The test-takers are consulting pocket watches with covers that snap open and shut.

161.26 the little preceptor

In 1904 Woodrow Wilson, then president of Princeton University, divided the faculty into twelve departments; a year later he hired fifty new instructors, or preceptors, who took over many of the teaching duties at the institution. These preceptors, most of them recently out of graduate school, increased the size of the faculty by one-third. They were often called upon to teach tutorial sessions for "conditioned" men—i.e., academically deficient students, like the protagonist of this story, who were required to pass make-up exams in order to continue at the university.

164.8 Carlyle's "Heroes and Hero-Worship"

Fitzgerald is alluding to Thomas Carlyle's *On Heroes, Hero-Worship, and the Heroic in History* (1841), a group of lectures in which Carlyle (1795–1881) argues for paternalistic government by strong men who will function as spiritual leaders of the world. *Sartor Resartus* (1833–34), mentioned later in the story, is Carlyle's spiritual autobiography.

166.1 "Mirrors of Shalott"

Fitzgerald might be suggesting that the preceptor views the world at second-hand, through his spectacles, rather as the Lady of Shalott observes life through a mirror in Tennyson's poem of that title, published first in 1833 and in a revised version in 1842. It is also possible that this is an allusion by Fitzgerald to Robert Hugh Benson's *A Mirror of Shalott* (1907)—a collection of stories about the supernatural. Fitzgerald mentions Benson in his review of *David Blaize*, annotated just below.

168.4 the broad steps that led to the campus

During Fitzgerald's years at Princeton, the train station was situated near the western boundary of the campus, at the foot of Blair Arch on University Place. One disembarked from the train and entered the campus by climbing a flight of broad steps and passing beneath the arch.

"'David Blaize'"

171.3–4 "The Varmint," "Youth's Encounter," "Seventeen"

Owen Johnson (1878–1952), who wrote novels for young men, published *The Varmint* in 1910. Johnson's best-known book was *Stover at Yale* (1912), which became "somewhat of a text book" for Amory Blaine in *This Side of Paradise*. The British novelist Compton Mackenzie (1883–1972) published *Youth's Encounter* in the US in 1913; Amory is much taken by the sequel, *Sinister Street* (1914), which he considers to be a "quest" book. *Seventeen* (1916) was a novel for young readers by Booth Tarkington, identified above in the notes for "Penrod and Sam."

171.4–7 E. F. Benson... Arthur C. Benson... Monsignor Robert Hugh Benson

The prolific British novelist and man of letters Edward Frederic Benson (1867–1940) is remembered today primarily for his ghost stories, of which "The Man Who Went Too Far" is the best-known. His brothers Arthur (1862–1925) and Robert (1871–1914) were also writers: A. C. Benson, an essayist and poet, was Master of Magdalene College, Cambridge; Robert Hugh Benson, who converted to the Roman Catholic Church in 1903, wrote science fiction, historical fiction, devotional works, and plays. The three men were sons of Edward White Benson (1829–96), Archbishop of Canterbury from 1882 until his death.

171.16–17 Ralph Henry Barbour

The boys' books of Ralph Henry Barbour (1870–1944) emphasized character-building and school spirit. Many of them were set at exclusive prep schools or elite colleges. Amory reads Barbour's *For the Honor of the School* (1900) in *This Side of Paradise*. Other Barbour novels were *The Half-Back* (1899), *Behind the Line* (1902), *The Crimson Sweater* (1906), and *Forward Pass* (1908).

171.21 Stalky's career

Stalky & Co. (1899) by Rudyard Kipling is a collection of stories set at a British boarding school. Kipling based the character Beetle in the stories on himself. Dominant concerns include the importance of friendship among the students, their rebellion against the masters, and their training to serve the interests of the British Empire.

"The Diary of a Sophomore"

174.2 Felt nervous

Fitzgerald is satirizing the swings of emotion among the Princeton sophomores during Bicker Week in March, when bids for the campus eating clubs were given. The clubs had distinct personalities and occupied well-defined status levels; sophomores who wished to join a club worried about whether they would receive a bid from the club they most desired. The "commons club" was an informal name for the body of men who chose not to belong to an eating club (or did not receive a bid) and took their meals in the campus commons.

"Tarquin of Cheapside"

178.– Cheapside

This section of London, originally known as West Cheap, was a center of trade and barter before the great fire of 1666. It was located near present-day St. Paul's Cathedral. Names such as Honey Lane, Bread Street, and Milk Street indicated what might be purchased at the shops and stalls on a given thoroughfare.

178.12 Calais and the Spanish marches

References to the invasion of The Netherlands in the late 1560s and early 1570s by British troops, who crossed the English Channel and landed at Calais. Britain was aiding the Dutch in their rebellion against Spanish domination.

179.31 The Legend of Britomartis

Fitzgerald quotes the first lines of Book III of Edmund Spenser's *The Faerie Queene*— "The Legend of Britomartis, or of Chastitie." Britomart, one of the most memorable figures in the poem, is the female knight of chastity. Book III recounts her infatuation with and pursuit of Arthegall, whose image she has seen in a magic mirror.

183.3 *The Rape of Lucrece*

Shakespeare's long poem of this title, published in 1594, was based on the story of Lucretia, the wife of Tarquinius Collatinus. Lucretia was raped by Sextus, the son of King Tarquinius Superbus; she admitted her dishonor to her husband and father and then stabbed herself. Her death brought on an insurrection in which the Tarquins were overthrown and banished; a republic was established to govern in their stead.

"The Prince of Pests"

184.10–11 the short one ... short leg ... long ear

Fitzgerald is playing on the fact that Kaiser Wilhelm II of Germany (1859–1941) was born with a short left arm, which he attributed to improper treatment given to his mother by the British doctor who attended her during pregnancy. This belief was said to have contributed to his enmity toward Great Britain and to his willingness to go to war in 1914.

"Babes in the Woods"

190.17 Vernon Castle-ish slenderness

The popular dance team of Vernon and Irene Castle brought their act to New York from Paris in 1912. They performed most often at the Café de l'Opéra, a New York nightclub, always at midnight. He was tall and slim, she trig and boyish with bobbed hair. They were best known for inventing the Castle Walk, a stiff-legged version of the fox trot to which they added a skip-step on the upbeat. Other dances popularized by the Castles were the Bunny Hug, the Turkey Trot, and the Lame Duck.

192.24 alluring Stutzes

The Stutz Bearcat, a two-seater sports car, was popular with young men of Isabelle's set before the First World War. Some Stutzes were fitted with cut-out mufflers in order to produce a loud, irritating racket.

193.30 "Babes in the Woods"

The lyrics that follow are taken from Jerome Kern and Schuyler Greene's "Babes in the Wood," a duet from *Very Good Eddie*, a popular 1915 Broadway musical. Fitzgerald has added an "s" to "Wood" in the title of the song and of his story.

"Princeton—The Last Day"

196.14 Heraclitus

This Greek philosopher of the fifth century BC believed that human experience was fleeting and mutable, and that all things were in continual flux. He was known as the "Weeping Philosopher."

"'The Celt and the World'"

197.1 Mr. Leslie

While a student at the Newman School in 1912, Fitzgerald had met the Anglo-Irish writer Shane Leslie (1885–1971), whose US publisher was Charles Scribner's Sons. Acting on Fitzgerald's behalf, Leslie submitted "The Romantic Egotist," Fitzgerald's first attempt at a novel, to Scribners in May 1918. Leslie was one of the dedicatees for Fitzgerald's *The Beautiful and Damned* (1922).

197.16 Dungal, Fergal, Abelard, Duns Scotus and Eriugena

The Irish monk Dungal (d. ca. 827) composed poetry on wisdom and the liberal arts. Fergus (d. ca. 730) was an Irish bishop who because a missionary, settled near Strageath in Scotland, and founded three churches nearby. Peter Abelard (1079–1142), a philosopher, theologian, poet, and musician, is most often remembered today for his tragic affair with Héloïse, an abbess, writer, and scholar. John Duns Scotus (ca. 1266–1308) was an important metaphysician and theologian during the High Middle Ages. Johannes Scotus Eriugena (ca. 815–77) was an Irish neoplatonist philosopher, a theologian, and a poet.

197.18 Pearse, Plunkett and the Irish Republic

Patrick Henry Pearse (1879–1916) and Joseph Mary Plunkett (1887–1916), Irish nationalist leaders in the Easter Rising of 1916, were both executed in May 1916.

198.3 "What doth it profit . . ."

Matthew 16:26: "For what is a man profited, if he shall gain the whole world, and lose his own soul?" (King James Version).

"Sentiment—and the Use of Rouge"

199.11 Seventeenth Sussex

The Seventeenth Batallion, Royal Sussex Regiment, an infantry unit in the First World War, was formed in France in May 1918.

199.13 Paddington Station

A major railway terminus (erected 1852–54) in the City of Westminster, served by the Great Western Railway and, after 1863, by trains from the Underground. The station was known for its glazed roof and wrought-iron arches.

204.10 Zeppelin

During the First World War the Germans used motor-driven airships called Zeppelins (after their inventor, Count Ferdinand von Zeppelin) for bombing raids and reconnaissance.

205.27 'Kreutzer Sonata'

Tolstoy's *Kreitserova sonata*, first published in the US in 1890 as *The Kreutzer Sonata*, was a controversial text addressing issues that are prominent in this story: whether sexual allure is by its nature deceitful, whether homosexuality is acceptable, and whether art can be a substitute for sexual involvement. Fitzgerald mentions *The Kreutzer Sonata* in *This Side of Paradise* and alludes to the work in his 1927 story "Jacob's Ladder."

206.16 train for Dover

Most of Fitzgerald's readers would have been familiar with Dover as the major embarkation point for British troops headed for the Western Front. From Dover it is approximately 20 miles across the English Channel to the French port of Calais. Dover is famous for the nearby white chalk cliffs, which rise as high as 350 feet above the Channel.

206.30 Rochester

This large town in Kent is on the River Medway, about 30 miles southeast of London. During the First World War, it was of strategic importance in defending the nearby Royal Navy dockyard at Chatham.

207.9 Zola . . . environment is environment

The French novelist Émile Zola (1840–1902), whose name is associated with naturalism in literature and art, emphasized the importance of environment in human behavior. Fitzgerald probably knew him as one of the most passionate defenders of Alfred Dreyfus and might have read his article "J'accuse" (1898).

208.17 Brighton

This British seaside resort on the south coast of England was a popular destination for military men (and their wives and sweethearts) just before embarkation for the war in France.

210.21 Westminster

O'Flaherty probably has in mind Westminster Cathedral, the seat of the Church of England, in central London.

211.28 Louisa M. Alcott

The American author of the popular girls' book *Little Women* (1868–69), and of the sequels *Little Men* (1871) and *Jo's Boys* (1886), all of which follow the lives of the March sisters—Meg, Jo, Beth, and Amy. Alcott (1832–88) wrote other novels for young readers, including *An Old-Fashioned Girl* (1870) and *Under the Lilacs* (1879).

212.29–30 a play where a man was born in a station, or a handbag in a station...

These are references to Oscar Wilde's play *The Importance of Being Earnest* (1895), in which the convolutions of the plot are made to come right in the end by the discovery that Ernest Worthing (or "Jack") was left as a baby in Victoria Station— in a handbag.

"'Verses in Peace and War'"

215.3–4 "Men, Women, and Ghosts" and "Sword Blades and Poppy Seed"

These two collections of verse by the American poet, critic, and editor Amy Lowell (1874–1925) were published, respectively, in 1916 and 1914.

"The Pierian Springs and the Last Straw"

224.4 Lauras... Petrarch

The Italian poet Francesco Petrarca (1304–74) first encountered a woman called Laura (possibly Laura de Noves, the wife of Hugues de Sade) at Avignon in 1327. She became the inspiration for his best-known vernacular love lyrics, including many of his most famous sonnets.

225.6–7 Andover... Y.M.C.A.... Williams

When Fitzgerald wrote this story, Phillips Academy in Andover, Massachusetts (est. 1770), was the oldest and most prestigious boys' prep school in the US. The Young Men's Christian Association (YMCA) was a religious and social organization with chapters on many American college campuses. Williams College, founded in 1793 in Williamstown, Massachusetts, was an exclusive liberal arts college for men.

231.34 Marc Antony and De Musset

Both were entangled with famous women: Marc Antony (ca. 83 BC–30 BC) with Queen Cleopatra (69 BC–30 BC); Alfred de Musset (1810–57) with the French novelist Georges Sand (1804–76). Fitzgerald might have known de Musset's novel *La Confession d'un Enfant du Siècle* (1836) and Sand's novel *Elle et Lui* (1859)—their separate fictionalized accounts of the love affair.

ILLUSTRATIONS

1 Cover for *Safety First!*—the third and last Triangle show for which Fitzgerald supplied the lyrics. Princeton University Libraries.

2 Shane Leslie, who encouraged Fitzgerald in his early literary ambitions. This is the frontispiece for Leslie's *Verses in Peace and War* (1917), which Fitzgerald reviewed in the *Nassau Lit*.

Chapter One   THE *Debutante*

      the Sixty-Eighth Street

      The time ~~is~~ february the place
a ~~little~~ large and dainty bedroom in
the Connage house -- a girl's room; pink walls
and curtains and a pink bedspread on a cream-
colored bed. Pink and cream are the motifs of
the room, but the only article of furniture in
full view is a luxurious dressing table with
a glass top and a three-sided mirror. On the
walls there is an expensive print of "Cherry Ripe",
a few polite dogs by Landseer, and the "King of
the Black Isles" by Maxfield Parrish.

      Great disorder consisting of the
following items: (1) seven or eight empty card-
board boxes, with tissue paper tongues hanging
panting from their mouths; (2) an assortment of
street dresses mingled with their sisters of the
evening, all upon the table, all evidently new;
(3) a roll of tulle, which has lost its dignity
and wound itself tortuously around everything
in sight, and (4) upon the two small chairs, a
collection of lingerie that beggars description.
One would enjoy seeing the bill called forth by
the finery displayed and one is possessed by a
desire to see the princess for whose benefit --

hunting   Look! There's someone! -- Disappointment! This
is only a maid ~~hunting~~ for something -- she lifts
a heap ~~from a chair~~ -- Not there; another heap,
the dressing table, the chiffonier drawers. She
brings to light several beautiful chemises and an
amazing pajama, but this does not satisfy her --
she goes out.

      An indistinguishable mumble from
the next room.   *alec's mother*

      Now, we are getting warm. This is
Mrs. Connage, ample, dignified, rouged to the
dowager point and quite worn out. Her lips move
significantly as she looks for ~~it~~. Her search
is less thorough than the maid's, but there is a
touch of fury in it, that quite makes up for its
sketchiness. She stumbles on the tulle and her
"damn" is quite audible. She retires, empty-
handed.

      More chatter outside and a girl's
voice, a very spoiled voice, says: "Of all the
~~stupid people~~ --

NOTE:—Many articles have appeared lately in our current magazines stating how simple it is for Germany to conquer this country. Is it? the TIGER asks. Read on, oh, gentlissimo!

The Conquest of America

(as some writers would have it.)

(Mr. Fitzcheesecake, who has written this article, needs no introduction. He has held numerous official positions: he was on three different beats in Trenton, and was for one year Deputy Garbage Man of Bordentown; and we feel that what he writes will be authoritative.)—THE EDITORS.

The American Atlantic fleet has been sunk. The Germans were coming in three thousand transports and were about to land in New York. Admiral Von Noseitch was swimming across with the fleet. Pandemonium reigned in the great city, women and tenors were running frantically up and down their rooms, the men having all left; the police force also, fearing to be called to the colors, had been in Canada for two months. Who was to raise and equip a vast army? The New York Baseball Team had finished in the second division, so Mgr. McGraw gave up all hope and volunteered; the new army, for secrecy, used a subway car to drill in. No help could be had from Boston, for they had won the pennant, and there was nothing on the front pages of the papers to warn the people of the imminent danger. General McGraw intrenched himself in the middle of Brooklyn for, so he thought, not even a German would go there. He was right, but three stray cannon balls came his way, and he struck out. The Statute of Liberty had been invested, New York's six million people were all captured; the Germans were upon them before preparation could be accomplished. Generals Von Limburger, Munchener, and Frankfurter held a consultation in Busty's the first

night: General Von Limburger was going to attack General Bryan and his army of the Raritan in New Jersey; General Frankfurter was going to take a Day-Line boat to Albany and thence to Canada, where three-fourths of the citizens of the U. S. capable of bearing arms had fled for a much-needed rest; while General Muncher with thirty picked men would hold New York. Gen. Von Limburger took the 7 P. M. train to Princeton, near which place Bryan was reported to have fled. Meanwhile all the United States had been captured, save this section of New Jersey. The Pacific Squadron, however, was intact; they had been taken for fishing boats and had escaped without any injury. The besieging army was fast approaching the city; preceptors could be seen running madly to and fro, mostly fro. Bryan drew up his army in the "TIGER" Office; they voted five votes to one not to let a German live.

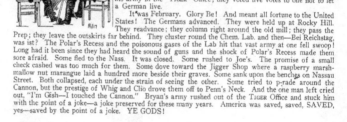

It was February. Glory Be! And meant all fortune to the United States! The Germans advanced. They were held up at Rocky Hill. They readvance; they column right around the old mill; they pass the Prep; they leave the outskirts far behind. They cluster round the Chem. Lab. and then—Bei Reichstag, was ist? The Polar's Recess and the poisonous gases of the Lab hit that vast army at one fell swoop! Long had it been since they had heard the sound of guns and the shock of Polar's Recess made them sore afraid. Some fled to the Nass. It was closed. Some rushed to Joe's. The promise of a small check cashed was too much for them. Some dove toward the Jigger Shop where a raspberry marshmallow nut marangue laid a hundred more beside their graves. Some sank upon the benches on Nassau Street. Both collapsed, each under the strain of seeing the other. Some tried to p-rade around the Cannon, but the prestige of Whig and Clio drove them off to Penn's Neck. And the one man left cried out, "I'm Gish—I touched the Cannon." Bryan's army rushed out of the TIGER Office and stuck him with the point of a joke—a joke preserved for these many years. America was saved, saved, SAVED, yes—saved by the point of a joke. YE GODS!

4 "The Conquest of America," by "Mr. Fitzcheesecake," from the Thanksgiving 1915 issue of the *Tiger*. The illustrations are by Alan Jackman, a classmate of Fitzgerald's. Mudd Manuscript Library, Princeton University.

THE PRINCE OF PESTS

A Story of the War.

I T was night in July, 1914. A man and his board of directors sat around a table in a palace at Berlin. The man was tall, with a moustache and a short arm. Who was he?—oh, reader, can you guess? He wore a military uniform, green with grey facings; his pants were blue with red facings.

"Your Highness," Von Boodlewaden was saying, "everything is ready."

The Kaiser shook his head sadly and folded his arms, at least he tucked the short one in with the other. Then he took his short leg and crossed it over his long one, and having scratched his long ear come to business.

"Nietzsche," he said, and waited for his words to have effect. Von Nicklebottom immediately sprang upon the table and led the customary cheer for Nietzsche—three locomotives with three sidels of beer on the end.

"Nietzsche," continued the Kaiser, "has said it. We will conquer by the sword." As he said this he ran his hand lovingly along his sword, then trying its edge on a bit of celery which he munched tentatively.

"Your Highness," cried Von Munchennoodle, "Belgium must be sacrificed."

The Kaiser bit his lip until the blood ran slowly down to the table where it spread into little livid pools of red and yellow liquid. His councillors dipped their fingers in it and reverently crossed themselves. Deeply affected the Kaiser pledged them.

"And what of America?" asked Pistachio, Chancellor of the Domino Club.

"America?" said the Kaiser, rising to his full height. "Charles II had his Cromwell, Caesar had his Brutus, and Wilson—"

There were cries of "plagiarism" and the Kaiser paused.

"Daniel Webster was a German," he continued, rather abashed. Turning to the man on his center,

Baron Badenuf, Chancellor of the Shakespearegoethe-teutonic League, he commanded him.

"Look him up, Baddy."

There was an hour while Badenuf looked up Webster, during which an absolute silence was maintained, broken only by the Kaiser as he ran his sword rapidly up and down his neck, where he had caught prickly heat the summer before playing leap-frog on the beach at Ostend with Czar Nicholas. Badenuf finally returned.

"I find in the life of Webster," he announced, "the relevant news that he once stopped at the Sauerkraut Inn while passing through Pennsylvania. This proves the case, for no one but a German would stop at a German Inn unless he has to, and Daniel didn't."

There were three wild cheers at this and according to the ancient German custom they prepared to pledge each other in the royal blood. The Kaiser tried his lip again but all the blood had gone out of it long ago. So he opened an artery in his leg with an olive fork.

They all gulped it down heartily while a German band played "Ach du lieber Augustine" and the Kaiser's valet strapped his paralyzed arm to his sword so he could have his picture taken.   F. S. F.

5 "The Prince of Pests," from the *Tiger* for 28 April 1917. These illustrations are also by Alan Jackman, class of 1917. Mudd Manuscript Library, Princeton University.

6 Music and lyrics for "One-Lump Percy," a song from *Safety First!* (1916). Princeton University Libraries.

APPENDIX

PROBABLE ATTRIBUTIONS

Fitzgerald pasted five unsigned limericks from the *St. Paul Academy Now and Then* into one of the scrapbooks in which he preserved his juvenilia (Scrapbook VII, p. 40, in the Princeton collection). Fitzgerald was likely the author of these verses, which appear below. These items were reprinted in the *Fitzgerald/Hemingway Annual 1975*, pp. 147–48. The first two limericks appeared in the *Now and Then* for February 1910, the other three in the issue for June 1910.

> There was a young fellow named Ware,
> Who was awfully proud of his hair.
> > One day he was shorn,
> > He looked lean and forlorn
> And felt like a chocolate éclair.

> Craw Brant's a studious boy,
> To him, to learn lessons, is joy.
> > He always gets "A,"
> > And then hollers "Hooray,"
> Then wastes all his time on a toy.

> There is an old lady next door,
> At baseball she gets awfully sore,
> > A policeman she got
> > And told him some rot
> (We don't play in the yard anymore).

> There is a young man who's not sour,
> In height he resembles a tower.
> > Mandolins he does play,
> > And cellos, they say
> (You've guessed by this time that it's Power).

Paul Briggs is a cute little (?) lad,
He seldom, if ever, is bad,
But one very dark day,
He got locked in, they say,
And fell in the ashes, 'tis sad.

•••

In 1968, John D. McMaster, a member of the Princeton class of 1919 who worked on the *Tiger* with Fitzgerald, identified the following short poem (from the June 1916 issue) as Fitzgerald's work. According to McMaster, Fitzgerald wrote the three-line lyric; McMaster then supplied the title. (Fitzgerald did not clip the item and paste it into one of his scrapbooks, however.) See Bruccoli, *F. Scott Fitzgerald: A Descriptive Bibliography* (Pittsburgh: University of Pittsburgh Press, 1987), rev. edn., entry C20. The humor derives from the title of the popular opera *Thaïs* by Jules Massenet, based on the novel by Anatole France. Thaïs, a great beauty, renounces her allegiance to Venus and enters a convent after meeting Athanaë, a monk of the desert.

Yais
Wouldn't it be nais
to sit on a dais
with Thaïs.